About the author

Marjory McGinn was born in Scotland and moved to Australia as a child, which later fuelled a passion for travel and writing. She became a journalist and worked on *The Sydney Morning Herald*, and as a senior feature writer on *The Sun-Herald*. In 2000 she returned to Scotland and worked as a freelance journalist, with stories appearing in leading British newspapers, including *The Daily Mail*, *The Times* and *The Herald*.

In 2010, together with her partner Jim and crazy Jack Russell dog, Wallace, she set off on an adventure to the Mani, in southern Greece, that lasted three years, which inspired her two travel memoirs, *Things Can Only Get Feta* and *Homer's Where The Heart Is*.

Marjory also writes a blog with a Greek theme on her website www.bigfatgreekodyssey.com and she can be followed on Twitter@fatgreekodyssey.

Homer's Where The Heart Is

Two journalists, one crazy dog
and a love affair with Greece

By Marjory McGinn

Sequel to Things Can Only Get Feta

Homer's Where The Heart Is

Published by Createspace Independent Publishing Platform, 2015.

ISBN-13: 978-1511896832.
ISBN-10: 1511896833.

Front cover illustration and design by Tony Hannaford. (www.anthonyhannaford.co.uk)

Editing, book design and author photograph by Jim Bruce. (www.ebooklover.co.uk)

Inside photographs © Marjory McGinn.

Dedication

For my parents, John and Mary, and Euphamia.

Author's note

This book is based on real events and characters. While I have kept the names of the villages involved, I have changed the names of most characters to protect their privacy.

My summary of events during the economic crisis was based on my experience of living in Greece during this time and through the people I interviewed, and my research in the Greek and international media. I acknowledge the excellent commentary in the Greek newspaper *Kathimerini*.

Note – Modern Greek

Modern Greek is complex and some word forms may confuse readers. Basically, articles, nouns, adjectives and most pronouns change according to gender, number and their position in a sentence.

The noun xenos, for example, meaning foreigner or stranger, in the masculine form, sometimes appears in the text in plural form xenoi, or feminine singular, xeni.

Masculine names that end in 'os', 'as' or 'is' will drop the final 's' in the vocative case (when addressing someone directly). The name Andreas, for example, will change when you say: "Andrea, are you listening?"

Contents

Prologue

IT was in a Kalamata bakery during the economic crisis that I understood for the first time that even though the Greeks invented the word stoical, they have their breaking point. Anger bubbled up unexpectedly at the bread counter between the volcanic village loaves and the crusty baguettes. And it was nothing to do with the prices.

I was in the Nostimo bakery, where we always bought provisions during our regular shopping trips to the city. I was on chatty terms with the normally pleasant young women who worked there. This time, however, the mood was different.

"Where do you come from again?" asked the young, curly-haired woman called Eleni, after I gave her my order. She looked hot and flustered.

"Scotland," I replied.

"Ah, yes, now I remember."

At least we weren't having the usual conversation we had in the rural Mani that started with "where's Scotland?" and ended with me having to draw maps of Europe on dusty roadsides.

Eleni wrapped my warm loaves of bread in tissue paper, and shoved them briskly into a plastic bag. As she passed it across the counter, she gave me a petulant look.

"Then go back to your own country. GO BACK!" she said, raising her voice.

At first I was slightly amused. After living in Greece for a year-and-a-half, I was used to the theatricality of Greeks, the way they could whip up a drama in seconds. Mostly it was meant to be entertaining, but this was something else. "Go back!" seemed to have 'get lost' as a subtext. Had I said something to offend her, so easy to do when you're struggling with a difficult language like Greek?

9

Other customers were entering the shop, shuffling impatiently behind me, showing the national aversion to queues.

"Why do you say 'Go back'?" I asked her, fumbling about in my purse for money.

Eleni wiped her hot, moist forehead with the back of her hand in the 30 degrees of late summer heat. She answered with a question.

"What? You don't want to go back? You WANT to stay here, in Greece? This is a terrible place to live now. Don't you know what is happening here?"

"I know what's happening in Greece," I said confidently, trying not to seem like the ill-informed *xeni*, foreigner, that she might have taken me for. I took my change and was about to bolt when the other young assistant, who had been stacking shelves with bread, pitched in as well.

"She's right. Go back to your *patrida*, homeland!"

I glanced quickly behind me and caught sight of a sweaty matron next in line, grimacing with too much heat and chatter. I feared if I stayed longer I'd get thumped with a brace of village loaves, round and hard, favoured by older people. But the assistants hadn't finished yet.

"Go back ... and take us with you, PLEASE!" Eleni pleaded, with big, mournful eyes.

"Yes, take us with you, to Scotland. Away from here," moaned the second assistant.

I hadn't seen this coming at all. "You're both joking, right?"

"No, we're not joking," said Eleni.

I stifled the urge to laugh, out of relief, mostly. At least I wasn't about to be frogmarched out of the shop. All the same, it was a strange way to convey frustration over crisis-ridden Greece.

"Sorry to tell you this, but we're not going home yet. When we do, you'll be the first escapees on our list," I said, trying to make light of the situation. They nodded.

I glanced behind me, towards our car parked outside. My partner Jim was peering through the side window, looking impatient. Wallace, our Jack Russell dog, was on the back seat, squirming about and whining.

I was about to leave when the pair started up again.

"Why do you want to stay here when the country's in such a mess?" said Eleni.

There were four people behind me in the queue, staring, waiting for me to answer, as if I were a team captain on University Challenge. My neck was prickling with sweat. The answer I was toying with was going to sound shallow to people who had begun to suffer the appalling effects of job and wage cuts, and new taxes. These were measures demanded by Greece's international lenders in order for the country to receive the huge bailouts that would prevent it from going bankrupt. I felt I had to offer some rationale for our on-going adventure in Greece. I proceeded as if words were eggshells.

"Despite everything … we love this country. And we love the people … that's why."

"Pah! You love Greece!" said an excitable old man in a dusty black suit. "But you are a foreigner. You don't have to work here, I imagine, or bring up children on a shrinking salary."

He nodded to the others and they all started talking at once, like a Greek chorus, with lots of shoulder-shrugging and hand-waving. The young women behind the counter were nodding their heads solemnly.

It was time to leave. When I said 'goodbye', Eleni's angry look disappeared and she offered me a tired smile.

"We mean you no harm, *Kiria*. You must understand how we feel."

"I do. Don't worry."

"*Kalo apoyevma*, have a good afternoon," she said.

I rushed outside, while the other customers started up again, berating the country, the government, the rising prices, and probably forgetting what they'd come in for. It was out of character for normally warm-hearted Kalamatans to be this abrupt with a foreigner. In other circumstances it might even have been funny, but not during the most tumultuous period of Greek history since the Second World War.

I was hot and flustered when I dived back into the car.

"You were a while. What was going on?" Jim asked.

I told him. He shook his head. "What a clumsy, daft thing to say, 'Go back'. Yeah, did you tell them it's only 10 degrees in Scotland today?"

I laughed as we drove off.

When we arrived at our rented house, 20 minutes later, we found Andreas, the landlord, wandering about the corner of the sprawling property near an old *spitaki*, the original dwelling. He and his wife Marina, whose family owned the property, spent much of their time at this stone house, slowly renovating it.

Andreas was feeding the cats and the big dog Zina, which was kept chained at the *spitaki* as a kind of guard dog.

He was a slim, handsome man with expressive brown eyes. He spoke very good English but occasionally mashed his grammar when excited. We told him about the scene in the bakery.

"They said that? You go back to your home?" Andreas held his arms out wide and very straight, to express disbelief.

"*Po, po, po!*" he added, meaning 'bloody hell!'

He looked at the nearby olive trees, as if seeking guidance amid their gnarled, stoical forms.

"It's beginning," he said.

"What's beginning?"

"Everything," he replied enigmatically. "Remember the terrible riots we saw on TV the other night, the young peoples fighting with the police?"

He was referring to the violent confrontations in Athens in October 2011 as the Parliament debated punishing new austerity measures.

"There will be a big domino wave," he said, meaning 'effect' I think. "And now it is starting. All this bitter fighting, and the people will be crushed, just like they were by the military *hounta,* junta, in the 1960s. We will see tanks on the streets again."

Jim and I looked at each other in horror. First the bakery incident, now this. Andreas may have exaggerated the link to the dark days of the 1960s and 70s, but many Greeks now feared that the increasing incidents of rioting in the capital could eventually spark some kind of military crackdown.

"I have a plan. When it gets very bad, I will move my family from Kalamata back to this property and we will all of us live here, grow food, harvest the olives. We will live simply. Damn those politicians!" said Andreas, raising a fist to the sky.

That night we sat on the front balcony of the big main house we were renting from the couple. We ate dinner and drank a few glasses of wine, while enjoying the view of the Messinian Gulf. The autumn sun was dropping behind the peninsula opposite, turning the sky an indelible pink.

We discussed the bakery incident while Andreas and Marina wandered around the property, checking things before heading home to Kalamata for the night. They were talking in hushed voices, possibly working out their plans for the months ahead. And what about us? Staying another year in crisis-torn Greece? Possibly with tanks rumbling along the city streets.

Perhaps we should have sensed we were in for a bumpy ride back in the spring. Not long after we moved into the house, we were engulfed by a terrifying storm and lay awake most of the night, with a mad dog on the bed … and something dark cowering in the bathtub.

1

It's raining chair legs!

THE storm peeled off the Taygetos mountains and roared down through the olive orchards. The wind was sharp and raw, strafing the stiff-brushed heads of the olive trees and bending their branches horizontal. Then the rain began all at once, full pelt, like a horse going into a gallop from a standing position.

For half-an-hour it rained *kareklopodara*, chair legs, as they say in Greece. It rained outside the house – and inside as well. The 25-year-old home, set on concrete stilts, was a wonderful summer house, with balconies on every side, and the main sea-facing balcony was wide and well covered. It was cool and breezy, built for everything, even earthquakes, but not stormy weather, like most homes in Greece. This heavy rain and wind from the Taygetos challenged the building. Water seeped under the front door and under balcony doors, along window sills and down the chimney as well, on to the iron grate below.

There was a frenzied knocking at the door and we opened it to find Marina outside, wet and cold, with an anxious face.

"Is everything all right here? Is there water inside?" she asked.

She didn't wait for a reply and rushed inside with proprietorial urgency, checking out the damage and rattling about in the bathroom, where the buckets and mops were kept. She started working her way through the house, room by room, with me following behind, a bucket and mop of my own, like the Sorcerer's Apprentice.

"This is very rare. Please don't worry. Only when the wind is blowing in a certain direction and the rain is heavy will you get this problem. I am so sorry," she said.

It didn't seem the right time to complain about the house's building flaws and I just took her word for it. The couple left quickly that afternoon in a state of panic because Marina said she was sure Andreas hadn't shut the windows in the basement of their Kalamata house, and the last time that happened they had a shallow swimming pool to deal with. Soon after they left, the thunder started.

Thunderstorms in the Mani are legendary: big, lusty, sky-cracking waves of noise that thump you in the chest as if you've been shot. And the storms brought not just a few forks of lightning but dozens. At night they zig-zagged down to the Messinian Gulf like a tracing of hot-wired veins against the dark sky.

I knew we were in for a bumpy night as Wallace, our dog, went bonkers with thunderstorms, roaring about the house, bunching up rugs, howling at the sky, head thrown back, legs planted defiantly. If the storms went on all night, so would he. It was like spending the night with a colicky newborn baby crossed with Shrek.

Wallace had been with us for 10 years and was a much loved pet, yet like any typical Jack Russell terrier, he had madness stitched into his genes. He had many behavioural quirks from his puppyhood, but while we'd been in Greece he had added to them. He had developed a phobia about noise. It started with insects, especially bees and hornets, but progressed to other things: cutlery chiming together, plates being rattled, doorbells ringing on television shows. With storms, his anxieties were ramped up to the max.

We lay uncomfortably awake half the night, listening to the thunder booming across the gulf. It was so strong at times we wondered if this house on pillars would go weak-kneed and collapse, and occasionally the noise even drowned out

Wallace's spirited barking. By 3am, however, the thunder finally started to abate. When all was quiet, Jim suddenly sat up straight in bed.

"What's that funny noise?" he said.

"What noise?"

"That scraping noise. Listen!"

I did, but Jim's ears are bionic and all I could hear was the sound of Wallace, cowering at the bottom of the bed, growling softly in anticipation of more thunder.

Jim leapt out of bed and rushed through the open-plan living room/dining room to the front door. When he opened it I could hear the rain hammering on the concrete steps outside, and a howling wind, like a malevolent spirit, swirled through the house. Jim was cursing.

The bedroom door faced the bathroom across the hall. Out of the corner of my eye, I saw a dark shape sloping past, heading for the bathroom. I sat up in bed as Jim reappeared.

"What was that I just saw in the hallway?"

Jim was shivering from the cold wind. "It's Zina. She's been outside all this time. That scraping noise was her at the door. The minute I opened it, she shot past me, soaking wet."

That was all we needed. Zina had apparently broken free from her chain at the smaller house, the *spitaki,* and was now in ours. I looked at Wallace at the bottom of the bed. I was expecting him to rush away for a territorial feud but he was quiet now, all stocked up on obsessions for the minute. I got out of bed and padded across the cold tiled floor, following Jim to the bathroom. He flicked on the light and there was Zina, hunkered down in the bath, head between her paws, trembling.

"Poor thing," I said, as we stared down at the solid beast, her wet brown fur giving off a musty, rank odour. I went to fetch some old towels and laid them over her. I didn't attempt to dry her though. Zina always had a slightly manic look in her pale brown eyes and she still seemed very unpredictable to us.

After our first year in the Mani, it was an English real estate agent in Kalamata who had suggested this house in the coastal village of Paleohora, when we were looking for a different property to rent. She had warned us, however, there were a few drawbacks, as there were with most Greek rental properties. First, there was Zina, the 'guard dog', chained up for most of the time on the property. The dog had once lived with Andreas and Marina, the landlords, in Kalamata but had now outgrown its city confines. Our worry was how Wallace would get on with Zina.

The first time we inspected the property, we took Wallace along to test the water. The two dogs went ballistic. Wallace ran the gamut of mad terrier behaviour and Zina strained viciously against her chain, barking. What would happen when she was off her chain, I wondered. She looked like she could eat Wallace for breakfast and then floss with him afterwards.

The second possible drawback was that the landlords would be more or less sharing the property, much of the time, working on the *spitaki* at the weekends, tending their garden and the olive trees. They would also come at least every other afternoon, when they finished work, to feed all the animals. It was an eccentric arrangement that could have swung either way, from entertaining to disastrous. It was difficult to tell.

The house was plain, like a white bungalow on stilts, with brown shutters, but the location was appealing. It was built on a low hill not far from the sea, and halfway up a dusty winding track called *Odos Elaionon*, the Road of the Olive Orchards. I was instantly seduced by the name and by the thick olive orchards on either side of the road. The property also had 80 olive trees, and some fig, lemon, orange and pomegranate trees as well.

The views from here were the southern region at a glance: the long sweep of the Messinian gulf from the front-facing balcony, with Kalamata city spread along its head, and views of the high peaks of the Taygetos mountains from the back of the house.

The Mani region of the Peloponnese comprises most of the middle peninsula out of the three prongs that hang like pulled roots from the southern mainland, with the Taygetos running down its spine to the tip. It is probably the more ruggedly charming of the three peninsulas, with mountain villages, historic tower houses and old Byzantine churches.

This northern section of the Mani coastline and its hinterland, from Kalamata down to the fishing village of Kitries, has long been revered for its physical beauty. But it had historic cachet as well, even in ancient times. Paleohora, meaning 'old capital', was first featured in Homer's *Iliad,* where it was called the city of Iri. On a high cliff at Paleohora there was once a temple dedicated to Asclepius, the god of healing. Later a Venetian castle was built here, though little of it remains today.

The modern village of Paleohora is a low-key cluster of mainly holiday houses owned by Greeks. It is vibrant in summer, with sheltered coves and busy waterside tavernas. In winter it is deserted, but with sea-lashed romance that makes you appreciate its Homeric links.

Despite the drawbacks of the Paleohora property, and the fact that it was slightly bigger and more rambling than we could possibly need, we took it. It was hard to imagine a more desirable location to continue our adventure that began in 2010.

@@@@@

We left our village in central Scotland in the spring of that year for what was to be a year's odyssey in the southern Peloponnese, to escape from an Arctic winter and a harsh restructuring of the newspaper industry, which had put both our journalistic careers in jeopardy.

In our first year, we settled in the hillside village of Megali Mantineia, where little had changed in centuries and most of its residents were goat farmers and olive harvesters. It satisfied our search for authenticity, in our bid to live as Greek a life as possible, and to turn some of our experiences into freelance features for British publications.

That year had been the most impressionable of our lives and it had also gone so fast that it was inconceivable we should return to the UK straight away. And so, in the early spring of 2011, we planned another year or two in the Mani, but in a different, yet nearby location, with a more comfortable house than the cramped stone property we had rented in the first year.

Paleohora was just a 15-minute drive from Megali Mantineia, practically next door, and we had the sea to enjoy all summer as well. It seemed like a perfect arrangement, except for one huge factor – Greece was sliding even deeper into financial misery, with swingeing austerity measures and social unrest, and at that time, we had no way of knowing just how much worse it would get.

But for now, at least, the only crisis we had to deal with was Zina, hunkering down in a bathtub in the middle of a storm.

In the beginning, Andreas had jokingly described her as a "she wolf" because of her size, her huge stamina and powerful jaws, but she also had the look and colouring of an Alsatian. After the first angry exchange between the two dogs before we moved in, we were still cautious about putting them together, fearing that Wallace wouldn't survive a dust-up with big Zina.

For the time being, we decided to keep Zina on her chain when Andreas and Marina weren't at the property and wait for the dogs to get comfortable with each other, at least from a distance. Now here they were, in the same house, both together on the crazy spectrum — Wallace barking at thunder and the brazen she-wolf a quivering wreck.

"Let's just leave Zina in the bath until morning and keep Wallace away from her," said Jim, as we shut the bathroom door and padded back to bed.

By dawn, the storm had passed and a pale rheumy light seeped through the worn slats of the wooden shutters. I turned my head away from the window, only to find a dog in my face: Zina.

She was leaning over the pillow, staring at me with glassy eyes, her tongue lolling, and the air filled with her pungent breath. I gasped. Yet she did nothing, just stared quietly. Then I remembered Wallace. I looked for him on the bed, hoping he wouldn't react. Luckily, he seemed to be finally asleep, underneath the bottom edge of the duvet, having bunched it around himself like a kind of panic room. Zina couldn't have seen him, he was so well-hidden.

Every dog has its duvet, I thought.

Some time in the night Zina must have crawled out of the bath and apparently opened the bathroom door, which wasn't impossible as it was old and only needed a light touch on the wobbly handle to open it. She must have pushed down on it with one of her big paws.

After eyeballing me for a few minutes, Zina skittered off to the sitting room and stood at the front door. As soon as I opened it, she rushed down the front steps and headed towards the back of the property, thickly planted with olive trees.

From the doorstep I could see a watery dawn spreading over the dark mass of the Taygetos, a row of lights still twinkling from the village of Ano Verga, clinging to a steep slope near the top of Mount Kalathio. The head of the gulf was just visible, the water churned and muddy at the shoreline, like a massive slick of café latté.

I went back to bed, and as I passed the bathroom, I saw a trail of sodden, muddy towels on the tiled floor, as if a gang of teenagers had just got ready for a night on the town. Jim was fast asleep, and when I slid under the duvet, my feet connected with Wallace's warm belly. I let him be. We'd had enough noise and canine theatricals already – and I was dog tired myself.

2

Custard pies and cowboys

STORMS in Greece are a lot like the people — their tempestuous outbursts are often short-lived and followed by good humour again. By 10am, when we finally got up, the only remnants of the storm were a strong wind blowing from the Taygetos and the messy heads of the olive trees.

After a late breakfast, we wandered around the property to see what damage the storm had caused. Not that you would have known really because the place was always charmingly messy, with old bits of farming equipment, olive wood and distressed furniture stacked under the main house and around the *spitaki*. Marina, who had a passion for arts and crafts, was deconstructing old folky pieces and rehabilitating them for use in the *spitaki*.

The place was also full of animals, a slew of cats – one male, three females (one pregnant), one scruffy thing of indeterminate sex, and Cyclops, whom we had brought with us from our first house in Megali Mantineia. We aren't cat people but had inherited Cyclops on the other property, an old male with a battered face and one eye missing, leaving just a tight ragged line in his fur. It was obviously a war wound from his macho younger years.

Despite Wallace and Cyclops engaging in gutsy steeple-chases around the property in Megali Mantineia when we first moved in, they fell into a kind of bickering Steptoe and Son relationship by the end. When we left the village house it seemed clear we should take the cat with us. I had a soft spot for Cyclops, a gritty old soul just managing to survive – a bit like Greece at that point.

At the Paleohora property, there were also chickens, part of Andreas's valiant attempt at self-sufficiency, an insurance policy against the fall of Greece. We were tasked with letting them out in the morning and shutting them in at night. The *kotetsi,* hen house, was like a cave set into a rockface with a wood and wire door. I don't know if it was from a defective diet, but the chickens laid the weirdest eggs we'd ever seen, with crinkly, paper-thin shells in duff shapes, like something crafted from Plasticine in a kids' art class.

There was a long wooden table outside the *spitaki* under a flourishing grapevine, with fig trees growing nearby. It was the centre of life on the property and I had visions of sitting here in the summer eating sun-warmed figs in the morning. That's where we were when the couple arrived from Kalamata that morning, carrying bags of shopping and a box of thick custardy *galaktoboureko* pie with a filo pastry topping.

"Good morning. Was everything okay in the storm, *paidia*?" asked Andreas, using the Greek word for 'children', his favourite nickname for us, which was cute as we were older than both of them.

"We didn't sleep much with the thunder," I replied.

"It was the same for us. And too much rain. The streets in Kalamata are full of water now."

"Wallace barked half the night. And Zina slept in our bathtub."

His dark brown eyes were wide with disbelief. "In the bath? Really? How does she get in the bath?"

"We found her during the night on the front step and she rushed inside."

"Did you hear that, Marina?"

That was one of Andreas's catchphrases. When we all spoke in English, he often translated things into Greek because he didn't want Marina to miss anything. Her English wasn't as good as his, but even he had some endearing mix-ups and mispronunciations. He had trouble with 'because' and always pronounced it 'becows', and 'perhaps' became 'peeerhaps', with a long emphasis on the 'e'.

Andreas was boyish-looking for a man in his late 40s. He liked wearing camouflage trousers and old black boots from his army service days a few decades earlier. Once I asked why he wore them.

"We must be ready for anything now, *paidia,*" was his ominous response.

"But I see what has happened with Zina. She was hiding before we left for the afternoon and we couldn't find her, but then we have to leave for Kalamata becows Marina says I have left windows open in the basement, and we will get flooding. And then I forgot to tell you about Zina and thunder and that she goes crazy with it," he said, making a claw of his hand and twisting it back and forth beside his head, the Greek gesture for anyone on the bonkers spectrum. "If she is off the chain in the thunder, she goes somewhere to hide."

"Like the bathtub," I said, laughing.

Andreas offered his other favourite gesture, making a windmill of his right arm, rotating it in lazy circles while comically biting his lower lip.

"Yes, like the bath," he said. "And Wallace? He was all right with Zina?"

"Yes, they were too obsessed with thunder to hate each other."

He laughed. "Don't be afraid, Zina will be good with Wallace. We have Zina since she was a puppy, in Kalamata. She plays with our children. Do not worry about Wallace," he said looking around for him.

"He's in the house," said Jim.

"Bring him down. I want to see Wallace now, please!" he said, pulling a comical face.

24

I hesitated, remembering that Zina was free of her chain and sleeping off the storm trauma in her big blue dog house under the steps of the *spitaki* that led up to its small top balcony. But then I thought: what could the two dogs do to each other now after spending the night together – in separate 'beds', of course? It would be fine with everyone around.

Jim went back to the house for him and Wallace came spinning down the dusty path that connected the two properties and sat under the table. Andreas had become fond of Wallace in just a few weeks and always ruffled the fur on his head and showered him with Greek endearments.

While Andreas was fussing over Wallace, Zina rushed over, and despite a boisterous skirmish at first, they seemed disinclined to eat each other. The main problem with Zina was that she didn't know her own strength and at least once I winced when she galloped past and scuttled Wallace into a sage bush, as if he were a ten-pin.

"Don't worry," Andreas kept saying, and yet I did. There was some unknowable twitch in Zina's eyes that told me that one day she would give in to to her wolf-minx destiny. And I was not wrong.

"Was your Kalamata house safe from the rain?" I asked Andreas, trying to forget about the dogs.

"Yes, I had shut the windows after all. Lucky for me, because Marina would be angry. *Po,po,po!* Never make Marina angry," he said, leaning in close so she wouldn't hear his teasing routine from the kitchen, where she was sorting out the shopping.

"Marina knows how to kill the chickens ... for the pot. She does it from a young girl, here on this property. She uses a knife, and she is fast, *paidia!*" he added, slicing a finger across his neck.

"I heard that, Andrea," she said as she walked over and placed a wooden tray on the table with the *galaktoboureko*, creamy and shimmering, on a big plate. She then made her own windmill gesture with an outstretched arm, which in Greece indicates surprise, disapproval − or anything you like really.

Marina was a petite woman, with warm, expressive eyes, and most of the time she was the straight guy to the playful Andreas. Like her husband, she had an easy manner about her, and they were like few Greeks we had met so far.

Although Marina had her roots in the rural Mani, she was quite cosmopolitan in her outlook and wore arty clothing, and modern jewellery, much of which she fashioned herself. She was also very thoughtful, and I guessed early on that she liked her free time at the *spitaki*, away from the troubles that beset every family in those days.

The *spitaki* had been in Marina's family for several generations. It had three tiny rooms and an ancient kitchen with a *soba* (wood-burning stove). Outside was the original *fournos*, oven, with a flat roof and heavy metal door, hanging on its hinges. It was a cavernous, dusty space and hardly used, but Cyclops the cat quickly usurped it as a bijou residence, with its clear view of the row of animals' food dishes below.

The house had mainly been used by Marina's grandfather and father during the months of olive harvesting. It had rough walls and flooring, a roof covered with old pantiles, some askew. In winter, the place felt like a colander, with wind rushing through its myriad cracks and holes.

"We're fixing it all up, you'll see. You'll be very jealous when we've finished," Marina told us in the beginning with a girlish taunt.

Somehow I doubted I'd actually be envious of this small house, plucked out of another era and brazenly raw, like those squat croft houses on waterlogged fields in Scotland that are often turned into folk museums, with box beds and acrid, peat-burning fires inside, to reproduce the past, but which instead make you realise why Scots down the ages have emigrated − to anywhere, really.

Marina left us to cut the custard pie into fat, wobbly slices, while she went back to the *spitaki* kitchen to make Greek coffee. This particular brand of *galaktoboureko* was so good, with its rich, sweet filling, that it had become a legend in Kalamata. Made by the Skiadas family, who have had a small shop in the historic centre of the city for several generations, customers would queue down the road for the pie on special holidays and feast days.

Its fame had travelled further afield as well. Sweet-toothed Hillary Clinton, during a state visit to Athens in the 1990s, had heard about it and requested that a box of the custard pie be sent to her hotel by taxi, a four-hour drive away. Maybe she planned to slap her famously lascivious husband in the face with it.

Marina brought out coffee in two large *briki* pots, the hot liquid crusting around their rims, and we huddled around the table, gorging on custard pie. Marina was usually quiet when we all spoke in English because she struggled with it, much like I struggled with Greek.

"Maybe tonight, when is more quiet, you will be see ools," she suddenly piped up in English.

Jim and I looked at each other. "Ools?" I asked, thinking ghouls, or fools perhaps.

"Yes, yes, ools."

"No Marina. Not ools! You mean owls," said Andreas.

Marina smiled over her language mix-up and we all lapsed into silence for a moment, enjoying the serenity of this outdoor space, warmed suddenly by the sun struggling through thin grey clouds. But the mood was suddenly shattered by a volley of ear-splitting gunfire. A cloud of birds flapped, squawking loudly, up into the air.

"That man!" said Andreas, slicing his hand sideways in the direction of a small ramshackle house a bit further up the hill, owned by our neighbour. "Always shooting, and is illegal now."

It wasn't often you heard that anything was illegal in Greece, from parking across the entrance to one-way streets, dumping broken white goods down ravines, to routinely failing to issue till receipts in tavernas.

"Illegal?" I asked.

"Yes, shooting must be stopped after March, to protect the birds and let them breed for next autumn."

Fat chance of that, I thought, as another volley of gunfire rang out through the olive groves.

"So, he's hunting birds then?" asked Jim.

"Not really. Every spring Orestes does this thing, he shoots at the thrushes becows they sit in his almond trees. He won't let even one bird sit in precious almond trees," Andreas explained.

I thought how comical it was that the man with the gun was named after the mythological character Orestes, the great avenger whose role in youth was to find the man who had slain his father, Agamemnon, and kill him. And this one was sniping at thrushes.

Marina was pouring more muddy Greek coffee into our cups. More decisive in her opinions, she gave the final word on the matter.

"No, Orestes just likes to shoot, that is all. *Ekopse tin alisida,*" she said in Greek, which Andreas translated.

"He's cut his chain, *paidia*, meaning, 'gone crazy'. It's a Kalamata expression."

The couple had many expressions for 'gone crazy', as most Greeks do, which was hardly a coincidence in a country that was, for most of the time at least, lovably bonkers and joyously maverick.

We were told Orestes kept goats, and a few sheep, on the slope behind his house and moved them to different locations, including an olive orchard below the couple's property. He often took his animals down the road past the main front gates. Andreas had told us early on that if we wanted to let

Zina off her chain during the day we must put her straight back on it again when Orestes was nearby with his herd, and to keep Wallace out of sight as well. When I asked him why, he just shrugged and looked uncomfortable.

"It is less trouble this way."

What trouble I couldn't imagine, and neither did he want to elaborate, but it confirmed the uneasiness I felt about Zina.

Our neighbour was a gruff old guy. Whenever he passed us on the road in his battered green pick-up truck he always gave us a narrow-eyed stare and occasionally barked a greeting. He never smiled. He must have smiled a lot once because he had masses of wrinkles about his eyes and his skin looked as parched as the Dead Sea Scrolls.

"I don't like the look of him," Jim had said. "We'd better not do anything to annoy him in future, that's for sure."

There was a final lone shot but nothing flew out of the trees, apart from bits of splintered branches. We grimaced.

"*Paidia*, forget old Orestes. You are going to see many more crazy things in Greece now. Have you read about the planned austerity measures for next month? We will have trouble. You wait and see," said Andreas.

Jim and I exchanged looks. Andreas quickly sensed our unease. "But not here. We are fine in Mani. And Maniots, we are tough people. Survivors," he said, not very convincingly.

We stood up to return to the house and Marina got up as well.

"Do you mind if I come with you? I want to get some things from the house."

When we opened the front door, she marched inside and made straight for the *apothiki,* the store room that had been created out of the third bedroom. This strange, cluttered room had come to typify in our minds the difference between the Greek property rental system and the British one. It was a part of the house that was forever someone else's, even though the key was always left in the door. It was a repository of the landlords' lives and would never constitute any arrangement in Britain with its tenancy laws.

Renting a house in Greece is an adventure in itself, as the process is far less regulated than in Britain. Even when you have a lease it offers little security under the law. Or as one Greek friend explained: "Taking anyone to court in Greece for a civil matter is useless, like extracting fat from a fly."

The house had been built by Marina's parents Yiorgos and Iphigenia. After her husband passed away, Iphigenia found the property too much to cope with, so she moved to Kalamata to live with the couple. Since then, Andreas and Marina had used the Paleohora house as a regular retreat, and as a summer house during the children's holidays. It was a good arrangement for everyone, until the crisis turned it into a financial liability, and they decided to rent it out.

It was let with all the family's furniture and their vast collection of memorabilia, and anything else that couldn't be squeezed into the *apothiki*, which was now starting to resemble Del Boy's lock-up.

While we bravely tried to declutter the house, we left the kitchen as it was, a kind of shrine to Greekness, with a heavy, folky bench seat, ceramic partridges on the wall that were the Greek equivalent of flying ducks, and old May Day wreaths. Yet the best thing in the house was also here, the grainy photo of Marina's grandfather selling fish at the seafront in Paleohora from a basket tied to his donkey.

The décor of the house ended up a curious alliance between the Greek family's lifetime possessions and our pared-down existence, with meagre items transported in our car from Scotland, and hardly added to. Yet it was a simplicity of lifestyle that I grew to love, filled with adventure and sensation, rather than personal acquisitions. It was all strangely liberating.

Marina came out of the *apothiki*, her arms piled high with things.

"In the summer, we will spend more time at the *spitaki*. Some nights, too. It's so cool and peaceful there," she said, beaming with pleasure.

Peaceful didn't spring to mind, especially when she told us Iphigenia, and Andreas's mother, who also shared the Kalamata house, would spend many summer days on the property, as well as the children on holidays from university, and other assorted friends and family. We were about to be annexed. Yet I thought it might be vaguely comforting to have the equivalent of a football team around us if Greece slipped into economic oblivion.

3

Saints and sizzlers

THE miniature white church was built on the hillside just above our old village of Megali Mantineia. It had room for only a dozen or so people to stand comfortably inside, but today there was a crowd of villagers and hardly enough room for the *papas*, priest, to swing a censer. Chairs had been set outside the church, in rows, behind an elaborate candle stand, a small forest of thin candles hunching against each other, an icon of Ayios Yiorgos fixed on the wall of the church. This was the feast day honouring this saint, known to us as St George, and it was also the name day for all those called George, or Georgia for women.

After the service there would be a *yiorti*, celebration, and a christening of sorts for the new wood-fired oven built on a terrace at the side of the church and paid for by the village council, which would serve many celebrations for years to come. It was a huge stone construction, with a heavy metal door. Already there were deep metal dishes inside, where lamb, goat and lemony potatoes were slowly roasting.

The chanting from the church reached a crescendo as we arrived. We squeezed into the last two chairs outside the church, where the women were sitting. The sight of Jim in the 'women's section' raised a few looks of quiet indignation as we broke with 500 years of Byzantine tradition. A cloud of incense reached us from inside, carrying the scent of flowers and rosemary. When one of the villagers opened the *fournos* door to check the food, the air also sizzled with the aroma of roasting meat. The women outside the church licked their lips and smiled.

"I think I'll stand with the guys," said Jim, touching his head. "If I sit here too long I think I'll faint."

Jim was feeling delicate that morning, probably from too much enthusiasm over a bottle of Nemea red wine the previous night. He got up and moved to the 'men's section', under nearby olive trees, where villagers were smoking, arguing about politics and waiting for the feast to begin. Our village friend Foteini moved over into Jim's empty seat and gave me a startling smile.

"Glad you came to the *yiorti*, Margarita," she said. Margarita was the name she gave me the first day we met because she couldn't pronounce Marjory, and the name had stuck, just as Dimitris had also replaced Jim.

Foteini was one of the most colourful characters in the village, a goat farmer in her 60s, who still rode her donkey and was what other villagers referred to as a *paradosiaki yinaika,* a traditional woman. When we first met her we were drawn to her instantly because she seemed so lovably eccentric, and was sometimes maddeningly so. She had a rather weather-beaten but handsome face and piercing blue eyes and favoured mannish layers of clothing teamed with an oversized straw hat in summer. Curiously enough, it was Foteini who set the course for our adventure in this wild Mani region.

Back in early 2010, not long after we had arrived in southern Greece, Jim and I had been strolling out of Megali Mantineia with Wallace, trying to decide whether to rent the small stone house we had just seen. Foteini came loping up to us on her donkey, keen to check out Wallace mostly, the small white dog with a black face that she mistook for a baby goat. It was an amusing encounter in which she cajoled us into renting the village house.

"Why not?" she bellowed. Why not indeed! Sometimes an adventure can start with this much simple logic. And for me, it was the beginning of one of the most unusual friendships of my life, with a woman I had nothing really in common with but who would challenge all my assumptions about life.

On this particular day she was smartly dressed for church as always: a black skirt and cardigan instead of the riotous work outfits she wore at her *ktima*, farm compound, with layers of plaid or paisley, sometimes all at the same time, welly boots and a hip holster for her pruning saw. I noticed how demurely she had hooked a shiny black bag over her arm, where normally she might have a dusty kid goat tucked under it, or a sheath of olive wood. It always amazed me how Foteini could keep these two completely different beings running in tandem and flip from one to the other with ease, like Clark Kent morphing into Superman at speed, but without the need for a phone box.

She leaned in closer, smiled sweetly and said in a hoarse whisper: "I thought you might like to take me one day to the olive press near Kambos to pick up some of my cans of oil. They've been there a while but I have a buyer for them. I'll treat you to a coffee."

Coffee would in no way compensate for the winding road that cut through the Taygetos mountains to this popular olive press, but Foteini was never embarrassed to ask for help when she needed it and in return gave us oil or goat's cheese, *myzithra*, which we hated – but it was the thought that counted. It was hard to say no. There was a slightly wily side to Foteini too, as there is with many village Greeks, born out of a need to survive, rather than anything at all sinister.

"Okay, just let us know when you want to go," I said.

Her eyes lit up and she patted my knee.

"Thank you, Margarita *mou*." My Margarita.

The smell of incense had increased and was dovetailing nicely with the meaty aroma from the oven. I licked my lips too. We hadn't had time for breakfast and it was now 10am. Papa Nektarios, the village priest, also seemed eager for the repast because he suddenly sped up the liturgy. After a final flourish of chanting, the service ended abruptly, like a door slamming in the wind. The *papas* strode out of the church, his black robe flapping around his legs like the wings of a giant crow. He gave us a thin look of acknowledgement.

We had been to many of the church services here and in some of the surrounding villages, where he was also the local *papas* because Greek priests have several churches to look after due to an apparent shortage of clergymen across Greece. We sensed that Papa Nektarios wasn't sure about us, or maybe it was *xenoi*, foreigners, in general, and he was probably frustrated by our lack of understanding of all the Byzantine rituals, like women on one side in church, men on the other, whereas Jim and I liked to mix it up. Or not knowing how to receive the consecrated bread, or what to say, or me talking at the wrong times with fellow churchgoers, which occasionally earned the women's corner a thick lashing of incense from an overzealous swing of his censer. Most of the expats in the village didn't go to church services and that was perhaps how the *papas* and the elders of the church liked it, even if the villagers had no qualms about it.

After a few moments of chatter with the congregation, Papa Nektarios strode towards a group of men sitting at small metal tables in front of the *fournos*. They were pouring local wine into paper cups and wishing *chronia polla*, many years, to all the Georges in their midst. A seat was vacated for the *papas*. Greek priests are wondrously charismatic in church in their long robes, and out in the community, also wearing their black stove-pipe hats, a nod to the past. And yet the rural priests are deeply rooted in local culture in a way I've always thought was refreshingly biblical. Like Jesus getting down and dusty with farmers and fishermen. Although Greek orthodoxy is lavish and ritualistic in the city churches, at grassroots level it seems refreshingly natural.

Foteini dived towards the baskets of blessed bread and came back juggling half-a-dozen chunks in her big hands, pressing a couple into mine and starting on the rest. She beckoned me towards the field at the side of the church.

"*Ela, koritsara mou!* Come my girl. We'll get a place on the tables."

I waved Jim over from under the olive trees and we both followed Foteini, who was sprinting towards the edge of the field. This flat space bordered by olive trees, with a glorious view down through orchards to the Messinian Gulf below, had been a gathering place for the village *yiortes* as long as anyone could remember. Four long rows of trestle tables had been set up, covered in the ubiquitous paper tablecloths used in tavernas. Greeks don't do queues and orderly seating, I'd discovered. Here, people were rushing to the tables to be with large family groupings, sometimes fighting over where to sit, as if musical chairs had been introduced to these outdoor gatherings but no-one knew the rules.

Foteini was heading to a table under a bountiful olive tree and one of the villagers, already seated, began to wave in our direction. It was Eftihia, whom we had become fond of in our first year in Megali Mantineia. She was with her mother Pelagia, an older version of Eftihia. Both were curvy and black-eyed, with the same kind of laughter. When they sat side by side, they were like adorable bookends. We settled ourselves beside them.

"*Ola kala stin Paleohora?*" asked Eftihia. Is everything okay in Paleohora?

"Fine. We like the new house, but you know that we miss the village."

She rolled her eyes at me. "Well, you could have stayed, you know."

It was a bit of a sore point that we had chosen to leave the village after the first year because the stone house we rented hadn't quite lived up to our expectations.

"Yes, maybe," I said, feeling uncomfortable. "But we couldn't find another suitable house in the village that we liked, for a decent rent. You remember how we tried. How we had everyone searching high and low for something."

"Yes, I remember. Don't worry, Margarita," she said, squeezing my arm. "You're here today, that's the important thing."

Pelagia nodded sweetly. "It's not far away, Paleohora, is it? It's not like you've moved across the gulf." She gave a big lusty laugh, her shoulders hunching up and down. "My husband moved down here from Altomira in the mountains when he was young and then to Kalamata and back to the village after the earthquake. Now that's what I call moving."

"Paleohora might as well be a foreign land to me," said Foteini, still chewing on bits of holy bread. "I never go there."

Foteini spent her days in her *ktima*, looking after her goats, then rode her beloved donkey Riko home at night and parked it near her old village house. She rarely went anywhere else, apart from the odd trip to Kalamata by bus. And she had never been out of the southern Peloponnese.

"You could ride along the old *kalderimi* from your *ktima* down to the sea, right to our house. I've seen the track," I told her, referring to one of the old cobbled pathways that criss-crossed the hills and had been used by farmers for centuries to get down to the coast.

She gave me an exasperated look. "Go down there with Riko? Pah! He'd never get down there and back. His knees are useless on a hill."

Everyone at the table laughed, and Foteini offered a mock look of disdain, brushing imaginary fluff from her skirt. Other people arrived at our table, and the young village boys, serving as waiters for the morning, started to hand out plates of roast meat and bowls of Greek salad. Glasses were set in front of each diner and carafes of pale village wine. The meat smelt succulent and we suddenly felt ravenous. Everyone piled up their plates.

There were two other women at our end of the table we didn't know, but also Angeliki, owner of the village *kafeneio*, the Kali Kardia (the Good Heart), whom we had seen regularly during our first year. She had been good company and helped me out with my Greek conversation. She often had a good laugh at some of my language gaffes and had a mischievous sense of humour.

"Your Greek has improved a bit, Margarita," she said.

"Just a bit?" I said, remembering some of my bigger language mix-ups, like confusing boy with cucumber, and worms with earrings, because the words in Greek for each set sound very similar.

She nodded. "It will get better if you give it another five years, at least."

"That long?" I said.

"Don't worry. We Greeks make mistakes too."

When we first arrived in the village my Greek was rusty, despite having started learning it years earlier, with the addition of some evening classes in Scotland. As our aim had been to live as Greek a life as we could and avoid being sucked into the local expat enclave, it meant getting my Greek up to speed quickly. I had boned up on all the old textbooks I'd brought from Scotland. Also, as a journalist, how could I write features about the real people of the Mani if I couldn't talk to them?

"What about Dimitri's Greek?" Angeliki asked, with a teasing look in her eyes.

"What's that they're saying?" said Jim, sipping wine and squinting in the morning sun.

"Angeliki wants to know how your Greek is coming along. I think you should say something," I said, nudging him with my elbow.

Jim had put a Herculean effort into learning Greek when we first arrived and finally had a few rudimentary sentences under his belt. The truth is he struggles with languages. He thinks a linguist is a kind of Italian pasta, washed down with a cheeky Chianti.

"Oh God, it's too early for Greek," he moaned.

"Go on, say something. Everyone's waiting."

I could sense his brain was trying to crank something out, but nothing happened.

"Use one of those easy expressions I'm always teaching you, like 'I'm fine as always, thanks'," I said.

"But I'm not fine. I've got a stonking headache coming on … Oh, okay, I know a Greek expression … give me a second."

Jim rubbed his forehead, deep in thought, and turned to Angeliki. The other diners seemed to go quiet. What was the *xenos* trying to say?

"*Den eimai kala… Angeliki …. Haliá … eimai,*" he spluttered.

Angeliki stared at him for a while, then suddenly roared with laughter. The others joined in. Jim looked helplessly at the group.

When she calmed down she announced: "So Dimitri's not feeling good today − he's carpets!"

"What's that she's saying?" he asked me, looking confused.

I was smiling, pleased that someone else for a change was thrashing the language to a pulp.

"You used the right word for feeling bad but the same word also means carpets when you put the accent on the final 'a' instead of the first − *hália*," I said, like some snippy class captain.

"Oh, for fu…!" he said, then laughed. "Well… not so fast, I do feel bloody carpets, I can tell you!"

And he repeated his sentence in a blather of reckless Greek, emphasising the carpets this time and thrashing his feet on the ground to convey the notion that he felt slightly sick and pummelled underfoot today. It was a vibrant piece of amateur dramatics and we were all intrigued to see what else he might come up with.

Angeliki laughed loudly and Yiorgos, Eftihia's brother, slapped Jim hard on the back and said in his colourful John Wayne-style English, learned from too many American cowboy films on Greek TV: "Good, Zim, everybody feel like blady carpets today in Greece. All people of Europe walking over us now in boots, eh?"

Yiorgos was a big man with a thick head of black hair, like his mother and sister. He also had a droopy Zapata moustache and big glossy eyes full of mirth. He slapped Jim again on the back.

"Buggit, Zim, buggit!" It was an expression he often came out with and was his take on 'bugger', unless he was slapping off an early mosquito.

Jim turned to me. "Oh, buggit, Marj! Let's have another glass of wine. Blady hair of dog, eh!" Then he raised his glass to Yiorgos. "*Chronia polla!* (many years), my friend."

@@@@@@

The meal was a boisterous affair and everyone ate a good share. Some of the men at our table had slipped away to join a group sitting around the oven, where Papa Nektarios was holding court. I decided to go for a walk before everyone left for the day and take some photos, mainly for the website blog I had been writing since we arrived in Greece, about our adventures.

When I came across the group of men at the oven, I knew it would make a great picture, with everyone in good spirits, talking and sipping wine. Papa Nektarios was slightly younger than most village priests, with his hair cut shorter, and was very photogenic. He had loosened the collar on his robe, and with this one simple gesture had suddenly become just another village guy having a laugh – until I came along.

When I asked him if I could take pictures, I received a beneficent nod, but I sensed he was uncomfortable about the photos – and not just because he was afraid of the 'off-duty' image he was projecting. I could see it more clearly when I looked at the images later, how he maintained a rather handsome but stoical demeanour, while the other men were falling about, laughing and playing up to the camera. They were lovely images, and comical, but Papa Nektarios's look should have reminded me that there are unknowable depths to Greek culture and it is so easy for a foreigner to step into the abyss. Later that year, I would learn this lesson, painfully.

When I got back to the table, everyone had finished eating, though there were still piles of food on the row of plates down the centre. It was too early even for Greeks to tuck into joints of goat and lamb. One of the women I didn't know got up to leave. She took a plastic bag from her pocket and began to fill it with leftover meat.

The others at the table watched her. She announced loudly: "I'm taking these for my dog, if that's all right." Another woman began to do the same, perhaps emboldened by the first. When they were walking towards their parked cars, and well out of earshot, Eftihia turned to me.

"These women always say that, 'Oh it's for my little dog'. They don't have dogs, I tell you. It's for their dinner. Pah! Why don't they just say it! There's no disgrace in not wanting food to go to waste, or not having money for nice cuts of meat."

The others at the table muttered and Angeliki piped up. "Soon we'll all be doing it, if the Government starts cutting our pensions, and forcing us to sign up to all the new business taxes. We'll all be broke."

Pelagia gave a sympathetic shrug and announced: "*Adia tsepi, zesti kardia.*" Empty pocket, warm heart." It was the kind of sweet-natured thing she often said.

Pelagia's family originally came from the villages deep in the Taygetos mountains and later moved down, seeking land, like most people here, in the more fertile areas such as Megali Mantineia and the plain near the town of Kambos. There was a gentle, slightly innocent quality to her, and a shyness that I had seen in many of the mountain people, including Foteini. Although life was hard in the Taygetos villages, they were spared much of the clan feuding of the lower Mani, as well as the Turkish raiding parties of past centuries. The mountain people had a slightly different take on life.

I liked Pelagia's family. They were solid, decent folk you could depend on, the kind of Greeks that few people outside the country would credit at a time when Greeks were being labelled lazy and work-shy in the foreign press. Yet these people were nothing if not hardworking, long suffering, and gracious with it. Before she left for the day, Pelagia made me promise to call by their house one day soon for coffee and *parea*, company.

The discussion about the two women taking leftover meat continued for a while and then turned to a general debate about the economic crisis, with everyone talking in fast, excitable Greek about how much worse it would get, with more austerity measures planned. There were very few people in Greece who weren't consumed by the economic crisis, and starting to feel stressed about the future. And this was a country where the general ethos was always one of healthy optimism and *kefi,* high spirits. Stress was an alien concept. But not any more.

The economic crisis had been brewing for at least a decade. After joining the euro in 2001, the Greek government had mismanaged its economy with a debt-funded spending spree, splashing out on expensive public projects like the 2004 Athens Olympics, which ran over-budget. As well as spiralling public sector funding, the country's GDP was hammered by deep-rooted tax evasion. In 2009, George Papandreou, leader of the socialist party Pasok, won a snap election, promising to tackle corruption and cronyism, and to get the economy under control. Yet months into his administration, with Greece on the verge of bankruptcy, Papandreou was forced to seek an international bailout.

In May 2010, the group that became known as the Troika (European Commission, International Monetary Fund and European Central Bank), as well as other eurozone countries, approved a bailout package of 110 billion euros, to be paid in stages over the next three years. In return, the government had to pledge — under the terms of the *Mnemonio*, the Memorandum of Understanding — to implement a raft of stringent austerity measures. By the start of 2011, more austerity was planned and Greece was entering a new and more devastating phase of its economic crisis, with an uncertain future.

As the villagers continued to dissect the crisis, one of the men who had been sitting further away moved closer to the group, carrying a small carafe of wine with him. Tassos had been a businessman, originally from Kalamata, and spoke good English, having lived for a while overseas. He had now retired to a villa on the outskirts of the village.

When the discussion began to peter out, he turned to us. "You picked a poor time to come to our country for an adventure, my friends, if I might say so. It's a great pity you weren't here a few years ago. It was heaven. No crisis, a property boom, lots of money, nobody paying any taxes, marvellous government wages. And I know that's not what we're supposed to say now, but life was good for a while, even if it brought us economic grief. We were happy. You should have been here then," he said, taking a mouthful of wine.

"So people keep telling us," I said.

"It surprises me how many foreigners there are in the Mani, particularly the British. And still they want to come here, like the pair of you, seeking…" Tassos opened his arms wide and shrugged his shoulders in a gesture of confusion. "What are you all seeking, even in this time of crisis? Tell me. I am intrigued!" He stared at us both.

"Escape from long winters, that's one thing," said Jim, pouring himself more wine. I could see he didn't care for Tassos's train of thought and took it as smugness.

"Yes, yes, my friend, I know you all come here for the weather and the beaches and Greek hospitality, and Greece is beautiful, of course. But I mean apart from that?"

"Isn't that enough reason though?" said Jim.

Tassos laughed. "Maybe, but if weather and the beach is the main reason, there are sunnier, and easier, places in the world to live than Greece. Like Spain, for example."

"Only if you like Spain," said Jim, sipping a lot more wine.

Tassos wasn't quite satisfied yet with our response.

"What do you really seek to find, my friends, in our country that you cannot find in your own? Forgive me, I mean no insult."

Jim lapsed into a glum silence but my interest was tweaked. What were we all seeking, those of us who came here for more than weather? It was a good question really. Along with: Why are we all so in love with this country? There had been enough of us coming to Greece from Britain, America, Australia, for starters, some from the early 1960s. And that was not counting all the legendary philhellenes: Lord Byron, Henry Miller, Lawrence Durrell, Patrick Leigh Fermor and Bruce Chatwin, whose ashes are interred near an old hillside church in the Mani.

"The answer is, Tasso, we don't really know," I said.

He smiled, but didn't push it further, satisfied, I imagined, that we were just idle dreamers, like most expats he'd encountered. Yet I had often pondered the almost obsessional feeling that many of us have for Greece and decided that while I had the time in the Mani, I would mull over Tassos's question a bit more and see where it led me.

When we made the decision to have a mid-life adventure in 2010, the choice of Greece was an easy one. Jim and I had enjoyed memorable annual holidays here after moving back to Scotland from Australia, where we were both living, in 2000. It was a joint decision, but much of the impetus for this particular odyssey came from me. I have had my own long love affair with Greece through many trips during my life.

My obsession, however, had not started, as it had for casual visitors, while chilling out in a quaint whitewashed villa by the sea, enjoying the sensuality of a Greek summer. My love affair was sparked in the crucible of one of the darkest periods of Greek history, during a year I spent in Athens in the early 1970s, when the country was ruled by a military dictatorship. It hadn't dented my love for the country, not long-term anyway. If anything, the uncertainty of the time, and the drama, only seemed to increase my fascination. Perhaps the current crisis was having a similar effect.

As we moved into our second year of the Greek crisis, increasingly I heard people refer back to the events of the 1960s and 70s with a kind of panic. Could similar days ever return as Greece teetered on the edge, with the risk of default and a return to the drachma always hanging over its head? I don't think that political analysts could see that happening but, in many ways, I also saw parallels between now and the 1970s, when I first came to Greece. These parallels would seem increasingly evident as time went on.

4

Athens, 1970s

I FIRST experienced Greece as a young woman on the long overseas trip from Australia that school-leavers in the 1960s and 70s undertook. More than an Aussie-style 'gap year', it was a rite of passage, mostly for the children of migrant families from Britain or Europe, seeking to go back to the 'old country' to hunt down their roots and fill themselves up with the culture they thought they were missing.

When I left on my youthful odyssey, I had no return date pencilled into my itinerary. With savings from several after-school jobs, I planned to be away for as long as I could, though I didn't breathe a word of that to my parents. I travelled first to Scotland, where I was born, to reacquaint myself with distant family and get to grips with why we'd left in the first place. That bit wasn't hard. Weather! Most of it bad. And there was also a grinding pessimism in that era which devolution, a few decades later, would help to shift.

After a few weeks in Scotland, my breezy Australian outlook was blighted and it was time to embrace the excitement of Europe. I had no doubt what my final destination would be — Greece. It would be warmer, for a start, but there was a more compelling reason for ending up there.

I had been introduced to Greek culture as a newly arrived migrant child from Scotland. My first friend at my Sydney school was Anna, a mainland Greek with a large garrulous family, with whom I spent many summer holidays and regular, long Sunday lunches. My fascination for the country and the people must have been set down in my childhood and never really left.

After a sight-seeing visit to London, I set off for Greece on an overland bus route with a Canadian boy called Rory, whom I had recently met in a youth hostel. He was looking for a travel companion and I tried to see him as nothing more than that, even though he was very attractive, with honey-coloured hair and brown eyes. Anything more than friendship would have been complicated for the young and carefree soul I was back then. Just as well, really, as we were different in personality and cultural tastes. His interest in Greece was no more than a desire to see the sights and tick off another location on his travel wishlist.

The bus arrived near the centre of Athens, four days after we left London, jolting along streets clogged with cars under a filthy brown sky – the *nefos,* smog, that blighted Athens and its antiquities in those days. Rory hated Athens on sight.

"It's just how I imagine Calcutta to look," he drawled disparagingly.

I couldn't agree. I was instantly smitten with the place. It was nothing I could easily define, but more a fusion of disparate things, all maddeningly exotic to my young mind: the incomprehensible street signs, the old people dressed in black, the coffee shops, the bakeries wafting aromas of freshly baked bread and *tiropites* (cheese pies) and all the other smells, even the bad ones – fetid drains and a city still staggering after a long summer heatwave. It all blended into a heady Levantine cocktail. Even today, if I shut my eyes and think of Athens back then, I can sense it, smell it. And in my mind I'm stepping off that bus again on to a city pavement.

As Rory and I walked towards the small hotel recommended by a fellow bus traveller, I caught my first glimpse of the Parthenon, way in the distance, beyond a long narrow street of apartment blocks. Its columns shimmered, even through the *nefos*, like a mirage, teasing you, reminding you of what you were still to discover about this multi-faceted city.

Rory and I had an easy friendship and I was grateful for his company, yet we never agreed on anything to do with Athens. He loathed it, I loved it. He was hanging about the city, visiting a few of the ancient sites, but was mostly considering his next move, scooping up the generous hand-outs his parents sent him regularly through American Express. It had a small office near Syntagma Square, next to Thomas Cook, with its poste restante facility that I was plundering weekly, but only for letters from home, not money. There was none on offer, but I liked my independence, knowing that once my savings ran out, I was completely on my own.

I spent those first few weeks walking around Athens, falling in love at every turn with the unexpected discovery of ruins and museums. My favourite neighbourhood was the old district of Plaka with its mix of neoclassical houses, tavernas, ouzeries and gift shops. Its highest levels were a labyrinth of narrow cobbled streets with small houses that have hunched up against the Acropolis from ancient times, though in different incarnations. Many are said to sit atop a hoard of undiscovered antiquities.

I frequented the city tavernas and the *kafeneia*, too. I knew they were men-only, but a foreign interloper, even a woman, was somehow given more leave to sit, on the periphery at least, watching the men drinking ouzo and gambling over board games. No-one ever bothered me. I liked the whole vibe, the Middle-Eastern click-clack of worry beads, the aroma of the coffee, the conversations that made no sense at all.

I tried to entice Rory to the favourite restaurants and ouzeries I'd staked out, but his favourite eatery was easily its worst – the Golden Gate Hamburger Restaurant near Syntagma Square, with Formica tables and the smell of cooking fat. It must have been a refuge for him, especially with its hubcap-sized hamburgers that could feed a whole family.

One afternoon I told him of my plans. "I'm going to stay on here and get a job."

"What kind of job?" he said, glaring over the top of his hamburger bun.

I had the *Athens News* with me, the English language newspaper that was an institution in the city back then (but closed in 2013 due to the economic crisis).

"There's plenty of work advertised here," I said, opening the pages with vacancies for live-in nannies and private English teachers. Most of the ads had a preference for English applicants because I suspected there was a certain cachet amongst the nouveau riche in having an English girl, particularly with a plummy accent.

He took the paper and read through the vacancies.

"You don't sound very English to me," he said with a sardonic grin.

"That's okay, I can bung something on. I can do Scottish at least. I'll be fine."

"Aren't you being a bit foolhardy? Don't you know there's a military dictatorship in power here, people in jail, freedoms curtailed? I read all about it before I came here. This is a dangerous place, especially for a foreign woman alone in the city."

I had read about it as well, as much as anyone read about overseas politics in 1970s Australia, at a time when foreign news was overshadowed by local party politics and sport. It never crossed my mind that living in a country ruled by a junta was going to impact on my small foreign life. Besides, among the Greeks I'd seen around the city, there was no outward sign of oppression, no threats of violence.

"It frightens the hell out of me, I tell you!" he said.

I often thought about that in the months that followed and wondered if that fear was the thing that marked Rory out, and later led to a situation that neither of us had expected.

"My advice to you is that you should try to look less like a foreign woman because this country is currently very anti-American, anti-West. You're quite young-looking, very girlish. If I were you I'd buy something in black, modest, with stout shoes. Become more of a shadow."

I laughed and nearly choked on my tasteless filtered coffee. Here I was on my first youthful foray outside Australia being told to dress like an old Greek woman. Most of my clothing was functional anyway, including the rucksack I'd bought from an army surplus store in London and I had a thick black coat bought for an outrageous sum at Selfridges. It was perfect for the Athenian winter, which I had been warned would be cold.

However, I later took Rory's advice and bought stout boots in the Monastiraki flea market. I got my hair cut shorter, which removed the sun-bleached highlights from Australia, turning my hair back to chestnut brown. I didn't look too obviously foreign, I thought. I was a not-unpleasant shadow perhaps.

I told Rory I was applying for one of the jobs advertised, working for an English woman who wanted someone to live in and look after her son, as well as improve his English. I assumed she was probably married to a Greek. Their home was on the edge of the north Athens suburb of Halandri, a posher part of the city, with its nearby suburb of Filothei, a quiet backwater housing foreign embassies.

Within a week, the job was mine and I moved out of the hotel. Rory said he was sorry to see me go but we promised to meet up regularly in the hamburger joint and exchange news, though I suspected he wouldn't hang around Athens for long. He was keen to tick a few more countries off his wishlist.

I was excited about working in Athens. Coming from Sydney in the 1970s, a city that felt like a big village, ringed with amorphous suburbs where some people still kept kangaroos in their backyards, and nothing much ever happened, this was pretty major. What the hell! If it didn't work out, I could go back to London and find a job there.

It didn't all go to plan, of course. Nothing ever does, especially in Greece, but it was the start of the long, inexplicable love affair with this country. And I would quickly find out that it would challenge me, right from the first crushing embrace.

5

Foteini goes large

WHEN I arrived at the gates of Foteini's *ktima,* she was milling about, ready to go. Her farm was ramshackle, with a sprawling collection of wooden sheds in the middle, some of which housed her baby goats. The sheds were covered in sheets of corrugated iron pinned down by a collection of old car tyres. There were piles of wood around, anorexic cats, and objects of doubtful usage.

She was dressed in baggy blue trousers, black shoes instead of her usual wellies, and a plaid overshirt. She had a dark floral scarf knotted under the chin. This was only a slight deviation from her usual *ktima* couture and the crazy layers of clothing. Before she locked the heavy gates she came up to the car and opened the back passenger seat and looked around, as if she needed to make sure everything lived up to her exacting standards. I leaned around from the driver's seat.

"Sit beside me at the front," I said.

"I prefer it here. It's safer."

What? The front of the car was less safe than her perching on the edge of a donkey while travelling on a village road, where cars and bikes hurtled along at crazy speeds?

"Okay," I said. After a year-and-a-half of knowing Foteini I accepted that you couldn't argue with her when she had a squinty idea in her mind. Much of her thinking was ruled by her rural superstitions.

She was still examining the car and must have come across some Wallace hair on the back seat. She started vigorously brushing the seat with her hand. I could hear her cursing under her breath. "Mother of God, that hairy animal..."

I smiled and waited for the amusing strop to pass.

"Wait a minute, *koritsara mou.*"

She scuttled back into the *ktima* and returned with a huge piece of sacking. It was dusty and looked like it had seen out 10 years of olive harvests. Yet she put it over the back seat and up the back, trying to tuck it into the headrest. Then she smoothed it down with her meaty hands. I couldn't help but smile at the idea that a sprinkle of dog hair to her mind was obviously a health hazard compared to her ramshackle farm. With the seat good to go, she padlocked the gates, got back into the car and settled down, every now and then plucking a hair off the seat and dropping it on the floor. I could see her in the rear-vision mirror, her face taut and edgy.

"Are you okay now, Foteini? You look nervous."

"Nervous. Me? No, I'm not nervous," she laughed uncomfortably. "What a funny idea."

"Put your seat belt on."

"This," she said, plucking the belt from the fold in the back seat, and letting it ping back.

"You've worn one of them, haven't you?"

"Yes, but I don't like them. You can't get out in a hurry, can you?"

How do you explain seat belts in Greek to a goat farmer? This was going to be a long day.

"Forget it then. I'll drive carefully."

I watched her in the rear-vision mirror, staring nervously out of the side window. As I gunned the engine and roared off down the road, her head rocked back against the headrest. I thought that might make her try the seat belt, but she seemed to have not the least inclination to do that.

"Where's Dimitris?" she said, as if she'd just discovered we'd left him behind.

"Dimitris has a new job for the summer."

"New job?" she said, screwing up her face. I don't think she'd ever got her head around what the old job was.

"Tell me."

I started to explain what he was doing and got myself hopelessly lost and tangled in unfamiliar words, all my efforts stymied by having to concentrate on hair-pin bends and Greeks driving erratically while chatting on their mobiles. The longer explanation would have to wait for another day, when I'd had a chance to strafe the Greek dictionary.

Near the end of our first year in Megali Mantineia we had discovered we needed to increase our funds if we were to stay on in Greece. We intended to keep up our journalism and sell freelance stories about our life in rural Greece to various British newspapers, but that proved harder than expected. Editorial budgets had been cut due to the deep UK recession, but many of our pitches were knocked back because section editors didn't want stories about Greece, a country they viewed as the basket case of Europe.

We also turned to the Australian market, as there were many Australian Greeks in the Peloponnese, and we saw an opportunity to collect some of their stories for possible features. We had both worked in newspapers in Australia and it was where I had started my career in journalism.

Jim and I had met on a popular Sunday newspaper in Sydney, where he was news editor and I was a senior feature writer, producing profiles on well-known figures in Australian arts and showbusiness. To some of our friends and colleagues, the idea of leaving great jobs in 'God's own country' was incomprehensible, never mind having an odyssey in Greece much later.

Although we liked Australia and its sunny lifestyle, we were both keen for a new challenge and decided to move back to Britain in 2000 to experience journalism there. We settled in Scotland, which made more sense than the cut-throat environment of the London media, and it had the second biggest newspaper industry in the UK, centred in Glasgow.

After 10 interesting years, however, newspapers in Britain were in ferment, with takeovers, redundancies, strikes and a general contraction of the industry that affected us both. With the chance to travel again, we struck out for a Greek odyssey.

After the first year of freelancing and battling for commissions, however, Jim was tiring of journalism and was keen to try something else for a while. He was unexpectedly tipped off by a British contact that an upmarket travel company, Apollo Adventures, was looking to expand into the southern Peloponnese.

The company wanted to hire someone with a range of skills, who could research and write information packs for visitors, liaise with villa owners, as well as being a travel rep, meeting people at the airport and sorting out their problems. In spring 2011, he was finally offered the job, which was a thrilling start to another year in Greece.

The first Apollo clients were now arriving in the region and Jim had his first airport meet-and-greet that morning. The only dark cloud hanging over this challenging new job was how healthy the bookings would be that summer, as Britons were reportedly frightened to come to Greece because of the crisis. They feared civil unrest, strikes and disrupted travel plans, especially with the knowledge that Greece might be sliding closer to an exit from the eurozone. Apollo Adventures wouldn't have anticipated any of that when the Peloponnese expansion was on the drawing board years earlier.

But Jim is the kind of man who throws himself into new initiatives, whatever the outcome, and he took up the Apollo job with immense energy, despite the obstacles. He looked smart and reppy that morning on his first airport gig, dressed in a dark polo shirt and beige chinos.

"I hope everything goes brilliantly," I said as he got into the small company car that was part of the deal.

"At least this travel gig will add another string to my bow, eh?"

"If you keep adding strings to your bow you'll be the New York Philharmonic in no time at all."

He drove off, laughing.

How to explain any of that to Foteini? I didn't. I just sat for 40 minutes listening to her curse at the automotive recklessness of her fellow Greeks. The olive press we were heading to was a co-operative venture, where Greeks brought their olives to be pressed using more modern methods than the old presses this region once had in abundance. When the pressing was done, the olive growers picked up their oil in sealed cans. Or they could sell it to the press for a lower price than it was worth on the open market.

Some older clients had their own arrangements and Foteini had left some of her cans of oil at the press to be picked up later when she found buyers for them, as she had scant room in her old village house to store the oil. It was late in the season to be picking up the oil and the press was virtually closed, apart from some routine maintenance jobs.

One of the workers brought out Foteini's six five-litre tins of oil, which was about all the small Fiat car could hold for the hilly journey back. He and Foteini had a short bantering conversation, while he dragged heavily on a cigarette. He eyed me up with curiosity, and asked Foteini who I was.

"This is Margarita. She's a *xeni* from Scotland."

"Scotland? You drink plenty whisk?" he asked in English, shortening the word and making the universal sign for a boozer, thumb jerking towards an open mouth. I always found it amusing that there were two things Greeks would always mention when I said I was Scottish: whisky, of course, generally assuming we started drinking it along with mother's milk; and the blue-painted face of Mel Gibson in *Braveheart*, a film that is, curiously, shown regularly on Greek TV.

For some reason Greeks seemed to strongly identify with Scots. Several times in the Mani I had been told there was a theory that Greeks had arrived in Scotland before the

Romans and had named the country after the Greek word for darkness, *skotadi*. And then, of course, the national flags are both blue and white. Some Greeks had preferred to think we were all 'brothers', or that the kinship might be milked.

He asked Foteini if I had driven her all the way to the press just to pick up her oil. She nodded.

He winked and said in Greek: "Ask your Margarita to find a good Scottish woman for me when she goes home. I like Scottish women."

She waved her big hand at him and told him to be quiet.

"Margarita's not going home. She's staying here. She loves the Mani," she said, like a doting mother.

He laughed heartily, his chest rattling. "She won't say that once the EU has finished with us, and we're under the German boot again." And as if to emphasise the point, he threw down his cigarette butt and ground it out with his foot, sending up a cloud of dust. It had the rough tang of a prediction about it.

"Pah!" said Foteini, calling him a daft goat, or words to that effect, and chivvied me along to the car. She was eager for her coffee stop in nearby Kambos.

Toula's was a small *kafeneio* on the edge of the *plateia* opposite a Byzantine church. The *kafeneio* also served a bit of food, nothing fancy, but with good prices that drew a regular clientele, including expats on a budget. Today there was a huddle of old men inside drinking ouzo, one or two of them rattling their *komboloi*, worry beads, as they watched crisis reports on TV.

We sat at one of the tables outside and Foteini ordered honey biscuits and coffee. Toula brought a tray to the table and sat down for a gossip. I could sense they had a bit to catch up on, so after drinking my coffee, I strolled away and called Jim on his mobile to see how he was getting on at Kalamata Airport. I couldn't hear him very well. There was a lot of background noise.

"How's work panning out, Jimbo?"

"You won't believe it. There's a huge fire across the road from the airport in those dried-out bamboo fields and it seems to be heading this way. I suppose we'll have to wait for the fire brigade."

Only in Greece would fields like tinder boxes in summer be left uncleared next to an airport.

"The family I've got to meet shortly have to make it all the way to Pylos today, which is a one-hour drive. They won't be pleased."

I could hear a lot of shouting in the background.

"Look, I have to go. It's just my bloody luck, isn't it? My first clients arrive and I've got a fire to deal with. I'll call you later."

I hung up. Excellent start to the new job, I thought. Excitement aplenty — and all his strings pinging.

When I got back, Foteini was still talking with Toula. Foteini had eaten half-a-dozen biscuits by now and was wiping away honey-covered sesame seeds from around her mouth with a man-sized spotted handkerchief. It made me wonder how other people viewed Foteini. I was used to her now; the way she often barked loudly when she talked, or slapped people hard but affectionately on the back. Then there was her thick rural accent, her funny ideas.

Being a goat farmer wasn't unusual in rural Mani, as every other person seemed to keep animals, but Foteini was slightly edgier than most farmers I'd met. Even I, with my poor Greek and my beginner's grasp of Mani life, could see that.

Foteini had plenty of *kefi* that day and after the coffee break she wanted to look around the new supermarket next door because normally she did all her shopping in the small general store in Megali Mantineia, or bought things from the hawkers who regularly passed through the village.

She wandered around the supermarket, squeezing everything, starting with the bread. She normally bought the volcanic village loaves that you could hammer nails in with, but here there were 'alien' loaves, long crusty baguettes. She picked one up and squeezed the length of it in her powerful hands. It splintered like a flimsy poppadom, the crusty bits showering the floor. She just ignored them, staring at the denuded stick, turning it this way and that, as if she'd never seen bread before. I looked around in case anyone was watching, then grabbed the baguette and stuck it back on the rack. She looked bemused.

"It's long. Who eats this stuff?"

"*Xenoi* probably, Foteini," I told her.

"Is that what you eat in *Scotia*?"

"It's a kind of French bread."

"French! Then what's it doing in Kambos?"

I smiled to myself at Foteini's innocent grasp of life beyond the boundaries of her *ktima*. After she'd picked up a volcanic loaf, I quickly steered her away from bread and left her to shop while I picked up some provisions of my own.

When we met up again I saw she had a bunch of *horta*, wild greens, in her basket and fruit. She was also holding a clear plastic box of Ferrero Rocher chocolates, wrapped in their distinctive gold paper. She held the box up to the light and gazed at it with wonder, and sniffed it as well. As I watched her, I could feel the start of a giggling fit twitching in my chest. I coughed loudly instead.

"I'm having these chocolates," she said, girlishly.

"Ah, you like chocolates, don't you, Foteini?" I said, remembering that one expat in the village, Bernard, had often brought her chocolates from London. But she never ate them all, especially not after she lost a couple of teeth biting into the hard ones. We were often given bags of squashed melted chocolates to take home.

"I'm going to keep these in my *kaliva* and when I have guests for coffee I'll bring them out. Offer them. *Kalo den einai?*" Good, eh, she said.

She turned towards the check-out and again I struggled to overcome my mirth. The idea of Foteini in her goat compound, where rickety plastic chairs matched her endearingly patched-up table, its central stand spiked into an old paint tin crammed with rocks, serving Ferrero Rocher chocolates, really got to me. It was endearingly mental.

When I dropped Foteini back at her *ktima* later on she made me promise to call by soon.

"Come on Saturday for coffee and we'll have some of those foreign chocolates," she said with an impish smile.

"I can't promise, Foteini, you know that."

"Ach, you're forgetting me already."

This was her favourite catch-cry since we had moved from the village. Before we left in May I told her we would visit her once a week if we could. Sometimes we couldn't keep to that and she would act like a child with separation anxiety. It was both endearing and frustrating, trying to explain that we had other obligations, including work. I realised early on when we lived in the village that although Foteini was an integral part of this close-knit community, was invited to every event and that many people looked out for her, she was something of a loner.

Later in the afternoon Jim returned to the Paleohora house, looking hot and trailing an aroma of burnt bamboo, his blue polo shirt a crumpled sweaty rag, his chinos all sooty.

"Bloody hell! What a day!" he said, opening the fridge and pouring himself a cold beer.

"Unbelievable. We were told at the airport that in half-an-hour the police would arrive and shut the road because it was too dangerous to drive out, so I had to rush around and help organise the family's hired people mover. Two adults and four children, going to a swish villa near Pylos. They weren't too impressed, I can tell you. The father, a wealthy London accountant, started to get tetchy. He said, 'I could have gone anywhere in the world for this holiday, anywhere, money no object, but I thought nah, let's go to Greece. I've always loved Greece. The crisis was worrying enough, but a fire at the airport on arrival? Appalling!'

"I waited until they drove out of the car park. The poor guy looked stressed. The kids were in the back, squealing with excitement. One of them was shouting, 'I want to stay here. I want to see the airport burning!' Honestly, it was almost funny."

"Did they get out of the airport okay?"

"With five minutes to spare. The flames were practically licking at the car as they took the turn towards Pylos. I got away a couple of minutes later. Thank God."

"At least the job's not dull," I offered.

"Not so far. Maybe these Apollo holidays will end up like a novelty tour: Come to Greece and experience a crisis first-hand."

Well, it wasn't far from the truth, and it made my day with Foteini seem pretty normal. And that's something I never thought I'd say.

6

Riots and revelations

THE first June heatwave came on a hot breath of wind from Africa. Even when the temperature dropped from 40 degrees to the mid-30s a few days later, the sky remained an indelible blue and almost cloudless for months. Overnight the lush grass and wild flowers around the house shrivelled, leaving hard, baked earth. We started to eat all our meals on the front balcony. It was like having the best box at La Scala, with a view of the gulf from Kalamata at its head and the Messinian peninsula opposite, where on a good day you could just see the castle town of Koroni at its tip. One morning we saw a pod of dolphins sporting around the coves below, making their way up to Kalamata. It was rare, we were told, and they even made it on to the local TV news programmes.

Every night we were visited by the pair of brown 'ools' that Marina had referred to. They parked themselves on the electricity cable that ran up to the far corner of the balcony. They seemed to be as intrigued by the *xenoi* pair as we were with them. It would have been hard for us to imagine a more glorious place to live. We felt contented here. As for what was happening in the rest of Greece, that was a different matter.

One night we took Wallace down the stairs for his evening stroll among the olive trees on the property. Andreas saw us and called us down to the *spitaki*, where we occasionally sat with the couple in the evening at their big table under the grapevine. They had a small portable TV there, with an electrical cable running across the ground into the kitchen. A few lights were strung up above the table, with what looked like dodgy wiring, but this was Greece, not the home of health and safety. As the months grew hotter, the couple stayed later, waiting for a faint breeze to blow up from the sea, to cool themselves down before their drive back to Kalamata.

They had finished their dinner and were watching the late news bulletins of the demonstration that had rocked Athens that day. The couple were sitting at one end of the table, a collection of cats at their feet, and Zina patrolling about, sniffing out half-hidden bones in the dry earth, snapping at the cats when they got too close. I couldn't see Cyclops, but I hoped he was safely tucked away in his *fournos*.

Andreas was waving his arm windmill-style as he watched the TV.

"*Po, po, po*! Look at this, Marina," he kept saying.

The scenes on TV were an uncomfortable sight. Around 20,000 protesters had gathered in front of the parliament building in Athens that day, jeering at politicians as they arrived by car to debate a second bill on austerity measures. In February 2011, EU finance leaders had complained that Greece had not gone far enough with fiscal reforms in return for its first bailout of 110 billion euros.

The new austerity measures now being debated were demanded by the Troika for Greece to receive the next slug of funds, totalling 12 billion euros, without which it was claimed the country could not repay debts maturing in the next few months. The new austerity demands, with severe spending cuts and new taxes, were also required as a precondition to further rescue funds being approved in the coming year.

This night would prove to be one of the most pivotal in the early years of the crisis, with Prime Minister George Papandreou also facing a vote of confidence in his reshuffled socialist government, which he would gain by the end of the night. The fear of default was a long way from the Greek mindset that night as the country faced more misery with the proposed new austerity measures.

The outspoken Greek economist Yanis Varoufakis (who later became the maverick Finance Minister in Alexis Tsipras's left-wing Syriza government in 2015) was offering sound-bites on the crisis. He explained to foreign media how tough these measures were for Greeks: "The first bailout was put to them 12 months ago and they said okay, we'll take the bitter pill. The bitter pill nearly killed them. And now they are being asked to hope for better results from a larger dose of the same pill, and they're simply not prepared to do this."

During the demonstrations, most of the crowd had been kept back behind barricades near the front of the parliament building, but on the periphery, fighting had broken out between riot police and demonstrators, with petrol bombs being thrown and the police retaliating with tear gas. It looked bad. It was the first time we heard a certain group of anti-austerity demonstrators being referred to as the "indignants" (*aganaktismenoi*), a largely amorphous but angry collection of ordinary citizens who could no longer remain silent at the way their country was being brought down by Troika directives.

Andreas turned to say something to Marina, but she seemed distracted and pale.

"I just think of my two children in Athens, that's all, and hope they don't get caught up in all this stupid violence," she said, getting up and walking into the small kitchen, where we could hear her washing the dinner plates vigorously in the old stone sink.

Andreas bent over the table towards us. "Marina is a very sensitive person. She doesn't want to think about what is going on in Greece. Many people like that now. Don't want to talk about the crisis. Everybody worried."

He mentioned his two children studying in Athens. Adonis was in his third year of a medical degree, while Iphigenia was studying arts.

"We worry they will be drawn into these riots. Sometimes I look at the television pictures and pray I don't see the children there. Ach! I am upside down about it," he said, using a funny translation of a Greek expression.

We watched the progress of the demonstration, then Andreas channel-surfed for a while, stopping at a news show with a discussion about the crisis. A TV anchorman and four commentators, one or two of them journalists, were taking part. It was a familiar scene on Greek television, where studio discussions never took place around a desk, but instead four to six people would be presented, each in a box on screen, as if they were in different locations and yet they each had the same background. They would shout and argue as if they were in an energetic game of the old British TV show *Celebrity Squares*.

Andreas laughed for the first time that night. "Look at these people. Always shouting. Nothing ever gets decided becows they know nothing."

We told him we didn't do TV discussions this way in Britain.

"Really. Not heads in boxes?"

"No. It's a bit crazy."

"Yes, peeerhaps! But everything in Greece now is crazy. Every time we get more money, we will have more cuts, more job losses. More demonstrations. More heads in boxes, eh?"

@@@@@

The heat of June brought the first of a series of earth tremors to the Peloponnese, which would continue throughout summer. It was as if nature were echoing the tension of Greek life and its shifting foundations. Everything seemed to be in a dangerous state of flux. The tremors came with such regularity that some people feared a serious event was brewing, like the devastating Kalamata earthquake of 1986. This was one of the region's worst earthquakes in recent history which killed 20 people, injured 330, and left 10,000 people homeless. The city centre was changed forever with 3,000 buildings destroyed, many of them elegant 19th century mansions.

The Kalamata earthquake still haunts the psyche of its residents, but in this instance Andreas believed the series of tremors we had that summer were nature's way of letting off steam, avoiding a major event. Either way, they were frightening.

We were sitting in the study after lunch one day. The study had been a second bedroom but we had converted it with some of the bits and pieces from the *apothiki*. A large wooden desk stood in front of the window, with a view over the olive orchards to the gulf. It quickly became our favourite retreat.

We had only one laptop with us, and on days when Jim wasn't working for Apollo Adventures and we were together in the study, we had to share it, sometimes arguing over the amount of time we each spent on it or waiting around until the other had finished.

While one person worked at the computer, the other sat on the single bed reading, with a floor fan in the middle of the room for coolness, and Wallace generally sleeping in front of it. When we got tired after lunch we often both squeezed on to the single bed and succumbed to the delicious necessity of a Greek siesta, to the sound of tinkling goat bells − and sometimes Orestes shooting at birds.

That day, I had been working on the computer and Jim was propped against the headboard, reading, when the house started to shake as if it were caught in a small twister. It seemed to last a long time and we stared at each other wide-eyed, terrified it would escalate.

The most sinister feature of these summer tremors was the noise, not the building (on its thick concrete stilts) shaking and rattling, but an eerie sound like wind moaning through the house, from one end to the other. It was as if we had been the victims of a poltergeist invasion. Moments later, the tremor would be over, followed by a preternatural silence. Sometimes another tremor would quickly follow the first.

"If that's a small earth tremor I'd hate to be part of a really big one," I said, trying to get back to the travel piece I was writing for a Scottish paper. My hands were sweaty.

Jim was looking serious, with his arms folded. He always does this when he's about to impart some piece of wisdom.

"I was reading a story on the internet recently about big earthquakes. Some scientists have shown that beforehand, fish will often disappear from their usual waters and domestic animals will begin to act strangely. So, if Wallace starts behaving oddly, it could indicate a big quake."

I was silent for a moment, then burst out laughing. "But how would we know? Wallace is always behaving oddly. Does that mean an earthquake is always imminent?"

"Yes, that was a stupid thing to say, wasn't it?" said Jim, unfolding his arms.

I looked at Wallace, who was lying on his back, with his legs in the air, fast asleep. Oddly enough, it seemed that of all the things that put Wallace into a panic, earthquakes didn't figure at all. I guessed there would be no early warning sign then from the crazy dog and we would simply have to perish.

In the weeks that followed, there were other tremors. One was so strong that things on the bookcase started to jump a bit, though not enough to fall. Only once was something dislodged and it struck me as being rather ironic at the time, slightly comical too. One particularly long tremor brought an icon that was badly hung on an old bent nail on the study wall crashing down into the wastepaper basket by the desk.

We contemplated whether this was some kind of sign, as the icon depicted Ayios Ioannis, the Theologos (St John the Theologian), who had written the Apocalypse, The Book of Revelation, predicting cataclysmic events.

"What does it mean?" Jim asked, rubbing sleepy eyes.

"I don't know. But an icon of the saint who prophesised how the world will probably end, falling in the study during an earthquake? Spooky!" I said, tapping away at the keyboard. "He's probably trying to tell us that we're in for a bumpy ride in crisis-ridden Greece."

"What was in the bin, just out of interest?" asked Jim.

I raked about. "Nothing much, apart from some ripped-up travel brochures I was using for this piece I'm writing. Maybe it's the saint's way of saying the feature's crap. Or that this freelancing business is going down the pan."

"We don't need a saint to tell us that, Margarita," Jim chortled. He had taken to calling me Margarita as well, but mostly he used it when he was trying to make a particular point.

I hammered the bent nail further into the wall and put the icon back. I had been slowly collecting reproductions of icons since I first started coming to Greece. They were small and inexpensive and this one was just a framed postcard of the Theologos that I had carried around for years because it was a favourite, and mostly because I had bought the card from the monastery in Patmos, which enfolds the famous cave where he had received his revelations from God.

This icon depicts a wise old man with his characteristic high, creased forehead, holding a scroll with the words: "In the beginning was the word and the word was with God." Just behind him was an eagle, which in Byzantine iconography is this saint's emblem.

I yawned and squeezed myself on to the single bed beside Jim, under a thin sheet. Wallace was still lying on the floor, his coat ruffled by the fan, sending his distinctive musky smell spinning around the room. It was at least cool here and I lay quietly, thinking about the Theologos and his story.

Originally, he was the apostle John, who had written one of the New Testament Gospels. He was expelled from the Holy Land after Christ's crucifixion and tramped around

Greece, carrying out missionary work, and ended up on the island of Patmos, off the coast of Turkey. He took refuge in a cave near the top of a natural acropolis, where he lived and received his communications from God, which were said to have been so powerful they cracked the roof of the cave with three distinct lines, said to be a sign of the Holy Trinity. He led an ascetic life, sleeping with his head on a rock, relating the prophesies to his own disciple Prochoros, who wrote them down.

I had visited this cave on one of my first trips back to Greece after living in Athens. The cave has a small church adjoining it, and is near a monastery dedicated to St John. Every half-hour or so the cave was deluged by tour groups from buses parked nearby. An old Greek priest had the vexing job of inspecting the groups at the doorway to the church, turning back those who were improperly dressed, like a prim head teacher. There was a lot of moaning from stroppy visitors, including girls in hot pants.

In between busloads of tourists, however, I found a 10-minute window of calm, long enough to sit alone in the cave, staring at icons, the rock bed where the saint lay, the writing 'table', a mere ledge carved out of the side of the cave, and I found it the strangest and most powerful place I'd ever visited. Why? I have no idea, but like so many holy places, it had a palpable calmness about it.

I have always been intrigued by the Theologos and think of him as the patron saint of journalism, the world's first 'celebrity reporter', surely, who got his apocalyptic exclusive straight from God. It just doesn't get better than that.

The other thought I've had about him is darker. A psychiatrist might say the Theologos was probably suffering from a mental illness, hearing voices, having visions about the 'end of all days'. To quote a joke I once heard on the radio: "When you talk to God, it's prayer, but when he answers you back, it's schizophrenia." Poor, dear saint! Until the world is about to end we will have no idea whether the revelations were for real or not. I played around with all these ideas, but in the end it was the superstitious side of me that felt uneasy about a saint's icon falling in a waste bin, especially this saint.

A week later, when I was visiting Foteini at her farm, I thought I'd run the incident past her, as she was superstitious and a mine of Orthodox knowledge. I was leaning on the doorway of her old shed, where she was about to make coffee at her *petrogazi* cooker. When I told her the story, she looked serious, rubbing her sandpapery chin.

"So, the icon falling," I probed gently. "It's not a good sign, is it, Foteini?"

She gave me a squinty look. "The Theologos and the Book of What? I don't have time to read books, Margarita. I've got goats to look after... and I can't get this *petrogazi* to light," she said, sighing and imploring me with her blue eyes.

Not for the first time did Foteini bring my doubts and musings down to a more manageable level.

7

Frugal hearts

IN mid-summer in Greece, everything seems to be pushed to its limit. The ground is baked hard, the air is thick and filled with the shrieking of cicadas, as if they're being cooked alive. Even the sea is dealt with, beaten to a fine molten sheen, *opos to ladi,* like oil.

Despite this agony of heat in July and August, the Greeks seem most content, as if ancient, sun-ripened wisdom has taught them how best to extract raw pleasure from high summer, how to make it a time of rejoicing and release, a time of *parea,* company. Mostly this happens at the sea. As wise Euripides once said: "The sea cleanses all mortal ills." This was especially true during the crisis, when Greeks poured down to the sea in droves, day after blistering day.

"How can we torment ourselves over the crisis when we have all this beauty around us every day? It makes up for everything we have had to go through," said one elderly woman in a broad hat, sweeping her hand majestically towards the indelibly blue waters of the Messinian Gulf. The fact that the coming winter would push the crisis to a new and more heartbreaking level made her comment all the more poignant when later I reflected on it.

In our time in Greece, we also sought out the goodness of the sea, and not just as an easy release from the heat. Some of our happiest hours were spent at the quiet coves around Paleohora, especially at sunset, when families were huddled along the shoreline, delighting in the arrival of a cool evening breeze. Often we would take a bottle of wine and some food and stay until late evening. How easy it felt to be happy.

The Greek writer Nikos Kazantzakis described this ethos eloquently in his seminal book *Zorba the Greek,* translated so beautifully into English by Carl Wildman. The maverick Zorba and the narrator of the book are sitting one evening on the beach by a brazier, roasting chestnuts. The narrator says: "How simple and frugal a thing is happiness: a glass of wine, a roast chestnut, a wretched little brazier, the sound of the sea. Nothing else. And all that is required to feel that here and now is happiness is a simple, frugal heart."

One day we went down to one of our favourite coves at Paleohora, which is hidden from the main road, like most coves along this stretch of the north Mani coast. Yet once you reach them, they offer the most expansive view: the head of the gulf and its mountainous hinterland, Kalamata city along the water's edge and the Messinian peninsula opposite. The coves are pebbled with clear water, and amid their somnolent beauty is a wealth of history, both ancient and Byzantine. There is recent history too.

In the cove we visited that day, I had once been told, several British soldiers hid among the rocks here after escaping from the Battle of Kalamata in 1941, when the heavily outnumbered allies fought a brave rearguard action along the city's seafront against the advancing German army. The men at this cove were later rounded up by German soldiers and sent to prisoner of war camps.

Yet to sit here on a sunny day, beneath the high curved wall of a derelict villa, overhung with fig and lemon trees, it was hard to reconcile that turbulent period of history with the peaceful arbour the cove was now — until Jim's work mobile phone chirped.

"That will be one of the Apollo clients," he said.

When he answered the call, I could hear a loud, frantic monologue from the mobile. Jim raised his eyebrows at me. Finally he managed to cut in.

"Try to calm yourself, Monty. I'll call the property manager right away and explain everything. And tell Casper I'm glad he's okay."

He ended the call. "Disaster! That's one of the actors from London, the pair staying for two weeks in a stone house near Stoupa."

"And they're called Monty and Casper?" I asked.

Jim smiled. "Monty's short for Montgomery Clift. Apparently his mother was crazy about the Hollywood actor. As for Casper. Inspired by Casper the Ghost? Let's not go there, Margarita!"

"What's happening then?"

"You won't believe it. As if they haven't had enough problems, what with the wi-fi cutting out all the time and the air-conditioning hasn't worked properly either. I've phoned the property manager several times but the luvvies say nothing's been done. They have to keep going down to Stoupa to use wi-fi in the coffee shops. They're not pleased.

"Now they've got a bigger problem. The front-door lock keeps jamming and this morning they were locked out. Casper got an old harvesting ladder from the olive orchard beside the house and climbed up to the front bathroom window that they'd left open. Just as he got near the top, one of the rungs gave way and he fell. He wasn't hurt, just some bad bruising. He landed on a thick lavender bush, which was lucky," Jim said.

I immediately thought of Foteini and the olive harvests we had helped her with for a few days. She always used a patched-up wooden ladder, with metal strips she had bound to the crumbling rungs with lengths of wire. Old ladders seem almost mandatory in rural Greece, where there is no fondness for health and safety. But Foteini knew how to navigate duff ladders as well as old olive trees.

"The luvvies are not happy, I tell you, and it's such a faff to get anything done at the house."

The place was owned by a Greek living in Athens, but was managed by a local property agent, who seemed to resent the constant calls, as if they were an intrusion on his precious time. Jim called him from the beach and insisted he get tradesmen out to fix the problems at the luvvies' house.

"Let's see what happens this time," Jim said, throwing the mobile into his beach bag with a sigh.

Early the next day there was another hysterical call from Monty. The property manager hadn't called round to see them and Casper was now feeling out of sorts after his fall. The lack of air-con was also making it hard for them to sleep.

"I don't blame them for being tetchy," said Jim after he'd ended the call. "But Monty's just threatened to write a letter of complaint to Apollo Adventures when he gets back to London. He says the house was a big mistake. They asked for something authentic and rural, but with all the heat, and now a plague of mosquitoes as well, Monty says they feel like they're starring in the movie The African Queen. You've got to laugh really. What else can you do? But Monty's parting shot was, 'I see now why Greece is in crisis'."

"I didn't know Montgomery Clift was in The African Queen," I said, sarcastically.

Jim smiled, but only for a moment. "Honestly, I thought this job was going to be a snip, but the way things are going, this could be my first and last year with Apollo."

It was easy to sympathise with the actors though over the way things moved to their own peculiar beat in Greece. If they moved at all. That summer we discovered a downside to the Road of the Olive Orchards – the water situation.

❦❦❦❦❦

The road was quite steep, though it flattened out briefly opposite our house. This was the place we jokingly called

'Pump Central', where a collection of raggedy pumps sent water to our house and various others further up. Near the top of the road was a slick apartment block owned by Athenians, with a green lawn and a swimming pool and its own 1,000-litre plastic tank and pump, located at Pump Central, even though the apartments were used for only a few weeks a year. As it was positioned to take water first from the mains supply, during the summer there was often a scant supply for everyone else.

It was the kind of crazy situation that we had got used to in Greece, where basic services were a hotchpotch, with little government money to spare. Andreas spent much of August, when all the Athenians had arrived, berating the 'water thieves' as he called them. There were days in summer when we only had a trickle of water.

On one such day, Jim was visiting Apollo clients. I went down to the lower gate at the side of the *spitaki*, where all the pumps were visible. I listened for a while but I couldn't hear any of them working, not even the pump for the large apartment block. Sometimes in summer the pipes along the main road burst and it could mean no water for hours.

All the animals had followed me down, looking for a bit of amusement, including Cyclops and some of the new kittens, born in the summer, and the chickens, which had started to grow on me, mostly for their eccentric behaviour. We had even given a favourite one a name, Aspro, not after the painkiller but the Greek word for 'white'. Aspro was the only white chicken in the russet-coloured brood.

Zina was also there, off her chain. We had slowly started to give her the run of the place during the day, while we were there. We had also started to feed her bones and other treats to supplement her usual diet, the provenance of which we had no idea, except that it was brought by Andreas and Marina from the Kalamata house and stored in the *spitaki* fridge. It was probably some heavy mix cooked up by the two mothers that had passed its use-by date. We never asked.

I decided to go up the hill and call on Orestes and his wife Roula and find out if they, too, had no water, as there was no-one else to ask. First, I chained Zina up at the *spitaki,* which was not an easy task as she was too powerful to hold steady while I snapped the metal ring on to her collar. It was at these times I appreciated her wilfulness and her stamina. I went back to the house for my sun hat and keys and set off.

The heat was oppressive and the road was baking, the cicadas chirping so loudly from every direction I felt I had stereo tinnitus. Swallows were wheeling about in the burning air currents above. There were fig trees along the route and I noticed how fat and purple the fruit was becoming. I plucked a fig down from a low hanging branch and carefully peeled off the thin skin to expose the delicate pith underneath. I split the fig in half to reveal the soft ripe inners and sank my teeth into its glorious strawberry-jam sweetness. Then I plucked down another two and ate them as I walked slowly up the hill, discarding the bits of skin by the roadside. My first figs of the season, well worth a year's wait.

I'd never been to Orestes' house and was afraid he might have dogs. Most people with small holdings had big, slathering dogs chained to trees. Further up the road from here, near a narrow gorge, was a small farm, though all you could see from the road was a mess of shacks, wood, and farm equipment, with a massive grey dog roaming inside. It was usually off its chain and when it saw you on the road it would bark maniacally and run back and forth behind the perimeter fence, spraying spittle everywhere. It scared the hell out of us, especially Wallace. But it was such a typical scene in this part of the rural Mani.

I reached a small gate at the neighbours' house and took the narrow path to the back of it, where the main door seemed to be located. There was a plastic table and chairs set to one side under a tree, reminiscent of Foteini's 'coffee spot' at the *ktima*. There were a few wired-off areas, with parched vegetables growing, but further away I could hear the tinkling of goat bells, which we often heard from our study room at the back. It was otherwise quiet here. Too quiet.

I knocked on the half-open door that led into the kitchen. At the far side of the room the pair were seated, having lunch. There was a strong smell of burnt meat. Roula got up from the table and shuffled to the door. I introduced myself as Margarita, the *"xeni* who lives next door", because that's how people still refer to foreigners, in the Mani anyway. It's a rather harsh word, meaning also stranger, outsider. Nothing inclusive about it. I apologised for disturbing their lunch.

She looked me up and down with narrowed, tired eyes. Over her shoulder I could see Orestes at the kitchen table, head down, seriously communing with lunch, forking chunks of meat into his mouth. He looked as grizzled as I'd ever seen him, and not in the mood for visitors, I imagined. Once or twice his eyes flickered towards the door with irritation, but he never missed a beat with the food.

"What is it then, my dear?" Roula asked.

"Can you tell me if you have water?"

"Water? Yes, we do."

"Ah, I see. It's just that we don't. I thought the water was running low now because of the apartments further up. You know, the 'water thieves'."

She smirked at that. Her husband grumbled something between mouthfuls of lunch. She shot him a wary look.

"We have a tank here, we get some water, unless things are really bad, so I don't know what your problem could be."

Then she did an odd thing. She grabbed me by the arm and pulled me forcibly away from the door, shutting it behind her and leading me out into the blinding sun.

"Look, Orestes doesn't like to hear talk of the water. It's a bad subject. Okay? He gets angry with talk of the water and the Athenians. Okay? And he hates to be disturbed while eating lunch."

"Okay, okay! I'm sorry I've disturbed your lunch."

Then she softened slightly, as much as a rock can soften, or a wingnut can melt. She had a sun-scorched face, lines, messy hair, stout legs, old sandals caked in dust. She looked scary. But more frightening was the thought that Orestes would get his hunting rifle and come outside, brandishing it, to get rid of the pesky *xeni* woman. I kept my eye on the back door.

"Look, *paidi mou*. Today isn't good, but come back another time for coffee, will you? In the morning is best. We can sit at the little table over there in the coolness. And you can tell me all about yourself. Margarita, was it? Lovely name. You're not Greek, are you? You don't look Greek. But you speak some Greek. Lovely. My cousin is called Margarita, such a lovely name. White flower, it means white flower..." She babbled on.

I held my hand up, like Moses pushing back the Red Sea.

"Yes, I know what it means," I said, feeling hot and faint. "Okay, I'll come back another day. We'll have coffee."

Roula shrugged and tipped her head towards the back door, as if to apologise for her annoying, anti-social husband.

"*Ti na kanoume?*" she said, shrugging again. "What can we do?"

It's an expression heard everywhere in Greece, every day of the week. Wallace's vet and our good friend Angelos in Kalamata, a humorous man who had spent time in England and America, explained the frustration of this expression one day while we were sitting in his surgery with Wallace.

"It drives me mad! It's like the Greeks are saying, 'What can we do about... the state of the country or our lives... only God can fix things. Our hands are tied'. You know in Greece

78

there's a joke, 'When a child is born the first words it says are not Mummy or Daddy, it's *'Ti na kanoume!'*" he said, laughing uproariously.

Roula was still shrugging manfully as I waited for the right moment to bolt. I doubted that a coffee morning in this place with this harpy woman would have any pull for me. Perhaps I had a better understanding now of why Orestes came outside sometimes and shot at trees. Before I had a chance to turn and go, she did another odd thing. She squinted at my face and took her forefinger, with a filthy nail, and wiped the side of my mouth with it. It felt like I'd been caressed by sandpaper.

"Figs, Margarita. You've got fig seeds on your face," she said, pulverising the seeds between thumb and forefinger, with a shrewd smile. I touched my face and, sure enough, I seemed to have fig syrup everywhere in my greedy gorging of them on the walk. I wondered if the trees were theirs. Most Greeks around here seemed to own half a hillside each.

I wiped at my face with the back of my sweaty hand. She wasn't done with me yet, however. After weighing up my appearance a bit more, she proceeded to pick Wallace's hairs off the front of my dark T-shirt, flicking them off with disdain. All this from a woman who smelt strongly of goats.

"I've seen your little white dog," she said, still plucking at the T-shirt. "He's very lively, isn't he?"

I didn't like her comment. It had an edge to it. I didn't respond but quickly stepped away from her and said goodbye, walking quickly to the road without a backward glance. I'd had all I could take from the goaty wardrobe mistress. On the way home I felt relieved to be on my own again. I snatched a few more figs off the trees. I hoped she was watching me this time.

It turned out that the water supply was okay, but this time it was a fault in the electricity power board in the *spitaki*, where a small tank and yet another pump were kept under the house to supply water to both houses on the property. So later in the afternoon I waited at the big table with Andreas and Marina while he called electrician friends on his mobile to get the problem sorted. One arrived within 20 minutes, which would have been a record in Britain. But Greeks know how to rally round each other in a given situation. It was a trait that served them well during the crisis.

I told Andreas about my meeting with the neighbours and their funny behaviour. He laughed.

"They are good people. Nothing to do with you, Margarita. Orestes gets angry with us becows of Zina. He doesn't like the dog becows he brings the goats and sheep down here a lot in summer to graze in the field below and he gets nervous with Zina. If you see him, you put Zina on the chain and take Wallace up to the house – or there will be trouble."

"What kind of trouble?" I asked.

He shrugged. "Nothing. Just keep out of his way."

I spent days and weeks expecting trouble – and sure enough it came. One morning I was collecting tomatoes from the spindly growth in the garden behind the *spitaki* because there was never enough water at any time to look after the plants properly, even on good days. I couldn't understand why the couple had gone to such lengths, digging out trenches, putting in spikes and shady awnings, buying dozens of small plants, just to see them shrivel and die.

I had been poking around the yard, squeezing the figs to see if they were ready yet, collecting lemons from trees and herbs from the pots that Marina had put around the property. It was part of the morning ritual at the house. I liked the yard, even though it was scrubby, with bits of Zina's gnawed bones around, overflowing tins for the chickens filled with old withered bits of vegetables and the fat rinds of watermelons, which they loved. It reminded me of Aussie summer days as a kid and the yards we had in various houses, big and rangy, full of adventure.

Zina was off her chain and Wallace was inside the *kotetsi,* annoying one laying hen with his snuffling and barking. The two dogs had fallen into an easy relationship now, which I never thought they would. Zina seemed fond of Wallace, wanting to bowl him into bushes for a lark, with Wallace always remaining just a bit aloof, unless he knew something that we didn't.

I heard goat bells nearby and went out to investigate. I saw Orestes' knife before I recognised him. The blade was long and thick and hanging straight down from his hand beside his leg. He had his back to me, smoking, but slowly he turned, looked at me, an ominous sideways stare, but he said nothing. First guns, now knives!

He looked angry and it crossed my mind that he was perhaps going to slaughter one of the goats in the field next door, unused except for olive harvesting in autumn, and he was annoyed that I'd sprung him. The minute Zina saw him she raced to the fence, leaping about and barking. The goats started to skitter and I thought of what Andreas had said.

I shouted to Orestes: "Don't worry, I will put the dog back on its chain."

He sneered at me and nodded, but kept the knife where it was. He suddenly looked like the hard-bitten bandit Calvera (played by Eli Wallach) in *The Magnificent Seven*, and not someone I wanted to mess with at the house, with not another soul about. I hurried away to get Zina. Surprisingly, she put up no resistance when I called her over to the chain underneath the *spitaki*. She obliged by holding still for once, while I clicked the chain hook on to her collar. Wallace was more difficult, dancing about the yard, and when he saw the goats, he started his loud, screamy bark, and Orestes frowned.

Since he was a puppy, Wallace has perfected this screamy bark, feet planted firmly, head thrown back, and uses it to fend off interlopers, or anyone he doesn't like the look of. As a Jack Russell, or Parson Russell Terrier to use his proper pedigree name, he thinks everyone else's territory is his anyway. It was just one of many mannerisms that arrived early on in puppyhood and which we failed to get to grips with, like the characteristic leaping up and down, so beloved of Masai warriors in Kenya, but more comical in terriers – and terrifying to cold-callers at the front door of our Scottish house.

He also had a tendency to kneecap visitors, by running down the hall as the door opened and leaping at their knees. This, together with a series of high jumps, scared the hell out of most people. When I once commented about Wallace's puppy behaviour to his delightful Edinburgh breeder Brigit, she told me: "Och, dear, they've got their own wee personalities these wee Jackies. Do we want to turn them all into poodles?"

But Brigit also explained that his eccentric, somewhat attention-seeking behaviour was probably in his genes, as Wallace was related to Moose, the first Jack Russell to play Eddie on the hit US sitcom *Frasier*, after an American bought one of Brigit's dogs and took it across the pond. She told us the dogs shared many cheeky mannerisms. Ironically, I used to watch *Frasier* in Australia and fell in love with the dog. That's why we ended up with Wallace. What was I thinking?

Yet taking Wallace to Greece had always been a risk. It was bad enough that domestic dogs were not commonplace in rural Greece, but a crazy Jack Russell was something else. In the village of Megali Mantineia few people had ever seen a Jack Russell before. Foteini mistook Wallace for a small goat or sheep the first time she saw him because of his colouring. Wallace has a white coat and big black patches around his eyes, that make him resemble a farm animal. But to us, he looked like he was wearing a Zorro mask, which suited his cheeky personality.

I doubt that Orestes had ever seen a dog like Wallace either, and I could tell he wasn't amused. Wallace was racing about under the olive trees, scattering cats like pinballs and making a spectacle of himself, yet there wasn't much Orestes could do about any of that from the other field, unless he had his gun with him as well and planned to shoot through the fence. That's when I remembered I had unchained the bottom gate that morning to go across and check Pump Central and hadn't locked it again. Orestes would have seen that. A guy like him notices everything.

Wallace kept up his mad sprint, with Orestes looking on. The idiot dog was determined to die.

There was no time to chain and padlock the gate. I needed to get Wallace into the house quickly. So I pulled out the big gun of dog obedience – and yelled "CHICKEN!" I only used the 'chicken' word in emergencies when all else failed with the disobedient Wallace. It was the one 'command' that always brought him to heel because of his obsession with chicken. It was all the fault of Brigit, who had a heart of gold but, unwisely perhaps, fed all her new puppies on chicken, thus creating picky eaters forever – like Wallace.

"CHICKEN!" I yelled again, and Wallace came this time. My hands were shaking but I managed to scoop him up under my arm and hurried back to the house, without looking back. The unchained gate would have to wait until later.

That night, when I was telling Jim about the day's drama, I wondered what might have happened if the dogs had somehow got out through the unchained gate and bothered the goats. The way Orestes looked, I knew he was capable of doing whatever it took to protect his flock. Quite right too, but I felt nervous having this weird cowboy living beside us. Another day in Greece on the edge? Or just another day in Greece?

I had been coming to Greece all my life since the early 1970s. I love the people for their spontaneous warmth, .charm, stoicism, all the things that came to the fore, even in a crisis, but I can't say I always understand the Greeks. They are a bewitching, complex, passionate, spontaneous, illogical race, hospitable to a fault, clever, funny, full of character, tough, fearless, but verging towards maverick, law-breaking, and some would say *poniroi*, cunning, a word that is heard often in Greece. Take your pick there, but the full-on Greek colossus is not a stereotype that sits easily with those who have a British temperament.

When we lived in Megali Mantineia, one of the gentlest of farmers, Leonidas, who helped us sort out several problems that our landlord couldn't deal with, once told me: "Even we Greeks don't always understand the things we do. So how can foreigners?"

He was right, of course. But my confusion over the mesmerising but maddening Greek character began a long time earlier.

8

Athens, 1970s

MY new job as a nanny and English teacher started in the autumn. Nikos and Deirdre Papadakis, lived in a salubrious part of Halandri, on Odos Lemonias, Lemon Tree Street. The lovely name had come about as there had been a huge lemon tree in the middle of the street for as long as anyone could remember and perhaps it was, in years gone by, part of an orchard. Ironically, once I moved to the apartment and started working for the couple, the job began to feel like a bit of a lemon.

When I went for the interview, I met Deirdre on her own. She was an attractive blonde, sensibly English, very capable, if slightly uptight, and perhaps it was no coincidence that her husband had been absent on that occasion. Nikos was diametrically different. He had a huge personality and was bold and charming when he wanted to be, which squared up well with his Cretan background, though there was little of the dashing *palikari* about him now as there might have been in his youth, when he was thinner and fitter. However, on his bad days, and there were many of those, Nikos could also be shambolic and cynical, all of which led to a lot of sniping between the pair. What myopic matchmaker had lashed these two together in matrimony was anyone's guess. It was Mary Poppins meets Zorba the Greek.

None of this seemed promising for a rookie from Australia, however, and in those first weeks I began to wonder if the job would last. Yet there were compensations. I liked their six-year-old son, Pericles. He was rather sweet and shy, with blond curls. He didn't look at all like a Pericles and at any rate he was called Perry at home.

Their flat was rented but it was big and pleasant, on the ground floor of a small L-shaped apartment block which, because of its layout, meant the apartment had its own entrance on the ground floor, leading off the main balcony. I had the bigger bedroom at the front of the house.

The wages were reasonable and I had most Sundays off, and every Tuesday, up to the late afternoon. Deirdre taught English in the evenings in a local *frontistirio*, private coaching college, and gave lessons at clients' houses during the day and on Saturdays. Deirdre had come to Athens as a graduate for a summer adventure in the 1960s, before the junta came to power. She ended up staying, found work as an English teacher, and met Nikos at a party, when life in Athens was more carefree.

Deirdre now worked long hours, which is why I had been employed, but she didn't interfere with the way I looked after Pericles, or with the English lessons I gave him. She also didn't care that my accent was more fruit bowl than cut-glass and laughed when she imagined how Perry might end up speaking like an extra on *Crocodile Dundee*. I wasted no time in teaching him a few funny Aussie songs and very soon he found the word kookaburra a lot easier to say than *koukouvayia*, owl.

The main problem was the antipathy between the couple. I tried to keep out of their way, which was easy with Deirdre because she was always out working, and difficult with Nikos because he never was. But because I saw more of Nikos during the day, I also learnt more about him than I ever did with Deirdre, who remained slightly distant. I began to realise that although Nikos was difficult to live with, he had earned much of his moodiness and cynicism. His youthful ambitions had crashed amid the disaster of life under a military dictatorship.

He had been a well-respected journalist on an Athens broadsheet until the military coup took place in 1967. The paper closed down rather than have to co-operate with fascists. It managed to pay out most of its staff, so there had been some money in the beginning for the Papadakis family, and the years that followed had brought various jobs offered by friends, but not much of it was journalism.

Five years later, with the dictatorship seemingly entrenched, Nikos had become embittered and decidedly middle-aged. His career was now just a pleasant memory. In terms of his marriage, I sensed the political problems had merely exacerbated an untenable relationship.

Nikos had a routine, even if it was a bad one. He left the house at 10pm, spent the night in ouzeries and bars with friends and came home early in the morning. He slept until midday, long after Deirdre had left for the day. They spent a couple of hours in the house in the early evening, but it was hardly together. Most of the time, when he wasn't in bed, Nikos sat in the boxy third bedroom that had a sofa and TV, smoking and drinking coffee, and Deirdre worked or sat reading in the kitchen, or on one of the balconies.

It was a curious, even depressing, arrangement that should have impacted on my young life in a strange and edgy city. And yet it didn't – not in the beginning, anyway. I was comfortably distracted by keeping Perry amused and up to date with his English, working our way through his vast collection of children's books. His English was already quite good, as it was the main language in this household. Nikos was pretty fluent in English because his father had run a successful business in Crete and there had been money for private classes.

During the holidays, Perry and I spent time walking around the neighbourhood, or in the park in the afternoons, where other expat nannies with more salubrious gigs — employed by bankers, lawyers and company directors — turned up with their charges and moaned about Athens, politics and Greek men. Mainly the latter.

On my free days, I roamed the city, visiting the Acropolis most weeks, wandering around the Parthenon and marvelling at my good fortune in being able to spend some of my youth in this glorious place. I also visited the museums, the flea market in Monastiraki and the gift shops, where small copies of the Parthenon sculptures vied for space with stripy cheesecloth shirts and worry beads.

The Agora was not far away. This was the gathering place where Plato and Socrates had regularly strolled and argued the toss about philosophy and politics, and despite being in ruins, it still had the weight of history about it. On some days you could stand in a wasted corner of the Agora amid fallen columns and the wind blowing through overgrown grass conjured up a murmur of voices, the sense of which had been lost in time. It wasn't hard to fall in love with Athens, with its mix of east and west, chaos and logic, mess and perfection that all seemed madly exotic.

I met Rory a few times in the hamburger joint and I wasn't surprised when he told me he was leaving soon for Turkey, and then possibly Israel to work on a kibbutz. I could tell he was keen to leave Athens, a city he had never grown to like. I knew I'd be sorry to see him go. We shared a special bond, having travelled to Athens together, the first real adventure in life for both of us. While we lunched on giant hamburgers, I told him about my mismatched employers.

"You sure picked the wrong job there. Those two will have a massive fall-out and you'll be stuck in the middle," he warned.

I laughed. "It's okay. If that happens there's plenty more work around. I'll be fine."

"Sounds like you're planning to be here a long time."

"At least until the summer. After that, who knows?"

I gave him the phone number at the house and he promised he'd call when he was in Athens again, on his way back to London.

In the next couple of months, life settled into a quiet routine. I motored softly around Deirdre and Nikos's domestic arrangements and their moods as if they were a couple of landmines. One day I asked Deirdre what had happened to the previous nanny.

"Ha! Nikos frightened her off with his disgusting habits. Hope he won't scare you off as well."

Nikos's moods were mostly related to his late-night carousing in Athens with his friends and he was often hung over and tired. Occasionally I heard him coming home at 3 or 4am, fumbling his key in the door, and then crashing about in the kitchen, fixing his dinner, as he called it. One morning I found Deirdre clearing up the remains of a chicken meal, the bones gnawed and scattered on the table beside an empty whisky bottle. Her face said it all, as she tidied up with grim determination.

Whenever Deirdre derided Nikos for "acting like a slob" he would shout: "Blame the fascist bastards who run this country, not me."

In the beginning of my stay in Athens, even as I learnt facts about life under the dictatorship, I found it hard to grasp the enormity of it.

I was brought up in a sunny, open place where people weren't sacked for their political beliefs, or dragged from their homes in the middle of the night and sent off to a distant island gulag and tortured. In 1967, when tanks were rumbling along the streets of Athens, I was a teenager hanging out at milk bars after school and learning how to body surf at Cronulla beach in Sydney.

In April that year in Athens, a group of officers, led by Colonel George Papadopoulos, engineered a coup. The reason for this swift and brutal 'revolution', as they called it, was to stymie the alleged infiltrations of leftist sympathies in the Greek judiciary, press and government departments and to overturn the political power of Georgios Papandreou Snr, who started the political dynasty that would dominate much of Greek politics for three decades.

Papandreou became Prime Minister in 1963 with his Centre Union party and had given a portfolio to his Harvard-educated son Andreas, who was a left-wing, outspoken opponent of US interests in Greece. There were fears that under this government, communism would have a resurgence. Papandreou was forced to resign in 1966 over an argument with the young conservative King Constantine II over reforming the military. With new elections looming in May 1967, a group of obscure officers carried out the swift and decisive coup. Both Georgios and Andreas were arrested, and George Papadopoulos declared himself Prime Minister.

The roots of the coup were complex and could be traced back to the bitter hatred between the Left and Right and the civil war which raged from 1946 to 1949. The war had been fought between Greek communists, fresh from fighting in the resistance movement against the German occupation in the Second World War, and the Greek government army, backed by Britain and America.

Once the colonels seized power, martial law was declared, civil liberties were suppressed and the press was censored. In the first few days thousands were arrested. The secret police tortured dissidents, and often their families too, in locations around Athens and on the infamous island prisons. While the CIA may not have engineered the coup, as many people have alleged, the regime was propped up by the US because of Greece's strategic position in the volatile eastern Mediterranean. There was strong anti-American feeling in Greece after the coup, but when the US formally recognised the dictatorship in 1970 it created another huge wave of antipathy.

Cultural life was suppressed by the colonels. Many books were outlawed, including the works of Aeschylus, Sophocles, Euripides and Aristophanes and modern writers Jean-Paul Sartre and Arthur Miller. All the works of composer Mikis

Theodorakis, who put modern Greek music on the map, were banned because of his left-wing sympathies.

In my first months in Athens, Nikos told me never to speak about the regime in public, never to mention or carry the books of the writers who were outlawed. Even humming the tune from the film *Zorba the Greek* (scored by Theodorakis) in a public place could end in arrest.

"Welcome to the home of democracy," Nikos told me.

Unless I indulged in outlawed behaviour, as a foreigner in Greece in the 1970s I had a small amount of immunity and some elements of Western culture were 'tolerated' by the regime, though none of this guaranteed a safe ride. For most Greeks, however, the situation remained grim and oppressive.

"We'll never get rid of these fascist bastards," said Nikos one day. "We might as well hammer a nail with a sponge, as Greek villagers say."

There were intervals of levity in the house, however. When Nikos was in a good mood he was a funny, mischievous soul. I had just started learning Greek from a phrase book I'd bought. Nikos took great interest in my progress and liked to goad Deirdre about it.

"Did you hear that, Deirdre, Marjory *wants* to learn the Greek language?" Deirdre didn't like speaking Greek and never spoke it at home, unless there was something she didn't want me to understand.

One Sunday morning I offered to walk to the nearby *artopoleion*, bakery, to buy some bread. I asked Nikos how to ask for bread in Greek. He told me and I practised it as I walked along the street. The bakery was busy. Several women were waiting to pick up their trays of cooked lamb or chicken with lemony potatoes, and the aromas were mouth-watering. In those days, few Athenians had ovens. Everyone took their trays of meat to the bakery to have them cooked in the giant *fournos*, on a Sunday morning especially. There were also big baskets of bread with their warm crusty aroma. When it was my turn, I said my piece, clearly and loudly.

The old baker threw his head back and laughed loudly – and all the women joined in.

I shrugged. *"Ti einai?"* I said simply. What is it?

One of the women spoke some English and said in a stage whisper: *"Paidi mou*, you've just asked the baker for a man's pinis," she said, with charming mispronunciation, pointing to her groin. I looked confused.

"No, that's not right? That's not what I said."

She nodded. "Yes, *psomi* is bread, *psoli* is pinis."

Everyone was laughing again and it dawned on me. Nikos had set me up.

"Whoever told you this," said the woman, *"Einai kakos anthropos*, he is a bad man. Now you must go back and tell him *dropei sou*, shame on you!"

With my two loaves of volcanic bread, I hurried back and dumped them on the kitchen table, saying: *"Dropei sou, Niko!"*

Nikos got such a laugh out of it, he nearly cried. Deirdre was hovering around the kitchen table and rolled her eyes.

"Niko, *malakas eisai*!" Wanker!

I learnt two lessons that day: not to confuse bread and penis again. Second, in the midst of national tragedies – and there have been many in this country – there was always great humour and eccentricity, without which Greece would probably never have survived.

9

Is there a rinse cycle for madness?

"YOU'VE forgotten me!" Foteini shouted down the phone when I answered a call one night at the Paleohora house. She said it so often now on the phone it had become her normal salutation.

Mostly it was amusing, but occasionally I regretted giving her our phone number. With rural logic, she simply couldn't understand why, when we seemed to be folk of leisure, without goats to herd or *myzithra* cheese to churn, olives to pick, and all the time in the world, we couldn't make it up the hill once a week as we'd promised.

Moving to Paleohora created the problem that I had anticipated in the first year when I started to befriend the villagers in Megali Mantineia. We would never be able to maintain the same level of involvement in their lives now that we lived down the hill and didn't see them as much, sharing in their day-to-day dramas. Yet the problem evaporated when we were with them because they were generous with their friendship and made you feel you had never left. As our village friend Eftihia would often say, bear-hugging us: "*I agapi paizei rolo.*" Love plays a role.

While Jim was working for Apollo Adventures I had more time on my hands and one Saturday, on a sweltering hot day, I drove up to the village to see Foteini at her *ktima*. I took Wallace with me, as I didn't want to leave him alone in the house in the heat. It always intrigued me how Wallace — despite his crazy behaviour at home, his aversion to bugs, rattling plates, the sound of doorbells on the TV and a host of other things — whenever we took him out somewhere, he generally rose to the occasion. More than that, Wallace was an incredibly stoical beast who could put up with more than we gave him credit for. The fact that he could sit quietly in Foteini's compound while it teemed with hyperkinetic goats, hornets and other hazards aplenty, not forgetting loud and barky Foteini herself, was a divine mystery to me.

When we arrived at her *ktima* I found it transformed suddenly from a ramshackle farm into a kind of old British bath house. Foteini had rigged up a large plastic tub on a table for washing clothes, with a hose leading into it and the overflow water sluicing down past her *kaliva,* shed, towards the back of her farm, bordering on a small gorge. On the way, the water formed puddles, the edges of which were patrolled by the worst kind of hornets, orange beasties with red, dangly legs that made them look like toxic jellyfish with wings. There were piles of clothes everywhere.

Foteini was singing loudly, dressed in her most bizarre outfit yet, a straw hat and her normal layers but with a big piece of plastic sheeting tied around her middle and up round her neck. She looked like she was cling-filmed ready to be shoved into a microwave oven, and she was steaming underneath it all, so that I fully expected to hear the sharp ping of an oven timer. Despite the water feature, the place oozed with heat, made worse by the fact there was a persistent, hot African wind blowing.

Foteini was wearing thick rubber gloves and when she turned and saw me she clapped her hands and danced around in front of the washtub, offering a song to my name, the old Theodorakis classic *Margarita Margaro,* which was amusing at least.

"See, I haven't forgotten you then, have I?" I said.

She smiled. "Have a seat for a minute, then I'll make the coffee."

But Wallace, who suddenly looked hot and bothered, had other ideas and pulled me over to where Riko the donkey was tied to a tree with an old industrial-sized feta cheese tin in front of him that was always brimming with water. Wallace plunged his face in it and slurped up some water, while Riko looked on. I heard the crackle of plastic before I saw Foteini beside me, puffing, hands on hips.

"You can't let the dog do that! The water's for Riko!" she yelled, as if we'd all gone suddenly deaf. It was one of her peculiarities. When she felt passionately about something, she shouted. She also showed her predilection for treating the donkey as if he were a minor deity, which was touching in its way.

"It's not for dogs. Riko could catch something. I can't do without Riko."

"What could Riko catch from the dog?" I asked, slightly exasperated, as I sometimes was with her rural superstitions.

"Things," she offered, with a shrug.

She then grabbed the donkey on either side of his face with her hands and kissed him lavishly on the muzzle, whispering endearments. His eyes flickered towards me, cartoonish and pained. After refreshing the feta tin from an old hosepipe, Foteini crackled back to her washtub. Behind her back, Wallace took another dive into the tin and slurped up some more divine Riko juice before I pulled him away. I could see this was going to be a day of madness, as if the planets were in some mischievous alignment. After a half-hour of this, I would want to dive into her giant washtub and swim a few reviving laps.

I sat on a thick plank of wood set between two rocks that constituted a seat at the side of the makeshift wash-house. I put Wallace up beside me, more out of devilment, and we silently watched the washing ritual as Foteini dunked clothes into the tub, creating tsunamis of water that cascaded all over the parched ground below. Then she smacked the items together in her gloved hands in a frenzied routine that went well beyond any heavy-duty setting on a modern washing machine. Foteini had a strange obsession with washing, and doing it outdoors at that. Not that she had much choice. There was no washing machine in her old village house, and anyway the thought of Foteini dithering over 'pre-wash' or 'delicate cycle' made me giggle. This extreme, rural wash was more her style.

There was so much about Foteini that was still unknowable to me because of the language barrier, and there were points at which I felt our friendship was stretched beyond comfort. But there was so much there also to admire. In the time I'd known here I'd seen her endure many hardships: the olive harvest for months on end, carting olive wood in a bundle on her back from the orchards to her *ktima*.

We had spent time with her, too, after thieves broke into her *ktima* and slaughtered three of her beloved goats for the meat, leaving a bloodstained butcher's knife at the scene. This left her distaught and we sat with her the day after in her village house, trying to cheer her up. It was the only time I had ever seen Foteini cry. I had thought her too tough for tears. But, of course, she wasn't. The incident had brought suggestions from other villagers that it may have been time for her to retire. But she was having none of that.

"Pah! Retire? What would I do then?" she once told us, with a mischievous glint in her eyes. "No, I'll just keep going until I fall out of an olive tree one day and die. That's my kind of retirement."

It would make a fitting epitaph for Foteini — "the woman who fell from an olive tree" — having seen her antics up in trees, never mind with wash tubs. During the olive harvest there was no-one more fearless.

She pulled off the rubber gloves and slapped them down beside the washtub.

"Come down to the *kaliva* and I'll make coffee."

There was a ritual to coffee with Foteini that you couldn't overturn. You were always placed at the rickety plastic table under the mulberry and fig trees, while she retreated into the shed to brew Greek coffee in a blackened *briki* on her old *petrogazi* cooker. The shed was old and battered and I had only ever glimpsed its dark interior from outside. The door, however, looked like it had never seen a lick of paint and was scrawled with names and phone numbers.

"Is this your phone book?" I teased her once. I could see numbers there for a taxi, a doctor, the names of different people in the village, farmers she regularly bought things from. The only peculiarity in this was that there was no phone here and she didn't have a mobile. She once asked if she could phone someone on my mobile. She knew how to use one at least, but it was comical to see her trying to jab at the touch pads with her breeze-block fingers. She gave up in the end and let me do it for her. I'd have liked to have seen her sending a text though.

The table outside had a rather jaunty addition to it now, an old blue and white beach umbrella that we had given her when she complained her 'outdoor area' was too hot. With typical ingenuity, she had jammed the umbrella pole into an old olive oil tin, filled with rocks. The area had a certain uncanny vibe about it and we had christened it Foteini's Kafeneio, even though it was like no other coffee spot on the planet and not likely to be up for a franchise agreement any time soon. And the world was a lesser place because of that.

I put Wallace on one of the scuffed plastic chairs in the shade and out of reach of the huge, mutant ants that were advancing on a pile of discarded banana skins on the ground. When Foteini came back out with the tray of coffee, she bumped it down on the table and stood staring at Wallace, her hands on her hips.

"Dogs sitting at tables now. What else can we expect?" she said, with a comical tilt of her head. "Would he like some coffee too?"

"Later on, maybe," I said, winking.

She brought glasses of water filled from the tap at a stainless-steel sink propped up on a plank of wood at one end and an ancient ironing board at the other, which was probably the zenith of invention on this eccentric farm and made me smile every time I looked at it.

"I've got nothing else to offer you, Margarita. Sorry!" she said with a pout.

"Not even the Ferrero Rocher chocolates?" I asked, teasing her. "You know, the ones with the gold wrappers?"

She gripped her lower lip briefly with her top teeth. "Ah, those. All gone. Can't keep them in this heat!"

I smiled. I expect they were never brought out for guests and doubted that Foteini would have many visitors here anyway, apart from a few goat farmers who came by to talk business now and then. I'd never seen anyone else from the village here. Even they seemed to feel the *ktima* was a world apart – and that was saying something.

While we sat sipping our coffee, she kept her gaze firmly on the dog. We didn't often take Wallace to the *ktima* because there were too many hazards for a pernickety dog like Wallace, not counting Foteini herself. But whenever we did take him, she seemed amused.

"Why don't you get a dog for your *ktima*? It would keep your goats safe," I said. She laughed loudly, her plastic apron crackling like a forest fire.

"What kind of dog, one like Vassie?"

Vassie was the name the villagers had given Wallace because they couldn't pronounce the English word.

"One that's scared of hornets and flies, sits on chairs and drinks coffee? That's all I need when the goat thieves come around with their knives."

I knew she meant no offence. It was just her rural cynicism about any creature other than a goat or a donkey.

"Ach! Dogs are too much trouble for me, and too expensive."

"Pity I couldn't lend you the dog that guards the property at Paleohora. She'd sort out your thieves."

She gave me a terse look. "You mean that big brown one, looks like a wolf?"

I nodded.

"I heard about that one. I know your neighbour in Paleohora, Orestes. His wife Roula comes from my village in the mountains. I see her sometimes in Kalamata market. She told me all about the big dog. *Po, po, po,* Margarita! I'm not having that one."

I couldn't decide what was more alarming – Orestes' wife gossiping about Zina, or the fact that Foteini had a connection with our crazy hillbilly neighbours.

"What did Roula say?" I asked.

She gave me the 'no-comment' gesture, that maddening thing that Greeks do, when they shut their eyes, tip their chins up and tut at the same time. It means 'can't speak, won't speak'. I let it go, as it was too hot to hear Roula's views on Zina. I kind of guessed what they were already. But I was curious, and when I finally left Foteini, pegging out all her washing on a rickety piece of rope slung up between olive trees, I decided to stop in the village on my way home and find one of the goat farmers who was the go-to man for any farming/animal gossip.

I found Theodoros in one of the tavernas, sitting with a farming companion, drinking ouzo. I joined them for a while, happy to be out of the hot sun. They asked me the usual question about life "down there" and about the house and how it must have been better than the tiny stone house in Megali Mantineia, which most of the villagers had agreed we paid far too much for, rented to us by an English expat.

I didn't even have to quiz them about Zina, as they started the conversation anyway. "How is Vassie getting on with the big brown dog?" asked Theodoros.

It amazed me, as it always does, how Greek villagers know everything that goes on within a 10-mile radius at least, and everyone, man and beast.

"You mean Zina?" I asked them, and they nodded. "She's a bit big and energetic for Vassie, but okay."

Their eyelids flickered heavenwards. No comment. Finally the other man, Panayiotis, broke ranks and said: "Your little dog will be all right, I think. It's the sheep that should be afraid of Zina."

"What do you mean?" I asked, and they told me a story that didn't delight me much. But neither did it surprise me, and it seemed everyone in Megali Mantineia knew this terrible tale.

A few years back, when Orestes kept a lot more sheep, he was grazing them in the pasture below our house. While he was away having lunch, a stray dog came down the Road of the Olive Orchards and spied the sheep. The dog moved fast and started to maul the sheep. Zina must have been watching from the property, and perhaps enticed by the smell of blood, she managed to jump over the fence at the bottom, near the lower gate, and joined in the killing frenzy.

By the time they had finished, 20 sheep were dead. When Orestes came back, running down the road after hearing the commotion, he was out of his mind with anger and the two dogs scattered when he fired a few shots at them, but missed. The stray dog never came back but Zina did, much later, and Andreas let her back into the property, mortified by what he'd heard about the incident.

"That's a terrible story. But Zina can't jump that fence. I don't know if you've seen it, but it's too high," I told the two farmers.

Their eyes flickered. "She was younger back then. She was a powerful dog," said Theodoros. "Still is."

"But it's hard to believe Zina has it in her to kill sheep," I said.

"All big, powerful dogs have it in them," said Panayiotis. "And it caused your landlord a lot of grief at the time, not to mention the payout to Orestes."

He held up his hand and rubbed his thumb and forefinger together with great emphasis to indicate quite a bit of money. I must have looked panicky, but they told me not to worry. "Just so you know," they said. "Just be careful."

I thanked them and wondered if I was better off knowing the story or not, and yet it only confirmed what I instinctively felt about Zina – that she was a bit wild and unpredictable. And to think she'd once slept in our bath during a thunderstorm.

I made a mental note that despite the way the two dogs were getting on, I would keep an eye on them when they were together on the property. I didn't doubt that Zina could kill a sheep, or even a small dog like Wallace, if he got in the way of her food bowl and her ferocious appetite. I now understood why Andreas kept telling us never to leave her off the chain when we weren't there. It was all fitting into place.

"That means she could still get out. I bet she can jump up to the side pillars on the lower gate," I said to Jim later that day when I told him the village story.

"Hmm. I don't see how. It's still a big jump for an old dog."

"But not impossible. And it explains why Orestes was standing in the field that day with a knife in his hand. He was expecting something perhaps."

"Have you ever thought that the story might not be true, a bit of village gossip, a wind-up?" asked Jim.

"Those two guys, they're not like that. They're decent people. But why didn't Andreas just tell us the truth about Zina?"

"Maybe he didn't want to frighten us. Maybe he was embarrassed and just preferred to keep it to himself," said Jim.

I laughed. "There's no such thing as keeping something to yourself in rural Greece. Everyone knows this story."

I remembered what Angeliki from the *kafeneio* had once told me: "Greek villagers can see into your very soul."

"It took place a while ago," said Jim, "I really doubt it would happen again."

Zina might have been too old now to tackle sheep, but even without the story the two farmers in Megali Mantineia had told me, I always had the uneasy feeling that Zina had it in her to play the minx one day — big style. That day wasn't far off.

10

Mani's best friends

IN Scotland, people are obsessed with the rain because there's so much of it, and so many types of rain. There's the cold persistent stuff that lasts for days and weeks, or the minx of all downpours, *smirring* rain, as the Scots call it, that falls like gossamer, feels like nothing at all but within 10 minutes you're soaked to the bone.

In Greece, the obsession lies with the winds: which direction, hot or cold, dusty, dry or moist, persistent, maddening. Only the fisherman can give you all their proper names. They are among the most lyrical words in the language: *tramoundana* from the north-west, *pounendes* and *maistros*, the west, *levantes*, the east. The most despised is the *sirokos* that blows from north Africa and is often weighted with the dreaded *skoni,* brown desert dust that darkens the sky and settles like cement on everything. The *sirokos* is the wind the Greeks say can drive you crazy. It makes you fit for nothing, apart from lying in a dark room with your eyes swathed in cucumber slices.

One Saturday afternoon, I was down at the *spitaki* with the couple and their children Adonis and Iphigenia, who were on holiday from their Athens universities. We were gathered around the big table under the shady grapevine, eating slices of watermelon, which seemed the only thing to do while the *sirokos* was blowing, hot and heavy, but not laden this time with dust.

The kids didn't seem to mind the wind or the heat. They were glad to be out of Athens in the summer and back home, particularly the handsome Adonis, eager to hit the party circuit after another gruelling year of medical studies in a university already suffering strikes, textbook shortages and other problems due to the crisis. The pair had been sleeping over some nights when the parents weren't using the *spitaki* because the Kalamatan house, to their young minds, was the uncool stomping ground of the *yiayiades*, grannies.

The kids liked the *spitaki*, as if it were the grown-up version of a tree house, a cute hangout where they sometimes brought their friends at night for innocent gatherings on the tiny top balcony under its vibrant grapevine, where fat bunches of grapes hung like an ornamental ceiling. They would light candles, sip a can of beer each and talk into the night, which would be the equivalent of a Bible-reading group in the UK.

Sometimes the friends would sleep over, but mostly only Adonis stayed at the *spitaki*. When the heatwaves of summer arrived he took a single bed from the *apothiki* down to the balcony, where he often slept under the stars, listening to Greek music on his CD player. Simple pleasures.

Marina had half-renovated the place, painting the tiny sitting room white, decorating it with memorabilia from the family, bits of donkey saddles, baskets, photos. It had a certain charm, but the lower bedroom, where Andreas and Marina often slept over, was dark and cramped. It was hard to fathom why they liked staying there so much when they had a comfortable house in Kalamata.

"In Kalamata, everyone is worried about the crisis, everyone stressed," Andreas once said. "At work the men talk about nothing else but crisis. How they will manage, how they will keep their jobs, and find work for their children when they leave school. Ach, for Marina and me, *afto einai to katafigio mas* (this is our refuge)."

That afternoon, everyone was subdued, including the animals. Zina was sleeping under an olive tree. Wallace was sitting on the bench beside me, panting hot, pungent breath.

Jim arrived home not long after the last slice of watermelon had been consumed. He'd been out most of the day, visiting some more of the Apollo clients. He'd never quite sorted out the luvvies earlier in summer. The air-con and the wi-fi never worked to their satisfaction and Monty had been bitten viciously on the face by mosquitoes. The poor man claimed he would need a kind of Phantom of the Opera mask for his next theatre production. The pair were so annoyed they were demanding compensation from Apollo Adventures.

Today's gig had been easier and comical too, Jim told us, slugging back a chilled can of beer from the *spitaki* fridge. A group of retired head teachers from England were having a week in a fabulous villa near Kardamili, with its own walled garden and swimming pool.

"These guys are all in their seventies and hysterical. While I tried to give them the usual informative chat about what to see and do in the area, the oldest guy sneaked inside, changed into a big baggy swimming costume and came roaring out through the terrace, shouting 'Last one in's a sissy!' Then he dive-bombed the pool, while the rest looked on, gobsmacked.

"I also heard an incredible story from a young Greek woman who owns one of the nicest villas on Apollo's books. Christina told me she was inside a couple of days ago, getting the villa ready for new arrivals. There was a knock at the door. She opened it and there was a guy outside, dressed in a sharp suit, holding a briefcase. There was a black Mercedes parked outside and a big guy at the wheel in flashy sunglasses, who looked like a chauffeur and bodyguard. The first guy told Christina he was Russian and asked her in broken English if the villa was for sale. She told him 'no' and that she ran a business there.

"He said, 'I know. I have heard your villa is excellent and I want to buy it from you'. Just like that!

"She said, 'It's not for sale!' but the guy wasn't put off. 'I can offer you any amount you like. I have cash in my briefcase. I give you whole amount now'. She told him to leave, and after a lot of persuasion, he eventually did, but reluctantly. She said the man frightened her. But just imagine, Russians carrying enough euros around with them to buy houses on the spot!"

Everyone suddenly became more animated. "*Po, po, po!*" said Andreas, slapping his hand on his thigh. "Did you hear that, Marina?"

She hadn't understood all the English and he explained it to her in Greek.

"Stupid Russians!" she said.

The family had a heated discussion about the story, which I couldn't quite follow.

"The Russians are the ones with money now. They are vultures waiting to prey on Greeks in crisis. They want the best houses, even some of the islands. Greece is for sale now," said their son Adonis, who spoke very good English. "It's good this Christina didn't want to sell. Plenty of Greeks would say, 'Yes, take my villa. What will you pay me?'"

"Would your family sell this property to a Russian?" Jim asked light-heartedly, in the spirit of the previous banter.

Marina understood and jumped in first.

"Ha! We die first than sell our house to anyone!" she said, her eyes wide with fury. "This is all for the children one day."

Iphigenia and Adonis were sitting side by side and beamed happily. Who wouldn't be pleased to inherit this huge property, among several others? It was also a peculiarity of Greek rural life that almost every family seemed to own a clutch of houses, often old village wrecks, left to them by family members, which is why so many Greeks are asset rich but cash poor. Despite the crisis, and new property taxes, it seemed that few families, in the southern Peloponnese at least, were in a rush to sell their spare properties. It was either a sign of economic madness or an indication of how deeply most Greeks feel about their ancestral lands.

Later in the afternoon we left the family at the table and decided to go back to the house for a siesta, as we both felt exhausted with the heat and the African wind, and the gulf had become too choppy for a swim. Wallace was asleep on the wooden bench.

Andreas saw I was about to call him.

"Leave Wallace here, sleeping. It is okay, *paidia,*" he said, smiling sweetly at him.

"Are you sure?" I said. "He might get himself into trouble."

"No! He is no trouble. When we leave for the day, if you are still in the house sleeping, I leave him with Adonis."

I knew that Adonis was planning to go out that night to a local club on the seafront with a group of friends, but I imagined we would be up well before then. I reminded myself that I worried too much about Wallace and, so far, Zina hadn't done anything to cause us alarm. In fact, they had fallen into a kind of slapstick Laurel and Hardy relationship, with Wallace as Laurel and Zina as the big bumptious one.

Up in the house, we immediately fell into a deep, dreamless sleep and didn't wake until the early evening, which was late for us. I started fixing dinner and Jim went outside to water some of the pots on the steps, where we were growing mint and basil. I could hear Jim calling for Wallace, but he never appeared.

"It's very quiet at the *spitaki*. They must all still be sleeping," he said when he came inside.

I finished cooking and set the table on the balcony, where we now ate most of our meals. The wind still felt hot but the sight of the gulf and the ever-changing colour of the water was soothing. The sun was beginning to set and the sky was streaked with pink and purple. The 'ools' had just arrived and settled on their stretch of electricity wire, hooting and nuzzling each other.

We had now rigged the TV up on the balcony, where there was an aerial socket, as this was the only place in the house we could sit at night comfortably. Greeks live on their balconies in the summer, watching TV and talking loudly, well into the early hours.

Jim went off to have a quick shower before dinner, and with everything prepared, I decided it was high time I went to fetch Wallace.

When I got to the *spitaki*, however, I was surprised to find the place in darkness. There was no sign of the family, their car had gone and the gates were all locked. There was no sign of Adonis either, or the dogs.

I returned to the house just as Jim was coming out of the shower.

"It's the oddest thing. There's no-one about and I can't find Wallace or Zina. Adonis can't still be sleeping, surely?"

"Maybe Adonis has left already and took the dogs to the bar with him," said Jim, smiling.

"Very funny, Jimbo! Zina and Wallace at a bar, ordering lagers and texting on their mobile phones? I don't think so! Have you had too much African wind today or what?"

"Probably," he said, ruffling his hair with his hand. "They do say it drives everybody mad."

"Or maybe the wind sucks things up into a vortex of *skoni* dust and they disappear. What about that?" I said.

Jim looked suddenly thoughtful. "Okay, I think I should stroll about the property and see what's going on."

"Good idea."

While I set the table for dinner, I kept peering over the balcony and saw Jim pacing around the front of the *spitaki*, calling out for Adonis, but there was no sign of him. Then he walked to the back of the property, through the olive trees, calling the dogs and now and then shouting 'CHICKEN!' That made me smile, but only for a moment. When he came back, he looked puzzled.

"I don't know. The dogs have definitely vanished, that's for sure. I'll have to call Andreas."

He fetched his mobile and called, but Andreas's phone was switched off. I then called the Kalamata house but one of the mothers told me the couple weren't home yet.

"They're probably driving back now," said Jim. Andreas was one of those rare Greeks who always switched off his mobile when he was in the car.

We decided to stay calm and have our dinner at least because, logically, the two dogs could never have got out of the property. Perhaps all would be revealed when Andreas called. It was dark when we finished our meal, but still we hadn't heard from him.

"I say we get the torch and go up the road and look for the dogs, just in case," Jim said.

The main gate to the big house was a heavy sliding contraption across the driveway. It had a small inset gate as well. Both were locked. We unlocked the smaller one and stepped on to the road.

"Either the dogs have been abducted by aliens or they've jumped over the fence somehow," I said.

"Even if Zina could jump over the fence somewhere, what about Wallace? He can't," said Jim.

I was starting to panic. What had gone on here?

"Okay," said Jim. "Let's go right up to the top of the road and see if we can find them."

We shone our torch along the edges of the road as we ascended, and also into the olive groves. Further up, beyond Orestes' property, there was only the Athenians' apartment block with a stout security gate, followed by the squalid farm and the big grey dog, barking and slavering as usual. Beyond this point was a heavily wooded ravine and more olive groves and fields all the way to Megali Mantineia. It was a big area roamed by a few wild dogs, foxes, and probably wild boars as well. There was no trace of the dogs.

We turned back and walked past Orestes' house. It was quiet there, too.

"Do you think we should just ask him if he's seen the dogs?" said Jim.

I was horrified, thinking of my last encounter with our neighbours. "God no! If he thinks the dogs are on the prowl he'll get the shotgun out straight away. Thrushes in the almond trees will be nothing to this, Jimbo."

"Let's just walk up the path to his house and have a look about."

There was nothing stirring on the property, apart from the snuffling sound of the farm animals in their pen at the back of the house, where the land sloped gently down into a gully. I tapped Jim on the arm and whispered: "I hope Zina hasn't led Wallace down there."

"Wallace wouldn't touch a farm animal. He'd be scared stiff. Remember how he used to run away from rabbits in the Scottish fields when we were out walking?"

While we were huddled together, whispering about the dogs, I felt something tap me hard on the shoulder. I squealed in fright and turned around to find Orestes behind us – with his gun in his hand. He was wearing some kind of hat. He looked like the movie fiend Freddy Krueger. My stomach did a spirited cha-cha.

"What the fuck!" said Jim loudly.

"What are you doing here?" Orestes snapped.

I panicked. "It's the water again. We've got no water. Have you?" That was all I could think of.

"Water? What is it with you *xenoi*? Always water. Can't you wait til morning? And why are you shouting? I heard you shouting something up the road."

It was true that when we got to the top of the road, where the undergrowth became thicker, we shouted "CHICKEN!" a few times to see if that would attract Wallace's attention, but there was no response. That had made me really worried.

"We weren't shouting," I said.

"Sounded like foreign words to me. Sounded like 'Zina' as well. You weren't shouting for those dogs, were you? Those dogs aren't out, are they?"

"Dogs? No, no, no! The dogs are…home in their…beds," I said, my mind a muddle of anxiety. He laughed loudly. It was a rough sound like a gate in need of oiled hinges.

"In their ships! The dogs sleep in ships? *Panayia mou*, holy virgin, what have we here?" he said, mouthing a few other colourful oaths.

For a minute I thought he'd flipped, but I quickly realised I'd had another language malfunction. I'd said *karavia*, ships, instead of *krevatia*, beds. Fear and anxiety was the cocktail shaker of my mixed-up Greek.

Orestes looked me up and down. His knuckles were white in the moonlight where he gripped his gun. We said goodnight and skittered down the path. We didn't turn round again but sensed him standing for quite a while, watching our retreat.

"Why was he laughing?" said Jim.

I tried to explain in haste but it occurred to me that even the right word 'beds' to Orestes would have been hysterical. To the rural mind, the idea of dogs in any kind of bed, and not on the end of a chain, would be outrageous.

"If he comes across the dogs in the night, I'm sure he'll shoot them," I said to Jim, with a tremble in my voice.

"No, he wouldn't dare, but I think we should go back home and call Andreas again. He will know what to do."

"Should we tell Andreas we know about Zina and the sheep?"

Jim rubbed his chin. "That's a tricky one. Perhaps not. He'll be embarrassed. Right now we just need help to find the dogs."

We walked down the hill past the olive groves, the dark heads of the trees with their sticky-up branches looking almost human, as if they were crouching, all ears, listening to us chattering on. Even dogs would feel unnerved out on this impenetrable hillside. I thought that if the dogs had had a good adventure outside they would want to come back at nightfall. They would have barked at the gate. They would bark now if they heard us. When we got back to the house Jim rang Andreas again, and this time he answered. He told Andreas the whole story but looked defeated when he hung up the phone.

"Andreas says the dogs were playing about with Adonis when the couple left and they were fine. He said he'd call Adonis on his mobile and find out what happened after that. He said Adonis must have left the property before we got up and in his rush to be with his friends he forgot all about the dogs – wherever they were." I could just imagine Andreas going: "*Po, po, po!* You know what the young peoples are like, *paidia.*"

"Andreas just keeps saying the dogs must be on the property somewhere because it's impossible for them to get out. He says we will have to wait until morning, and if they haven't come back to call him again."

We sat on the balcony watching TV but every time we heard a noise outside we got up and peered over its side edge, with a view of the front gate, hoping the dogs were back. There was nothing.

"We couldn't expect the couple to come over right now and help us. They've both got early starts in the morning," I said. Andreas was a manager at a food supply company, west of Kalamata, and Marina worked for a government health department in the city and, like everyone in Greece, they both feared for their jobs.

"There must be something we can do. How can we go off to bed when Wallace is out there? I think I'll take the torch and go along the road for another look."

Jim was out for at least half-an-hour. He looked tired and worried when he got back.

"Not a thing. I don't even want to think what's happened to them."

We felt helpless. Greece is one of those places where you fall on your own reserves when things go wrong, and people survive by having good friends and contacts. There are few support groups, especially to help animals. And calling out fire brigades to rescue cats from tall trees would be an act of lunacy here.

We went reluctantly to bed and even though we were exhausted, neither of us slept much. Several times I got up and wandered out to the balcony when I heard the sound of barking, though none of the dogs had Wallace's screamy delivery. At least once I heard gunshots but couldn't tell whether it was from Orestes' property or further up the hillside, and I tried not to think of the chilling possibility that the dogs had wandered into his animal enclosure. I don't think I had passed a worst night in Greece.

We were both awake at 7am. We felt exhausted but needed to get up and see if the dogs had come back. While I fixed some coffee, Jim went outside to check at the front gate and returned with a long face.

"Nothing."

The home phone rang. I picked it up. It was Andreas, wanting to know if the dogs had returned.

"Not yet," I told him.

"I work this morning, but as soon as I can, I am coming to help you find them. And you must wake Adonis now, he will help you." I didn't bother to tell him that Adonis had not come back to the *spitaki* after his clubbing night, as far as we could tell. Missing children were a step too far.

We got ready to go out again on another search but just as we were walking down the front steps we saw a red pick-up truck stopping near the big gate. We gasped when we saw Zina leaping out the back of the truck. I couldn't see Wallace, though. We reached the small gate just as the driver was getting out. I was overjoyed to see it was Yiorgos, the brother of Eftihia from Megali Mantineia.

"*Kalimera filoi mou*, hello my friends. Are you missing a dog?" he said, pointing to Zina.

"We've lost Wallace," I said, ignoring Zina for a moment.

"Ah," he said, earnestly twiddling his big moustache. "You mean this little guy?" He leaned into the back of the truck and picked up a filthy grey bundle of fur, depositing it on the ground at our feet. I felt sick with dread. A lifeless Wallace.

"Come on, little guy," said Yiorgos, and Wallace finally shook himself and got up slowly. He was almost unrecognisable, but I was mighty relieved to him again.

"We've been looking for this pair since yesterday. How did you find them?"

"I was driving down the English road from the village," he said, smiling. He called it by the name the villagers had jokingly christened it because it had been settled mostly by English expats six years earlier, when a local builder had sold plots of land for 'dream homes'.

"I see the two dogs running on road. I did not know the brown one but I see Vassie, even though he is carpets, eh my friend," he said in English, slapping Jim on the shoulder. "*Xaliá* remember?" That was his favourite joke now and he wouldn't let Jim forget it. "You are lucky you get them back. Someone might have stolen, or shoot with gun. Mani, all cowboys."

"Come in for coffee, Yiorgo. I've just made some fresh," I said.

"Sorry, but I'm on my way to do some pruning work for a friend," he said to me in Greek. "But why don't you call by one afternoon to the house to see Eftihia and my mother. They will like that and Pelagia hasn't been very well."

"Oh, I'm sorry to hear that. Nothing serious, I hope."

"Ach, Margarita, my mother has had some health problems for a long time, but she's doing fine."

"Tell them I will come and see them as soon as I can."

When Yiorgos left we set to work on the dogs with a bottle of shampoo. We tied them to one of the concrete pillars of the main house, where there was a water hose. The two dogs were filthy but there were no signs of blood – theirs or other animals'. They stood side by side, moaning and shaking under the jet of water, until the job was done.

They were now at least the best of friends but it was clear that Zina had been the boss of this Colditz escape operation. What surprised me was that Wallace, who was afraid of flies and bees, had the nerve to disappear from the house and have a sleep-over on a Mani hillside with a she-wolf sheep-slayer. Was Wallace becoming a fully-fledged terrier after all, getting in touch with his inner rebel? Was this the terrier equivalent in Greece of riding a motor scooter with a trombone in one hand and a take-away cappuccino in the other? You think I haven't seen that in Kalamata?

Andreas was mystified by the break-out and that evening when he arrived at the property with Marina, he scoured the perimeter fence, scratching his head, walking about and making lots of windmill gestures to express his amazement. As for where the dogs had been all night, he had no idea.

"It never happens before, Margarita. Zina out all night. I think they fly off somewhere and come back in the morning. Magic! Becows can't be nothing else."

It would take quite a while before we discovered how the dogs had escaped – and it was nothing like we had imagined. It also confirmed my belief that Zina was a rebel with paws.

11

Greeks in a lather

ONE Saturday morning in late September, Andreas knocked at the front door, looking very animated. "Come quickly, *paidia*! Marina's mother is down at the *spitaki* making soap. Take some pictures if you like."

The first thing that jumped into my mind was how bad things must be getting in debt-ridden Greece if people were now making their own soap. What would it be next? Tooth-paste, loo paper?

Andreas was excited, saying it was the first time he'd seen this rural practice. And two hours later, he swore it would probably be the last. But this was not an invitation you could refuse, so I fetched my camera and notebook. Even Wallace scooted out the door, keen to see what was bubbling away below.

We were used to seeing the old house in various states of makeover and had seen Marina on many weekends painting old furniture in folky hues and hanging baskets up around the wooden beams of the kitchen, with sheaths of dried lavender and other herbs. But what awaited us here was like a scene from Shakespeare.

A huge black *kazani*, cauldron, with long legs had been set up on the concrete terrace in front of the *spitaki*. It had a fire roaring underneath and Iphigenia senior was stirring the pot with a long stick. She was curiously well dressed for the occasion in a smart woollen skirt and blouse but wearing stout rubber gloves and a straw hat. She had strong features, a commanding presence and was handing out orders.

Andreas rolled his eyes towards his mother-in-law. "She's the boss with the soap. Do exactly as she says, *paidia,* becows it is trouble if we don't."

While she stirred, Iphigenia told us this soap-making method had been passed down through the generations of her family and was taught to her as a child, growing up in a nearby old property on a cliff top that we could clearly see from the balcony, but which was now crumbling on to the cove below, its roof caved in. In this one small coastal area, it seemed as if the skeletal remains of Greek family dwellings lay everywhere, beyond help, heaped upon Homeric ruins.

Iphigenia used the same four ingredients her mother had used: old olive oil, water, caustic soda and ash, which apparently helps the mixture to bind together. This unappealing combination all went into the pot, where it had to be stirred continuously until it went from a runny yellow mess to acrid soupy consistency. It looked like something the Maniots might once have poured from the top of their famous stone towers on to the heads of marauding Turks below.

Iphigenia was stirring the mix, peering at it closely.

"It will be ready when dark bubbles rise to the surface," she said, with portent, like Lady Macbeth in box pleats.

Andreas took a turn at stirring the mixture. It was fiendishly hot and gave off a stinky aroma. After 20 minutes he looked like he'd just run a mountain marathon.

"*Po, po, po!*" he said, wiping rivers of sweat from his forehead.

"If Greece goes bankrupt you might have to be doing this all the time," I said, winding him up a bit.

"Ach, not me. I will refuse to wash."

Iphigenia smiled at this younger Greek attitude and the idea that life was tough now, with all the austerity measures.

"When I was young, growing up in the Mani, we had *real* austerity," she said with emphasis, sounding more like a tough Yorkshireman with a handle on comparative miseries. "We had to make do with the things we made ourselves, like soap. And before anyone had a washing machine, we all washed our clothes in a *kazani*, like this one."

When I told her that in Megali Mantineia, Foteini still washed this way, or had done until her cauldron was stolen, Iphigenia's eyebrows pinged skywards.

"Margarita and Dimitri know all about village life up there," Andreas told Iphigenia in Greek, pointing towards the hills behind, and then explained that we went to the village a lot to see our Greek friends. Although the Paleohora house was a 15-minute drive from Megali Mantineia, it seemed like another world to the couple, and one they had no urge to investigate. Too raw, too many reminders perhaps of how their ancestors had lived. Yet rural life in Greece wasn't a thing of the past, it survived in a kind of parallel world.

The thought occurred to me once to take the couple up to meet Foteini, but even they would have been shocked at how rugged her life was. Making soap with the mother-in-law was as far into the past as they were willing to go, unless the crisis got much worse.

When the mixture had thickened, it was poured into wooden drawers from an old cupboard, lined with sheets of plastic, where it would stay for a few days inside the *spitaki*, ready to be cut into large blocks – about 80 or so. It seemed to me like a massive faff when a bar of soap was pretty cheap, but I think Marina, with her endearing penchant for turning the *spitaki* into a small folk museum, was keen to keep this tradition alive.

While Iphigenia and Marina finished storing the drawers inside the *spitaki*, we sat at the big table with Andreas, drinking beers and enjoying the warmth and solitude of this leafy property.

"See what we have to do now?" he said with a wink. "But seriously, we are lucky here. We can live quietly and cheaply.

We can do things to help ourselves. We can make oil from the trees, and we have the garden. And all this."

He waved expansively down towards the gulf, with its calm blue water. A bright blue and white caique was describing a huge lazy circle across its surface, a fisherman dropping a yellow net in the water to be retrieved later. When you live in Greece what you come to appreciate most are the simple rituals of life: old men drinking coffee in a village *plateia*; the harvesting of olives; the iconic image of a caique.

And the components of life here are also simple and eternal.

The distinguished 20th century poet Odysseas Elytis once wrote: "If you were to take Greece apart, in the end all you would have left would be an olive tree, a grapevine and a boat... and with these things you can rebuild Greece."

Andreas started to outline his money-saving ideas.

"Marina is going to stock us up with more fresh chickens," he said, slicing his finger across his throat.

"No," said Jim, "not the chickens. We've just got used to them. We've even given them names."

"Really? You give chickens names?"

He called Marina over to the table. "Marina, did you hear that, the *paidia* have given the chickens names."

Her eyes were dancing with amusement.

"What names?"

"Oh...different things," said Jim, looking bashful. "But our favourite is the white one called Aspro."

"Ach, *paidia!* See the one over there by the *kotetsi*?" he said, pointing to one of the russet-colour hens. "It has a red thread tied around its leg. That's Marina's method. She marks the one she's going to get next."

He cackled for a while, enjoying the wind-up. "Marina is good with a knife. Iphigenia taught her. Be careful! Marina and mother-in-law. They are dangerous!"

Marina told him in Greek he was being ridiculous. "Is just a kitchen, after all," she told us, using her mixed-up word for a chicken. She strode off back to the *spitaki*.

Andreas put his finger over his mouth, and lowered his voice again. "I am sorry for the jokes, but maybe I tell her to spare Aspro for now, okay?"

"Is she going to slaughter them all?" Jim asked.

He nodded. "They are old anyway. We have them a long time. The mothers in Kalamata make nice soup with them. But we will buy baby chickens in spring, so we have more and more chickens, and maybe a few roosters too."

Why not add noisy roosters to the mad mix of cats and dogs, I thought? It all seemed rather normal to us now.

"And another mummy cat will give birth soon," said Andreas, smiling.

But we drew the line at more cats. We have never been cat people and the ones in Greece are generally bin scavengers, through no fault of their own. Cats in tavernas were a sore point with tourists and some seemed to be on a mission to save them all. We once saw a well-meaning English woman in a taverna raiding the tables after diners had left, taking plates of leftovers out to the street and scraping food on to the ground.

The taverna owner was not amused. "Why you do that?" he asked her, pulling a face.

"I can't bear to see a hungry cat."

"Then don't come to Greece. It's full of hungry cats. And hungry people now. Can you save them, too?"

While I wasn't partial to cats, I liked Cyclops. His name refers to the mythical one-eyed giants, the *Kiklopas*, the fiercest of which was Polyphemus, who was blinded in a skirmish with Odysseus in Homer's *Odyssey*. These were wild, lawless creatures, as I expected Cyclops was in his earlier life.

Cyclops was a battered hero, looking more than usually dusty and off-white from his first months of hiding in the *fournos* at night and having to scrap with the other cats for food. Despite Marina bringing food for the animals on her regular visits, they were always ravenous.

As it grew hotter Cyclops moved to the orchard across from our kitchen balcony. Here there was dry grass and bushes of lavender to hide beneath, and there was some hunting to be done there. Many times I would see him sitting alone under an olive tree, his one eye turned mournfully towards the house, waiting for a treat. Once I made the mistake of putting food out for him on the kitchen balcony, but when the other cats got wind of it they climbed up and finished it off.

I got into the habit of waiting until Cyclops was alone in the orchard and would hurl bits of food across to him. He had a ragged dignity and I knew he couldn't have a lot of years left, but at least the last era of his life would be peaceful enough. In my mind, Cyclops had become, increasingly, a metaphor of survival. If he could navigate his way through this edgy adventure, then so could the rest of us.

In September, not only was Greece in difficulty with high levels of debt, but also Italy, Spain, Portugal and Ireland, and there was a shadow hanging over the whole Eurozone. It was reported that the IMF was running out of funds to save more EU countries from a debt crisis.

Greece had not performed well that year in its bid to cut the deficit and the Troika was pushing Greece to accelerate fiscal reforms and implement its privatisation programme, or the next tranche of bailout money would be withheld. And while the Troika had agreed to give Greece a second rescue package worth 130 billion euros, the negotiations had already broken down and the package would need to be renegotiated.

German Finance Minister Wolfgang Schauble, who had taken a consistently hard line on Greece, was highly critical of rescuing countries, including Greece, which had been foolish enough to pile up mountains of sovereign debt, arguing that "profligacy shouldn't be rewarded". This harsh stand by the Troika and criticism from the Germans was unhelpful and opened the way for the international press to further blame Greece for the ills that had befallen it. In a short time, Greece had become the most vilified nation on earth.

Tourists started to avoid the country for fear of riots and strikes. German travellers had become particularly nervous. One villa owner in Stoupa told Jim his bookings were generally down and one large group of German tourists had cancelled their holiday for fear of being beaten up by Greeks, even in the rural Mani, because of the increasing hostility towards Germany.

Apollo Adventures, despite having a healthier number of bookings mid-summer, suffered a slowdown by the end of the season, which is traditionally still a popular time with British tourists. There was even some doubt over whether the company would need a rep in this region the following year. To make matters worse, the company had lost one of the best villas on its books.

The villa was a luxury six-bedroom property by the beach and near the new, upmarket Costa Navarino resort. A business tycoon from Kazakhstan had rented the villa for a month, at 1,000 euros a night, and liked it so much he bought it from its Greek owner, who announced that, henceforth, he could be found sailing his new yacht around the Med. Strange times indeed.

We tried not to worry too much about what would happen the following year, as the Greeks were worrying enough for everyone. But however hard we tried to live absolutely in the minute, like the Greeks, we couldn't. It wasn't in our genes. Like most westerners, we were future-centric. Greeks are imprecise about the future. "If it hasn't arrived yet, how can we talk about it?" said Foteini one day. Simple laser logic.

And there is a popular Greek saying: "When humans make plans, God laughs."

In late summer, while Jim was working, I had plenty of time on my hands and I decided to start writing a book about our adventures in Megali Mantineia in our first year. It had seemed that the way of life we encountered there couldn't last forever, especially when the crisis began to change the fabric of Greek life, as austerity took its toll. And the Greek character was changing, too. Many Greeks remarked to us as the crisis increased: "We used to be happier."

I wanted to capture this way of life before it disappeared altogether. Once I started writing the book, it became an enjoyable task and the characters and situations leapt on to the page unbidden, most especially Foteini, with her big personality and unique way of life. I hoped that during the long, cold nights of the coming winter I would be able to crack on with it. But it wasn't just the Mani that had given me the idea to write a book about Greece. The seeds had been sown in Athens. It's just that it took me more than three decades to get around to doing it. And, in a funny kind of way, it wasn't even my idea.

12

Athens, 1970s

GREECE has always been at heart a genial, laid-back place, even in the midst of a political upheaval. But when you throw Greek bureaucracy into the mix, there's a set timetable for anxiety. Mine came in the form of a residency permit after being in Athens nearly three months.

Nikos told me one day that I would have to go to the Aliens Bureau in the city to organise a permit. The bureau was run by the police, as it still is today, and Nikos said he would have to go with me, as few police there spoke much English and under a dictatorship there was more need than ever to follow the right procedures. Before we went, he told me he would do all the talking, apart from the odd Greek pleasantry on my part. I wasn't to say that I was working for the family but that I was a friend of Deirdre's from Australia. Work permits were almost impossible for foreigners to gain.

"We'll say you're a *filellinas,* philhellene, and you're here on a cultural mission, soaking up our history, visiting the antiquities. I know, I'll tell them you're writing a kind of travel book about Athens and you're staying with us while you do your research," said Nikos.

"A book? Yeah, sounds good," I said. In my last years at high school I had toyed with the idea of becoming a journalist one day, if not an author, and I was writing a diary while in Athens.

The Aliens Bureau was housed in a stark, functional building. Permits were issued in a large, busy room with old-style wooden desks arranged in a U-shape. At each desk a police officer was interviewing applicants. We waited in a ragged line that constituted a Greek queue.

Nikos seemed to have a particular officer in mind and when he was finally free, Nikos nudged me in that direction. He had a quick word with the officer and we sat down on hard metal chairs. The officer looked like a boxer gone to seed and seemed to overflow the boundaries of his chair. His desk was messy, with a large scribbled-on blotting-paper pad, an overflowing ashtray and rows of chewed pens. There were rubber stamps and an ink pad and all the other hallmarks of creaking Greek bureaucracy, things that you can still see today in some government offices, such as post offices.

Up to that point I'd had nothing to do with Greek authority figures and being in this tawdry, testosterone-charged hub of law and order was unnerving. The name of the place was bizarrely off-putting for a start, 'Aliens Bureau', as if those who found themselves here were Martians, left behind after an ill-starred mission to Earth, who now had to be dealt with by the local authorities. Even the Greek word for a foreigner, or even just a stranger, is harsh enough, 'xenos', as if we are entirely another species.

There was a bit of easy banter to start with and then they got down to business. I assumed the first question was why I wanted to stay in Greece for another three months. Nikos replied and turned to me, patting me on the back, engaging in a small theatrical scene, in English.

"I'm just telling the officer here how much you've enjoyed your stay in our country and that you're writing a book, *ena vivlio*." He did a scribbling sign with one hand, prompting me.

"So you like our country?" the officer asked me in Greek, with a tight smile.

"*Malista. Para poli.* Yes, very much," I said, using the polite word for 'yes' that would guarantee I kept on his right side. But I stopped right there lest I ventured on to a trail of words that would result in an embarrassing language mix-up. And anything to do with bread was definitely off-limits.

The whole thing was mercifully over in no time and I was handed my *adeia,* the flimsy piece of paper folded in the middle that served as a resident's permit. It was rubber-stamped. I thought how easily Nikos had dealt with this small rite of passage, though it wasn't quite that simple. Nothing in Greece ever is. The last bit of the formalities was done so quickly I might have missed it, but as we got up to leave there was a quick darting of Nikos's hand under the blotting paper – a flash of bank notes. The officer didn't react. We all said goodbye and were out the door.

"Ach, let's go and have a drink. I know just the place," said Nikos, walking on ahead of me through streets I had never visited before.

Finally, we came to a narrow staircase that led to the kind of small basement taverna called a *koutouki,* which was popular then. It was a low-key kind of hangout that served simple dishes and barrelled wine and occasionally might have a bouzouki player late at night and a singer courting danger with banned ballads. Men were huddled at wooden tables, eating from little plates of *mezedes,* snacks, which in those days usually accompanied a drink. Nikos was on friendly terms with the owner and waiter and I assumed this was one of his regular haunts. We drank an earthy, yellow-coloured wine from a chilled metal carafe. It tasted of honey and rural hillsides. It was good and soothing after our Aliens Bureau experience.

"Did I see you slip that guy some cash?" I asked Nikos.

He put a finger over his mouth, which seemed funny as no-one here spoke English, I imagined.

"That's the way it's done in Greece. It greases the wheels," he said softly.

Decades later in crisis Greece, I would hear people talk about the same thing, even while the government was trying to change the culture and stamp out corruption. Now it's called the *fakelaki*, the little envelope, that is stuffed with money to make sure that doctors, lawyers and anyone who can make a difference to your life does what they are supposed to do, and expeditiously.

"Do I have to go back and do the same thing over again when the permit expires?"

Nikos nodded. "It will be easier next time, or else they'll just say no. I don't need to tell you these are shit times we live in." He glanced around as he said this. "The government doesn't care about foreigners as long as you keep out of trouble. And just be careful. Don't walk around late at night where it's too quiet; don't draw attention to yourself, don't discuss anything political in public, all right? Become a shadow."

I had heard this so many times that I wasn't listening, enjoying the slightly maverick feel of this subterranean haunt.

"And this is important," said Nikos, tapping the back of my hand to get my attention. "Never, ever get into an argument in a public place with a Greek. You won't win. There are many ordinary Greeks who hate foreigners right now, particularly Americans. But any foreigner could be a target. If you get into a scrape with someone, walk away. Okay?"

"Yes, yes," I said, sipping my yellow wine. I was half-listening as it was something I had already picked up on, that most Greeks hated Americans for supporting the coup in 1967, but there was a general suspicion about foreigners. Several times in the city, in shops or tavernas, I was asked if I was American and the reply "Australian" always brought a look of relief and a sense that we were almost family because there were so many Greeks in Australia. Years later in the Mani, I would have the same experience when I met Greeks for the first time, with them pointedly asking if I was German, mainly because of its harsh role in the austerity programme.

"Remember, no-one is safe in Greece now," Nikos said.

He ordered more wine and small plates of food: *loukaniko* sausage, *dolmades*, stuffed vine leaves, and tiny *tiropites*, cheese pies. It was delicious. I could see him physically relaxing now, as if good Greek food could salve a multitude of anxieties. Certainly the wine was having that effect. He picked up his refilled glass and clinked it against mine.

"And here's to your book on Athens. One day, I want a signed copy – and you can post another one to the Aliens Bureau," he said, guffawing.

13

Fermor's firmament

DURING our second summer in the Mani, we began to see how this joyous season had a string in its tail. We knew our summers would be limited in number and our big fat Greek odyssey would never be Homeric in length. One day we would have to return to 'normality' in Britain. It's a thought that occurs to most foreigners here, sooner or later. Some circumstance, usually health, will take the most 'permanent' of settlers back 'home' in the end, and few want to go.

The impermanence of life in the sun cut a little deeper in the summer of 2011, when we heard that the great British travel writer and philhellene Patrick Leigh Fermor had died from cancer, aged 96. Since the 1960s, he had spent most of his time in the Mani, in a monastic stone house in the seaside village of Kardamili, an hour further south from Paleohora.

Fermor had a lifelong passion for Greece, dating back to the Second World War, when he was in the SOE (Special Operations Executive), stationed in Crete during the Nazi occupation, where he famously kidnapped German General Heinrich Kreipe, commander of Crete, in 1944 – and sealed his romantic and daredevil destiny for ever more.

'Paddy' Fermor had first come to the Mani in the 1950s with his wife Joan. He described the region in his seminal travel book *Mani* as having "survived in a fierce and enchanting time warp". The Mani in those days was remote, cut off from the rest of Greece, due to bad roads and the inhospitable rocky spine of the Taygetos mountains running the length of the peninsula. It was only when he reached Kardamili, a place steeped in ancient lore, that he fell in love with the wild beauty of this area, one he often referred to as "Homer's Greece". The couple eventually bought a swathe of land on a rocky promontory and built the now famous stone house where Fermor preferred to live, even in his great old age.

Before we set off for the Mani in 2010, I had optimistically toyed with the idea of setting up an interview with Fermor for a freelance feature article. However, when I contacted the publicity manager at his publishers, John Murray, she doused my enthusiasm for the project, saying Fermor was a daunting interview subject now, mostly because he was quite frail in his old age, with hearing and sight problems. It all seemed too much of an imposition, so I let the idea go, not realising that one day Jim and I would find ourselves in his wonderful home to write a very different kind of feature, but sadly Fermor would no longer be there.

Ironically, we learnt after his death, from friends and contacts in Kardamili, that the convivial Fermor was more approachable and accessible than most people knew. On his name day every year, his house was open to all the villagers, and frankly anyone who cared to drop in. Fermor had been given the name Mihalis during the Cretan operations and celebrated his name day on November 8, the feast day of Ayios Mihalis.

Some of the expats in Kardamili told us stories of meeting Fermor at his house, and we heard at least one amusing tale of how, even outside of his name day, if you knocked on his door during sociable hours you would have been well received.

An English couple had been out one afternoon in a sailboat in Kalamitsi Bay, below Fermor's house, when their boat capsized. They managed to swim to shore, wearing nothing but their swimming costumes, but with no means of getting back to their holiday villa in nearby Stoupa. The man knew that Fermor lived in the stone house by the beach and decided he would throw himself on his mercy, helped by the fact they appeared to have a writer friend in common. The couple scrambled over a stone wall and up through the garden, where they found Fermor and Joan on the back terrace. The man introduced himself, emphasised their mutual friend and then anxiously told him: "Our boat's just capsized and we nearly drowned, can you help us?"

Fermor needed no introductions and took them inside, first plying them with large, reviving whiskies. The man later said this was about the last thing they needed, but they didn't like to be impolite. The ever chivalrous Fermor offered the couple some dry clothes and later drove them back home.

While the villagers mourned the loss of Fermor after his death, they were also concerned about the future of his house. It had become a part of the cultural landscape of the place, partly due to the cast of illustrious visitors over the years from the world of arts and literature, including Nobel Prize-winning Greek poet George Seferis, Poet Laureate Sir John Betjeman and famous Greek painter Nikos Hadjikyri-akos-Ghikas. Sophia Loren is said to be one of the signatories in the guest book.

There were stories that the house was now falling into disrepair. Years earlier, Fermor had bequeathed it to the respected Benaki Museum in Athens, with the stipulation that it should be used as a writers' retreat. With its monastic style and heavenly setting, overlooking Kalamitsi cove and a nearby small island with an ancient chapel, this was a perfect use, some might say. After his death, however, the Benaki's bosses were slow to reveal how they planned to honour Fermor's wishes.

While visiting friends in the area, we decided to pass by the house and see if the stories about the state of it were true. The side of the house is visible from the track down to Kalamitsi beach and it was easy to spot the rotting shutters hanging off their hinges. Also the perimeter stone wall near the beach had crumbed and it was easy to jump over it and ramble right up to the back terrace of the house, much as the capsized couple had done years earlier.

We contacted the Benaki Museum, hoping to write a feature about the future of the house and its current state. Although the museum initially agreed to a visit, there were months of procrastination, unanswered phone calls and emails. With the economic crisis worsening by the day, it appeared the Benaki, partly funded by the Greek government and also by private donations, was feeling the pressure and the house was understandably low on its list of priorities. The problem for the Benaki, it seemed, was that no funds had been allocated for its upkeep and refurbishment in Fermor's will.

However, we finally got approval for a visit in the autumn and what we found there became the basis for a feature published in *The Daily Telegraph* the following year, under Jim's byline.

The day of the visit was glorious and warm. When we entered, through thick wooden doors that led into a shady garden at the side of the house, we were met by a ferocious-looking Great Dane that barked and pranced around us and which we took to be a guard dog. However, it belonged to a Benaki representative called Aristotle. He had been staying alone at the house, mostly, cataloguing Fermor's collection of 7,000 books, and had brought the dog along for company.

Another doorway and side passage took us to the fabulous walkway with stone arches, through which there are bewitching views down to the sea and the wooded slopes at the side of the bay. With most of the rooms of the house opening on to this walkway, it is this aspect that gives the house its monastic feel, the rooms like the small cells you find in Greek monasteries. At one end of it there's a secluded nook with a wooden table, overlooked by a headless Grecian statue in a carved recess on the wall behind. It was one of the many quirky touches of this house, which reduced its monastic grandeur to a more human scale.

We drank Greek coffee with Aristotle and tried to discuss the future of the house, but from what he told us it seemed the plan for a writers' retreat hadn't progressed much at all. He said the Benaki would take time to get the house in the right order first before it decided on its best use, either as a writers' retreat, or even a museum of sorts, which was the option that would have best pleased the villagers. That's as far as we got on that score and to date nothing much has been done by the museum to push the plan forward, though one British organisation at least has galvanised Fermor aficionados and money has been raised to help renovate the house.

Aristotle, however, was a gracious host and left us to trail about the house as we wished and take photos, while he tagged loosely behind. He told us we were lucky because the house had not been disturbed much since Fermor's death – a unique window into his inimitable world. More than that, there was a feeling that not much had changed in this house since the 1960s. It was like a house in a time warp, and lovably messy, a curious mix of English country house, with a dash of Levantine charm and bohemian shabby chic thrown in. This was especially true in the sitting room, where tall built-in bookcases dominate, with a dazzling mix of travel, history, wildlife, cookery, and many novels spanning centuries.

Aristotle told us: "Paddy had a huge range of interests and was a real Renaissance man. He couldn't bear to throw anything away – all his books, letters and documents were stored around the house."

The books are one of the rich legacies of Fermor's life, which was why the Benaki was cataloguing them and removing many of the more valuable and rare, which included a large collection of Fermor's own first-edition books and ones with inscriptions by other writers, such as Lawrence Durrell and Bruce Chatwin. Aristotle plucked one from a two-foot stack on the floor, all waiting to be catalogued. It was a first-edition book of poetry by Sir John Betjeman, one of Fermor's great friends and a frequent visitor. The humorous inscription in the book, titled *High and Low,* read: "For Paddy and Joan, inscribed with undying devotion by the pile-ridden poet John, 1969."

The sitting room and adjacent sunny 'winter chamber' overlooking the cove below was obviously the heart of this house. It was built with reverence for the Greek landscape and its light, but most of all it was designed for conviviality. It wasn't hard to imagine soirees in this room around the impressive dining room table, consisting of one decorative slab of marble. The drinks 'cabinet' had a large tray on top, displaying a collection of bottles: whisky, ouzo, vodka, and many were half-empty. There was a sense here that Fermor had just stepped out for a minute on some errand and would be back soon. The house was still imbued with his presence.

But it was joyous to wander about the house, among the milestones and pointers of this man's life, who began to feel less and less like a stranger. In the separate studio block, which had been Fermor's study, and according to his housekeeper of 11 years, Elpida Beloyannis, his favourite room for reading and writing, there were piles of letters and postcards on the mantelpiece, left ill-advisedly to chance.

Most revealing of all was a photo, tucked behind a sketch of his wife Joan. The 'hidden' photo was of Fermor's long-time friend and correspondent, the late Deborah Cavendish, Duchess of Devonshire. The picture showed the young 'Debo', as he called her, on 1954 Grand National winner Royal Tan at Lismore Castle in Ireland. It seemed a tantalising sign that the rumours about the pair having had a more intense relationship, spanning decades, may have had a grain of truth in it.

For me, one of the most bewitching mementoes was Fermor's ancient travel trunk, which must have seen a slew of continents by the looks of it. On the lid was written: Patrick Leigh Fermor, DSO, OBE. Travellers' Club, Pall Mall, London. In just a few words it conjured up this man's life: its privilege, its high-brow attainments, but also its gloriously itinerant chic and bonhomie.

A lot has been made of Fermor's charmed life, mostly due to his association with wealthy friends and his marriage to Joan, nee Eyres-Monsell, whose family was wealthy and well-connected. But his own small bedroom at the back of the house was devoid of prestige. It was monastic, with basic furniture and curious, rather dreary etchings on the wall. This was the room that Aristotle, rather shyly, informed us was his quarters during the cataloguing and he had left much of Fermor's personal possessions as he had found them, like the writing paper and pencils on the bedside table.

"Paddy left these things all around the house to grab when he suddenly wanted to write something down," said Aristotle.

Before we left, we called in at the kitchen, one of the rooms off the arcade. It was large and homey, and pots were bubbling on old stove, tended by Elpida Beloyannis. Her family had known the Fermors since the 1960s. She had been his housekeeper but later also became his personal assistant and finally a nurse at the end of his life. A rather shy, unassuming woman, Beloyannis had probably been closer to Fermor in his great old age than anyone, but because his death had been so recent she didn't want to discuss him.

"He was a wonderful man, a good friend and employer. I don't feel it would be right to talk about him. I just want to honour his memory," she said.

While researching the feature about his house, and Fermor's relationship with people in Kardamili, we spoke to other loyal villagers and friends, including the Greek children's author Maria Morgan, married to a Welshman. Maria was a close friend of Paddy and Joan's for 20 years as a child growing up in Kardamili and had visited the house many times.

She cleared up one of the points we had noticed on our walk through the house – the lack of any modern appliances.

She laughed when she told us: "Paddy and Joan liked to live a traditional life there. They didn't want anything in the house that was modern or made of plastic. They did have a television but they only bought it to watch a documentary about Paddy on Greek TV – and never switched it on again."

Maria said the couple were very approachable and kind. During her many visits to the house they helped her when she started writing. "I caught the writing bug at their house."

She also spoke very touchingly about Paddy's last days before his death. It completely overturns a few of the rare, negative sentiments we heard from some villagers after Fermor died, the slight bitterness over the fact he had preferred to be buried in England rather than the country he seemed to love the most – Greece. It confirms Fermor's love and affection for the people of Kardamili.

Maria said: "At the end of Paddy's life he had throat cancer and it severely affected his voice, so he could not talk. He knew the end was near and he expressed a wish to return to England to see a couple in their 80s who were close friends, so he went back, but sadly he never got to see them before he died.

"We spoke to him on the phone from England but he could not answer us. He was in tears. Many other villagers from Kardamili also phoned him. We were his best friends and his family, but he could not talk to us because of the cancer. It upset him greatly. He was an honest friend to the villagers. I think he would have given his life to help any of them."

For me, Fermor's house offered a poignant sense of the last days of his life. When I stood on the back, cobbled terrace of the house, looking towards the island opposite that the athletic Fermor regularly swam to, it wasn't hard to imagine the thoughts that must have weighed heavily on him as he prepared for his very last journey. Not only taking leave of a gloriously accomplished life, but leaving all of this behind … the searing beauty of Greece, on this leafy promontory especially, that he had once described as "a promised land". To never set eyes on the Greek sun again. It was something that made me feel uncannily close to a man I never had the good fortune to meet.

14

"Greece has no maaaney!"

EFTIHIA'S tiny kitchen was "the house" effectively. It was where she and her mother Pelagia spent much of their time, sitting side by side, watching Turkish soaps, which was the curious new obsession of Greek TV viewers. There was also something bubbling away in the slightly anachronistic pressure cooker on the stove top, with heavenly aromas fizzing out of it.

On the day we visited the family, a strange noise was coming from the fireplace. Yiorgos was hovering over it, admiring the dozen or so new-born chickens squeaking in a box, with a small heat lamp rigged above, as if this was the most normal thing in the world. These were chicks the family had bought a few days earlier from the many hawkers who regularly drove through the village, their crackling loud-speakers announcing incongruous produce: chairs and chickens, watermelons and beach umbrellas.

"Beeweutiful, yes? And look, see, lamp above. They having little Greek holiday in sun," Yiogios said in English, chortling.

Eftihia elbowed him out of the way. "They need some warmth, Margarita. We had a couple of cold nights up here and the chicks are so small," she said, fussing over them.

The kitchen was cramped and plain but possibly the homeliest kitchen I'd ever seen, which had become a kind of walk-in centre for other villagers nearby, who came to chat, drink coffee, or moan about the state of Greece. We always saw at least one other person there whenever we called by. In that respect it was a typical village house, but Eftihia and her mother were among the warmest people in Megali

Mantineia, and the most entertaining. However, Eftihia had another gift that put her in great demand. Her mother and she had long-term health problems that meant they had to have regular injections of various medicines and Eftihia had learnt to give injections and administer first-aid. On many occasions other villagers with health issues came to the house for treatment with syringes and drugs bought from local pharmacies. It seemed to take communal living to a whole new level.

Naively, I asked Eftihia if villagers couldn't get a doctor to come out to see them, especially for a chronic condition. She shook her head.

"It's a lot of trouble to get someone out. A private doctor might come but not everyone can afford the fee. It's easier to drive straight to Kalamata Hospital. Many people in Greek villages know how to do these injections. We have to," she said.

Again, I was reminded just how stoical these Greeks were. There are only a few state doctors in the Mani to service the whole area and many won't make house calls – unless it's a life-or-death situation.

Eftihia and her family had quite a large house but they all lived on the bottom floor, with the top floor left unoccupied. She once explained that the top part of the house had been set aside for her brother Yiorgos when he married. But still a bachelor in his forties, remarkably for such a striking and considerate character, he chose to live below. It is often the custom in more traditional societies for the elder brother to remain unmarried if his younger sister has not married first, so he can look after her. In this case it meant he had the care of both women.

The crisis had affected them badly, as it had all the villagers, especially now that a new property tax, the *haratsi*, had been introduced on to electricity bills and calculated on the size of the property. In the beginning, if payment wasn't forthcoming, the electricity would be cut. This was to become the most contentious and loathed of all the new taxes in Greece. Even farmers as poor as Foteini were forced to pay *haratsi* on old village dwellings, which was a hardship.

Yiorgos had seen his work diminish during the crisis. Like other fairly unskilled workers in rural Greece, he had fewer opportunities, especially with the painting and decorating work he had done for years during the boom time, when opportunistic developers had sold village land-and-house packages in the area to British expats. Now the building work had dried up and many expats were heading home. Even the Albanian stonemasons, who had thrived before the crisis, were leaving.

Yet Eftihia and her family were generous to a fault. We had been invited on that particular day in the autumn for lunchtime *mezedes* and there was a vast array of little dishes on the table: salads, stuffed cabbage leaves, cheese pies, cold meat and *tsikles*. We avoided the *tsikles*, the little pickled thrushes with their heads left on that are so loved by the Maniots.

Pelagia laughed. "You don't like the *tsikles*, Margarita, I remember!"

She was referring to a summer lunch we had once been invited to at the house with their family and we had been coaxed into trying the birds, much to the amusement of the others at the table. We only managed a few morsels of the delicacy.

"They are tasty but not my favourite. I'm sorry," I said.

She held up her hand as if to say, 'don't apologise'. "I don't like them much either. It's Yiorgos who likes them and Eftihia makes a good job of pickling them."

Eftihia slapped Yiorgos on the back. "He's the hunter in the family."

Yiorgos poured his home-made, honey-coloured wine into our glasses. It was quite strong and went straight to our heads.

"I am cowboy now, shoots everything, eh?" he said.

Yiorgos was always good company and liked a good laugh. In Chrisanthi's taverna in the village, where we still came for regular meals, the farmers gathered most evenings to talk about the crisis and olive yields. Yiorgos liked to lighten the proceedings with banter and a few good jokes. He made people laugh and even with his limited English he was amusing. His favourite English expression was: "Greece has no maaaney!" He would say it while holding his hand high and rubbing his forefinger and thumb together.

"Shooting birds very soon, and rabbits. Many things. *Ti na kanoume?* Greece kaput!" he said, laughing, his big shoulders hunching up and down, though I could tell by a certain frustration in his eyes that the latter part was no laughing matter.

Not long after we started eating lunch, we heard the familiar voice of Foteini outside, coming back from her *ktima* for a meal. A place was made for her at the table. She was wearing her usual layers, though her wellies were replaced by shoes.

"You didn't come to see me for coffee, Margarita," she said.

"That's because they're here," said Yiorgos, with a look of impatience. I sensed he sometimes felt aggrieved being surrounded by so many women in this corner of the village.

Foteini put one or two things on her plate. For such a big, solid woman, she ate rather sparingly and daintily and favoured the vegetable dishes over the meat. She was quiet during the meal but near the end she suddenly came to life.

"Are you going in to Kalamata soon, *paidia*?" she asked us.

"Maybe."

"You know those lovely soft olive-harvesting gloves you got me last year?"

In fact she had the pair stuffed in the pocket of her big plaid shirt and pulled them out and showed everyone. Yiorgos rolled his eyes.

"Can you get me another pair?"

"What's wrong with those?" asked Yiorgos.

141

"Ach! They're worn out now," she replied, holding them up. The gloves were made of thick cotton but the palm area had a kind of rippled, rubber surface for grasping branches. You could see they were slightly threadbare after harvesting some 200 trees and when we had helped her for a few days the year before we had seen the gloves in action.

"Can you get me another pair like this, from the shop, wherever it was?"

"We'll try," I told her. "But what if we can't find the exact type?"

She shrugged. "I don't want the hard ones. They're no good."

Jim and I looked at each other. Hard ones, soft ones. How would we know?

"Why don't you come in with us the next time we go to Kalamata and you try some out for yourself," I said.

Yiorgos gasped. "*Panayia mou!* You're too kind, Margarita and Dimitri, offering to take Foteini shopping," he said, and then switched to English so she couldn't understand presumably, garbling it all up, in a most diverting way.

"You go craaaazy taking Foteini to shops. She takes you all over city. No buy. Complain, complain, complain! No buy. More complain. Drives man crazy!" he said, palm-slapping his forehead. We started to laugh. Foteini sat silently, biting her lower lip.

I well remembered my own shopping trip with Foteini in a supermarket, where she demolished a baguette in seconds.

"You've been shopping with Foteini then?" I asked Yiorgos.

"Oh yes! Yiorgos been shops with Foteini. *Panayia mou!* Not ever agains. You go alone with Zim. No take Foteini. You buy any gloves, whatever you wants. See gloves. Looks good. You buys. Too hard, too soft. You buys for Foteini. *Kalo!*"

He slapped his hands together energetically to indicate some finality in the endeavour and we all laughed, except for poor Foteini.

"What you say?" Yiorgos slapped Jim on the shoulder. "Shops no bladdy good for mens, eh? Buggit Zim! Woman wok!"

I laughed heartily at the 'wok'. Listening to Yiorgos speaking English was a pure delight. Pelagia was giggling but Foteini said nothing. She ate her lunch with a beatific grimace.

Before Foteini left to go back to her *ktima*, I told her I would look for her soft gloves. When she was well out of earshot, Eftihia told me: "She's got lots of pairs of gloves, I tell you. Plenty of soft ones. I think she's collecting them. Don't bother yourself, Margarita. You've got better things to do."

I agreed but knew that I'd probably end up trailing around Kalamata looking for gloves anyway.

Yiorgos got up and went off to chop some olive wood, and Jim offered to help. I passed a good hour with Eftihia and her mother, looking through their photo albums, old pictures of the family in Kalamata before the earthquake and before they had to decamp to the village when their house was destroyed. Eftihia had pictures of village weddings, *paniyiria*, and funerals. She also took delight in pointing out people in the village now and what they looked like when they were young.

It was easy to see how village life had aged some people. Though most old villagers were still fit and spry, with some their hardships were etched deep on their faces. It was a pertinent reminder not to sentimentalise Mediterranean village life as if sun and olive oil could work miracles, turning Tutankhamens back into Peter Pans. Pelagia, now in her mid-70s, had also had a hard life but there was such brightness and sweetness about her face, and when she smiled you were drawn to her.

"Come again, any time," she said when we finally left for the day. "But you don't have to keep bringing us things."

Eftihia also chided us. "Just come as you are."

"It was only a cake we brought this time," I said, laughing. "Not a diamond."

She shrugged. "If you bring us a diamond, it won't make any difference. It's the *parea*, company, we like."

Pelagia nodded in agreement. Yiorgos and Jim had just returned from their wood chopping and heard the end of the conversation.

"Margarita, don't listen to silly women. Bring a diamond sometimes and Yiorgos will be happy. He'll never have to work again!"

The two women laughed heartily at Yiorgos's comment as we all left the house, and the noise swirled though the warm afternoon air. I knew that if we had still been living in the small stone house across the fields and visible from Eftihia's terrace, we would have heard that joyful sound clearly as we sat on our back balcony. It would have mingled with the melodious sound of goat bells and the soft rustling of olive branches as a breeze swept up from the gulf below.

It was a sound I always found comforting, and one that would have been worth staying in Megali Mantineia for. In a few months I would have even more reason to think it.

◎◎◎◎◎

On October 19, Athens was gripped by a two-day strike and demonstrations of up to 150,000 people as the Parliament met to approve yet another raft of swingeing austerity measures in order to receive the next instalment of 8 billion euros, which EU finance ministers had held back on due to Greece's poor fiscal performance, and for negotiations to progress on the second rescue plan.

The new measures would include more tax hikes, spending cuts, the suspension on reduced pay of some 30,000 public servants and the shelving of collective labour contracts. Without the latest instalment it was said that Greece would run out of money by mid-November.

We watched the day's events on TV. What had started out as a fairly peaceful demonstration of unionists and 'indignants' became increasingly more violent as gangs of youths, anarchists and left-wing groups joined in. They hurled bits of marble paving stones, ripped off the street in front of the parliament building in Syntagma Square, and threw petrol bombs.

Three thousand police were dispatched to the area and retaliated with rounds of tear gas and stun guns. The night would end with the austerity bill winning approval in Parliament, but the next night MPs would again meet to vote on the details of the new measures. The two days of riots would involve around half-a-million demonstrators and become the biggest and most violent the city had seen in decades.

On the night of the 20th Andreas and Marina had come up to the house. Andreas had been fixing a few things around the property and afterwards we all sat down in the living room to watch the latest developments on TV. We made a night of it at least, opening a bottle of wine and bringing out snacks as if we were watching a good movie – though there was nothing entertaining in what we were seeing. Again I was struck by how different the landlord/tenant situation was in Greece to Britain, to the point where it was hard to think of Andreas and Marina as anything other than friends.

The scenes we watched were as unsettling as the previous night, as violent clashes continued between protesters and the police in Syntagma Square and on the road outside the Hotel Grande Bretagne, which had seen many historic battles in its history. The violence later spread through the back streets of Athens this time, as black-clad protesters hurled fire bombs at police and set fire to the industrial-sized refuse bins that were piled high with rubbish after a strike by council workers. Most of downtown Athens resembled a war zone.

"Look at that, *paidia!*" said Andreas, every time a fresh wave of violence swept across the screen. He kept shaking his head and now and then the couple exchanged their thoughts in rapid Greek.

"This is terrible," he said, pointing at the TV. "Look what is happening to Greece now."

A few days after we watched these scenes on the TV with Andreas and Marina came an event that was etched in my memory for months afterwards. It was the day I had gone into the Nostimo bakery in Kalamata to buy bread and I was confronted by the strangely hostile pair of assistants who were normally very pleasant.

They warned me to "go back to your *patrida*, homeland!" because Greece was such a mess. I had to convince them that going back wasn't on the agenda for us then, which angered them more.

"What? You *want* to stay in Greece? This is a terrible place to live now!"

While the curious incident ended on a friendlier note with the two women comically asking me to take them back to Scotland when we finally left, to escape Greece in crisis, the scene was unnerving all the same. And when we got back to the house that afternoon, Andreas came out with his chilling prediction.

"It's beginning," he said. "Remember the riots we saw on TV the other night, the young peoples fighting with the police? All this bitter fighting and the people will be crushed just like they were by the *hounta*, junta, in the 1960s. We will see tanks on the streets again."

It sounded like a far-fetched idea at the time, even though back in February 2011, the EU Commission president Jose Manuel Barroso warned that crisis-torn countries like Greece and Spain could easily fall victim to military-style takeovers.

By November 2011, the takeover theory had gathered a bit more strength, however, when stories began to circulate in the Greek press that the top personnel of the Greek armed forces had been reshuffled by Prime Minister George Papandreou to stamp out any possibility of military intervention during bouts of civil unrest.

At the very least, most Greeks feared they were becoming the unwilling victims of foreign policies and international pressures in this strategic corner of the Mediterranean. There was a strong sense that Greece was no longer in charge of its own destiny.

This was hammered home in January 2012, when a leaked document from Germany showed 75 per cent of Germans were in favour of a fiscal tsar in Greece to oversee economic reforms because the country couldn't be trusted to do it properly, a proposal which most Greeks vehemently opposed.

It was not difficult for me to draw some parallels between the tensions and paranoia of the 1970s and the present day. I had experienced anti-western hatred in Athens in the 1970s. With Greeks feeling the pressure during the crisis, how easily could an anti-foreign resentment, and an illogical hatred, flourish in these difficult times?

15

Athens, 1970s

NIKOS Papadakis warned me many times after we went to the Aliens Bureau for my residency permit to keep a low profile around the city. He told me that although things looked okay to a foreigner's eyes, there was a "parallel world" in Greece, where even teenagers could be snatched from their homes for having communist sympathies and taken to a police station, tortured, sent to an island prison. Every family, he said, knew someone with a story of loss and terror.

Even in salubrious Halandri, a suburb I don't think he liked very much, he claimed there was a secret detention centre, where communists were held and tortured, though it was a story that no-one else ever corroborated. Although it made the dictatorship seem more inimical in my imagination, and brought its torment closer to home, I felt that Nikos's dislike of Halandri had its roots more in ancient history.

Nikos took great delight in telling me the area had a mad, sinister back story. In ancient times it was known as the *deme* (borough) of Phyla and the centre of a strange cult dedicated to Rhea, the mother of the Olympian Gods. Devotees were said to have sung songs to Dionysus, a kind of luvvie god of theatre, wine and wild behaviour. The cult's summer ritual involved much frenzied dancing and howling. Once, when Deirdre was lecturing Nikos about a particularly long and boozy escapade in Athens, he cackled majestically and said it was all to do with living there, under the influence of that wag Dionysus.

"*Malaka!*" she shouted, which was easily her favourite description of him. "Only you could blame your drinking habits on a Greek god. Pity you couldn't have fallen under the spell of a more abstemious god instead."

In my mind Nikos was less Dionysus and more Hermes, the god of writing, cunning wiles and persuasion, and of course, the messenger of the god Zeus, with winged feet and a helmet. In this capacity, Hermes also protected travellers. It was Nikos more than anyone else who tried to steer a safe path for me in Athens, while I did my best to ignore all manifestations of the dark side. When my parents wrote from Australia, asking if everything was okay because of things they had read about Greece, I told them the politics didn't affect foreigners. It wasn't our fight. But I was soon to discover it was everyone's fight.

In the spring, I had a letter from Rory, who had gone to Israel to work on a kibbutz. He was on his way back to London and stopping off in Athens for a week or so. I smiled, wondering how hard he would have found it, living in a commune without access to fast food. Of course, we met up in the Golden Gate hamburger joint. Rory looked lean and tanned from his days working in orange groves. He seemed tougher and more assertive, too, for someone who appeared to be a bit aimless when I first met him. I admired him for it, if not his diet.

"You've had hamburger withdrawals then?" I asked him.

"Yeah, you could say that," he replied, biting into a burger the size of a small occasional table. "I tell you though, I'm not enjoying Athens. It's just the same chaotic place as ever. And the vibes are real bad. People look stressed. Don't you see it?"

To tell the truth I didn't, not outside of Nikos and Deirdre's house. They were stressed enough for all of us.

"If it wasn't for the fact that I'd left some stuff here in Athens, and that I promised to see you, of course, on my way through, I wouldn't have come back," he said.

I was flattered. He gave me a coy smile. I had the fleeting notion that perhaps I was slightly attracted to Rory and wondered if he was to me. Or was it just that he was feeling confident and happy on his travels.

We left the restaurant and started walking down towards Monastiraki. Rory wanted to see the ancient Kerameikos graveyard with its tombs, some dating to the time of the Battle of Thermopylae in 480BC, and the remnants of the Sacred Way that once led to ancient Eleusis. Like me, he had studied ancient history at school, possibly one of the few things we could agree on.

Instead of walking straight down Ermou Street, that starts at Syntagma and leads to Monastiraki, we detoured down some of the side streets, with their curious old-fashioned shops, *kafeneia* and ouzeries. We reached a T-junction and were just crossing the road when an expensive-looking car roared towards us to do a right-hand turn. The driver must have seen us ahead but didn't slow down and forced us to jump back on to the pavement out of the way.

Rory's reaction seemed a natural one, for a guy. He raced over and banged his hand down on the boot of the car when the driver finally stopped to do the turn. I guessed Rory wanted to show his anger at nearly being run over.

I expected the driver to gun his engine and roar off – but he didn't. He flung his door open and leapt out, approaching Rory and shouting in Greek, something about harming his precious car. A small crowd of passers-by began to gather on the corner. The driver tried to slap his palm on Rory's shoulder and Rory deflected it with a deft uppercut of his right arm. The driver wasn't pleased and, anticipating a fight, I told the guy in my fractured Greek that we meant no harm. We were foreigners, as if he hadn't sensed that already.

"Where from?" he snapped, switching to English.

"Australia," I said.

"What about you?" He pointed at Rory.

"I'm Canadian, if you must know. And hey, buddy, don't get aggressive. You nearly killed us a minute ago."

"You don't criticise, okay. This is my city, not yours," said the driver, his arms held out rigid, a sure sign that a Greek is feeling agitated.

Rory was looking tense and all signs of his sunny adventure in Israel were now draining away. But neither Rory nor the driver seemed inclined to move on, as if they were weighing up their options, or working up a bigger head of steam, and neither were the bystanders keen to budge. They were beginning to bicker loudly among themselves, about what, I couldn't be sure. I was starting to feel nervous.

"Please, let's not argue. We meant you no harm," I said to the driver, tugging at Rory's arm at the same time, trying to get him away from the corner.

The driver was quiet for a while, sizing us both up, and maybe in the end he didn't think we were worth a fight. I was relieved to see him turn and walk back to the car, even though he had to have the parting shot. It wasn't a stream of oaths but a gesture, the palm of his hand directed in a sharp movement towards Rory, which in Greece is a curse, and has more power than a punch.

The driver got back into his car and took the right-hand turn with a squeal of rubber.

"Can you believe that guy?" said Rory, watching the car roar dangerously down the street.

I thought we were out of danger and relaxed slightly, until I realised the crowd was still plugged into the incident, talking loudly together. We were about to move away from the corner when a male voice rose above the others, speaking in English: "You say you're Canadian, but you're an American really, aren't you? You sound like an American."

It was then that I thought about Nikos and all his damned warnings. Don't pick a fight with Greeks. Walk away, he

would say. I also thought about all the anti-American sentiments I was hearing about the city.

I took Rory's arm again, but more forcefully this time.
"Come on, Rory, we have to go!"

But he wanted to correct the error, as Canadians do when
they're mistaken for Americans.

"No, man, you're wrong. I'm Canadian."

But to these people what difference would it have made
– Canadian, American – when they were spoiling for a
fight? They didn't care if the Greek driver was in the wrong
or not, what mattered was that we were foreigners in the
wrong place. I suggested we head back the way we came
towards Syntagma Square, where there were more people
about.

As we turned to leave, Rory's hand caught the edge of a
small metal 'lollipop' parking sign that was used in those days.
It clattered into the gutter. We ignored it and continued
walking, but it took only a few seconds for the metal sign to
be retrieved, with its base grating over the pavement, and
there was a rasp of laboured breathing that made us both
turn around in fright.

I don't remember much about those few seconds, only
that the sign came crashing down on Rory's forehead,
sending a spurt of blood down his face, on to the pavement.
The attacker was middle-aged, small but stocky, his face
crumpled with anger. He let go of the sign and again it
clattered loudly on to the road. The others gasped and
started arguing, and shouting. Rory put his hand over his
forehead. He looked pale.

"Why the fuck did you do that? I've done nothing to you,"
he said to the attacker, who shouted back in Greek, something I couldn't quite understand, but it sounded bad.

An older woman in the group seemed to have some sense
and tried to calm everyone down – but it had little effect. I
wondered how this was going to end and if nearly six years

of terror and oppression would see this little group venting their frustrations completely on an Athens back street.

"Come on, Rory, we'll have to get you to a doctor. I think you need stitches." I tried to sound calm but my stomach was squirming. I had no experience of street violence to call on, or dictatorships, for that matter.

Before I could propel Rory away from the junction, I saw two other people joining the fray, two young guys aged about 20. I watched them, waiting to see if the metal lollipop would come up for another strike. I was still holding Rory's arm but he seemed disoriented and I wondered if the blow was more serious than it seemed at first.

"Rory, let's go!" I shouted.

Too late. One of the boys had stepped up to us and grabbed Rory by his other arm. He was tall and good-looking. Too nice to be a thug, surely.

"Quickly, come with us," he said in English. "You must get away from here. If someone calls the police, you're in trouble."

"We're not Americans," I blurted out, as if that made any difference.

"We know, we heard. These are crazy people. They make you trouble. Come."

I felt a wave of relief flow over me as we managed to direct Rory along the street, each holding an arm, with the other young guy walking behind to scout for any more trouble. We made good progress and by the time we turned into Ermou Street again we had all broken into a jog. Rory was struggling though, holding his head.

When we were nearly back at Syntagma Square, one of the boys managed to hail a taxi. We were bundled inside. I saw the guy who had first spoken to us giving the driver money.

"He will take you to the hospital," he told me. "Go, get out of here! *Sto kalo.*"

It was the first time I'd ever heard this heartwarming Greek farewell, which is a shortened form of *na páte sto kalo*, 'may you go to the good'. If ever I needed to hear those words it was that day in Athens, when I finally got some measure of the hateful undercurrent of life under the Colonels.

I didn't have time to thank our two guardian angels, who slipped away down a side street. I took Rory's hand. He smiled but I could tell he was feeling bad. His face and his clothes were spattered with blood.

"Scarred for life now," he said, trying to smile, but his head lolled against the back passenger seat. "I should have stayed in Israel."

The taxi guy drove like a maniac, doing mad turns, never giving way, shouting the word *gamoto!* (fuck it!) at frequent intervals and telling other drivers they were *malakes!*

Trembling with nerves, we eventually arrived at a city hospital, though I had no idea where it was exactly. We waited in A&E and eventually Rory was seen by a young doctor. He organised an X-ray and the results showed no skull fracture, but he needed four stitches and they decided to keep him in overnight because he had slight concussion.

The doctor explained to Rory that he was very lucky and that if he'd caught the blow on the back of his head, low on his skull, which was where the lollipop guy had been aiming just before Rory had turned, the outcome could have been much more serious.

"I see the irony now of us heading down to the ancient boneyard of Athens when this happened," Rory said, with a grim smile.

When I got back to Halandri later in the afternoon I told Nikos about the attack. He was furious.

"You were lucky those two *palikaria* came by and helped you out. Now you see why I've been warning you all these months. Next time I hate to think what could happen."

It seemed an odd thing to say, as if he were expecting another Athens altercation. But next time, my enemies would come from closer to home.

The following day I went back to the hospital to pick up Rory and found him with a slab of dressing over his forehead. He looked pale and tired. We got a taxi back to his small city hotel. I managed to talk Deirdre into giving me a few days off so I could spend more time with Rory, as I was the only real friend he had in Athens.

I took him on a low-key tour of the sites he hadn't seen already, including Kerameikos, finally. But everywhere we walked we felt guarded, not speaking loudly, keeping ourselves to ourselves. I also persuaded him to sidestep hamburgers for a change and eat proper Greek food. I took him to my favourite tavernas in the Plaka. After a few days of eating giant slabs of moussaka, fried octopus, souvlaki and lusty mounds of Greek salad, washed down with plenty of local wine, he started to chill out again. His antipathy towards the city was beginning to thaw, but his opinion of Greeks had nosedived.

I kept making excuses for them, saying the ones we met that day weren't typical and that generally they were among the most kind, honest people you could find anywhere. It was understandable, I told him, that after these years of oppression, some would be on the edge. However, he had no sympathy for Greeks. He said they got the junta they deserved, that was all. I scolded him for being flippant. I tried to explain, as much as I understood it then myself, that Greece was complicated. A history of war, occupations, reprisals, vendettas. One disaster had perhaps spawned another. It was easy to be critical of the country.

"Okay, the Greeks may be victims of history, but if I were you I'd still get the hell out of this place," Rory said.

I sighed. "I know how you're feeling right now, Rory. You could have been killed. It was unforgivable but, as for me, I can't help it... I just...."

"...can't help loving this place," he said, finishing the sentence for me, with a shake of his head. "You know what I think? Your passion for Greece is a bit like having an intense affair with a stranger. Exciting, but very risky."

When Rory had his stitches out the scar was a raw gash above his left eyebrow. "My Greek souvenir," he called it. But at least he was able to laugh about it now.

I saw him off at the city bus station. He was going back to London to work for a year or so, if he could manage it.

"My father's tired of sending me money via American Express. For the first time I guess I'm on my own."

"You'll manage, Rory, you're a smart guy."

I was sad to see him go finally. We kissed each other on the cheek. He bear-hugged me and I felt a strong urge to tell him not to go. I wondered if he felt the same.

"Let's catch up when you get back to Britain. Keep in touch in the meantime. And remember, don't stay here too long, Marj. I fear you're not seeing this place for what it is. It's a bad scene here."

"Thanks Rory. I appreciate your concern but, as I keep saying, Greece is complicated."

But here's the thing: it still is.

16

The Papas

PAPA Lambros seemed to float across the cool marble flooring of the church like an apparition. In his traditional black robe, he was statuesque and strikingly handsome. His black hair was tied back in a knot just above the nape of his neck and his beard was slightly flecked with grey, which made him seem prematurely wise. Everyone turned to look at him as he made his way through the church to the sanctuary, behind the *iconostasis*, stepping inside for a moment.

An Australian writer friend Geraldine, who had lived in the southern Peloponnese for nearly three decades, had mentioned Papa Lambros when I was looking for unusual subjects to write about for Australian newspapers. There were many Greek Aussies in the southern Peloponnese who had come back to their homeland to settle before the crisis, and many were now struggling with economic hardships they had never experienced before. There were, I imagined, many interesting stories among this group.

All I had gleaned from Geraldine was that Papa Lambros had given up the good life in Australia to move to Greece to become a priest, which was a fascinating tale in itself. She said she hadn't seen him for years, however, but thought he was based at a well-known church across the road from the city beach.

A quick call, answered by the church deacon, informed me he was the senior priest there and the best way to meet him was to turn up on a Monday night for his regular 'church clinic', where he was happy to talk to anyone about the church, or anything really. It seemed a very Aussie kind of set-up and augured well for a possible story.

157

I arrived early for the evening 'clinic' and was directed to a row of chairs in the corner beside a table with a computer on it, which was a curious touch amid the formality of this large Greek Orthodox church, decorated on every wall surface with frescos of saints. As I waited for the *papas*, I watched many people come and go, lighting candles and pressing them into the ornamental candle stands, and kissing icons. It was no surprise that in troubled Greece, the church seemed increasingly like a refuge from the outside world.

For me, the great strength of the Greek church lies in the fact that it has changed so little in the past 500 years. The spirituality of the distant past, its stories and mystery, is still very much in evidence, not refracted by changing beliefs and modernity. It seems both ancient and accessible. And compelling: the icons, the chanting, the incense. All your senses are engaged here.

A sound broke my reverie: feet pacing over cool marble, the swish of a long robe. I looked up and Papa Lambros was walking towards the computer corner. I had never spoken much to Greek priests, apart from Papa Nektarios, briefly, in Megali Mantineia. I had always found them slightly intimidating.

Papa Lambros also looked quite austere. When he reached me he held out his right hand and I might have been expected to kiss it, which is customary here, but I decided on a warm handshake instead. After a formal greeting in my best Greek, I dispensed with the language too and told him in English I was a Scottish/Australian journalist currently living in Greece. The word 'Australian' made his eyes sparkle with interest at least.

"I didn't catch your name?" he said in English with a sunny Aussie inflection. It was incongruous. We might have been in a church on the Kalamata seafront but the accent was pure Bondi Beach to me.

"Margarita," I told him.

"That's not a Scottish/Aussie name?"

"It's my Greek name," I said.

"Well. I guess if you've got a Greek name already you're more or less Greek then," he said, smiling broadly, revealing dazzling white teeth that seemed to light up his face. It was easy to see how he might have earned his ecclesiastical name of Lambros, meaning 'bright, shining'.

I sat down, feeling more relaxed, and waited until he'd taken a few items out of an old leather briefcase and placed them on the big desk where the computer, with its black screen, suddenly looked like a grumpy interloper. Papa Lambros pulled out the desk chair and sat opposite me, arranging his thick black robe elegantly around his legs. Even from the beginning, he had an aura about him that was captivating.

"So, Margarita, tell me what it is you wanted to talk about today?" he said, quietly.

I explained that I wanted to chat about his life with the possibility of writing a feature for a paper in Sydney, where we both happened to have grown up. He seemed quietly surprised, but not averse to the idea.

I had no idea then what the angle would be, apart from what Geraldine had already told me, which was great for starters and, of course, he was also very photogenic. I felt he might also have some thoughts on the economic crisis. In fact, his story was much more intriguing than I could have hoped for and revealed a complex individual torn between countries and careers.

Papa Lambros had a typical Greek/Aussie upbringing in an inner-city suburb of Sydney, where he was born, but at the age of 10 his father decided to relocate the family, including a brother, back to Kalamata, where he was originally from. He wanted his sons to reconnect with their own culture. It was a tough time, the *papas* explained, going to Greek school and dealing with a culture that was much more strict and rule-bound than his easy upbringing.

"I remember early on, going to a mountain village in the Mani with my parents to meet one of our grandmothers for the first time. We knocked on the door and this really ancient woman, completely dressed in black, opened it slowly and to our eyes anyway she looked like a witch and my brother and I shrieked and didn't want to go inside. I remember thinking is this what parts of Greece are really like?" he explained, laughing and again showing his strong teeth.

Papa Lambros, however, never really settled well in Greece as a teenager and while his parents decided to stay, he returned to Australia at 20 to get a better education. He went to university and became an IT specialist, working for some prestigious companies. He then married and had the first two of his four children. The Aussie dream had kicked in – or had it?

Papa Lambros admitted that despite early career success, he had obviously been searching for something more in life. What he was leaning towards, however, was the priesthood.

"During my teenage years in Greece, I had what you'd describe as a calling from God. I knew I wanted to do something spiritual with my life. I never forgot that but unfortunately I had put it aside to get on with practical things," he said.

But the pull towards religion finally became too strong and despite having the good life in Sydney, at 30 he walked away from it all. He moved back to Greece again, with his new family this time, settling in Athens, where he studied to become a priest. He admits it was a difficult decision and the financial prospects in the priesthood were modest. In the Greek church, priests can marry, but once they have made this decision they can no longer rise further than parish priest level. The better paid, and higher church orders, are only open to celibate priests.

After he was ordained, he moved to Kalamata, where he took up a position at this seafront church, and was, I imagined, a popular addition to Orthodoxy in the city, with his open, inclusive manner. However, by 2010, just as he was beginning to find his true path in life, in his mid-40s, he was hit by the austerity measures imposed during the crisis. His life was suddenly turned upside down again.

He smiled a lot during our chat and also tugged at his beard now and then. I sensed that God had led him on a merry chase with his career path, but I didn't say it. I didn't have to. It was as if he had caught my drift.

"I would say God has tested me quite a bit," he said, lapsing into silence for a while before touching on his biggest challenge yet – a possible move back to Australia with his wife Polixenia and his children, who were now mostly in their teens. I was full of awe for this man and his Moses-like wanderings back and forth between continents and cultures. And here was another perilous sea to part.

This time the move back to Australia would be for the children, mainly, to provide them with better opportunities, with Greece now suffering 50 per cent unemployment for young people, a figure that would soon rise to over 60 per cent. Priests' salaries had also been cut during the crisis.

"The problem for Greek priests is that we are paid by the government and the public service here has been the hardest hit. The salary for priests has always been modest, but with four children I find it's now challenging. My salary has already been cut by 20 per cent," he told me.

In Greece, the relationship between the church and the state has often been an awkward one. Yet under a special treaty, the state agreed to pay priests' salaries in exchange for a large chunk of church property, which is said to have amounted to the transfer of most church land to the government over the past few decades.

The 10,000 priests and bishops on the payroll were now costing the Greek government more than it could afford, which meant cuts had to be made. But with the average wage for a parish priest around 1,000 euros a month, any cut in salary was going to seem severe. The government had also stipulated that it would now fund only one new priest for every 10 who retired or died.

During the crisis the church was stripped back to the bone and yet, ironically, in a country that generally does not support the idea of charitable organisations, it was the church that impoverished Greeks were having to fall back on more and more.

Even before the crisis, Papa Lambros had to take up a part-time teaching job in high school to provide a better life for his family, but the salary for that job had also been cut.

"If there are more cuts on the way I think we won't be able to manage," he said.

Papa Lambros had a fascinating story, though I hadn't expected the interview to touch so significantly on the economic hardships of Greek priests. In a country where the Church has been the mainstay of its culture and belief system since the Byzantine era, this seemed a tragic circumstance. It was a subject the *papas* felt strongly about and it was clear to me now that this should be the main thrust of the story, and he agreed.

I asked him if he was serious about a move back to Australia.

"If I go back, I would be able to work full-time as a priest in the Greek Church without having to hold down a second job. I am torn between two countries now and waiting to see how bad things might get in Greece. I'll leave it in God's hands. If he wants me back in Australia I will get a sign," he said, giving me a vibrant smile. Clearly this was a person who took life's trials in his own sunny way and he had a nice sense of humour as well.

Before I left for the evening he asked me a bit more about myself and why I had left Australia and a job on a Sunday paper in Sydney, to go back to Scotland. I realised that my life had been just as peripatetic. I too had been torn between two places: Scotland and Australia. We were both migrant children condemned to feel that home was somewhere else, shimmering in the distance like a mirage. I told him I was rather conflicted about leaving Greece one day, a country I had always loved, but more so during our Mani odyssey.

He looked at me thoughtfully for a moment, tugged on his beard and laughed.

"Scotland, Australia, and now Greece? It seems to me that you're ahead of me then. What I need is a third country to be torn between. Perhaps I'll think about a move to Britain. That should do it."

His laughter reverberated around this almost empty space. It was a strange sound in an Orthodox church and not something you ever seem to hear. But Papa Lambros was not someone you meet every day in Greece, and there lay the great heartache for his congregation.

"They will miss you," I said. He nodded and his face clouded briefly with anxiety.

"I know, and I would miss them too, and I know that most of them are also suffering through the crisis, some much worse than we are. My suffering is very small in comparison."

The time had flown and I had enjoyed my talk with Papa Lambros. He was a deeply religious man and a thoughtful character, and it was impossible not to feel drawn to him. I told him I would send out a pitch to papers in Sydney. If one of the publications was interested I would come back for a Sunday service and take some photos.

My only anxiety about this kind of feature, I told him, was that his thoughts on the crisis and the priesthood might annoy the church administration. Would that be the case?

"No, I don't think so. The head of the Messinian church here, Bishop Chrisostomos, is a very cosmopolitan, educated man. I think he would agree with the sentiments. I'm only speaking the truth."

I mulled that over for a moment, reminding myself how many times as a journalist I had discovered that the truth is often no defence. I consoled myself with the thought that Bishop Chrisostomos would probably never see my Aussie story. But as it turned out, he wasn't the one to fear.

When I got up to leave, I remarked on the church frescos, which were particularly beautiful. Though not old, they were painted in the strict Byzantine style and flanked along the walls like foot soldiers.

"Why are there so many portraits of the saints in the Greek Church?" I asked him.

"I agree, there are a lot," he said, smiling up at the rows of serious faces. "It reminds us that we are being looked after by these saintly people who have gone before us. And they will be waiting for us when we pass out of this life. I find that a comforting idea," he said.

Never before had the Greeks needed such a refuge in these venerable old folk.

@@@@@

At the end of October, EU finance ministers finally negotiated the second bailout for Greece, worth 130 billion euros. They also struck a deal with private creditors to accept a 50 per cent write-down on their Greek bonds (worth over 200 billion euros), which became known in Greece as the *kourema*, haircut. Later on, that figure would rise to 70 per cent. But in return, even more austerity measures were expected of Greece and more implementation of fiscal reforms.

A few days later, however, Prime Minister George Papandreou surprised the Greek and international communities by calling for a referendum on the second rescue plan, saying the Greek people had already suffered enough and they should decide whether they wanted to endure more austerity.

He said: "The referendum will be a clear mandate and a clear message in and outside Greece on our European course and participation in the euro."

Papandreou had not consulted EU leaders before this referendum proposal. Jean-Claude Juncker, head of the Euro Group (eurozone finance ministers), said if the referendum should reject the bailout, it would mean bankruptcy for Greece. The referendum sparked heated debate in Greece and overseas, with critics saying Greece only had itself to blame for the mess it was in by not collecting taxes and avoiding fiscal reforms.

Liana Kanelli, the husky-voiced, outspoken member of the KKE, the Greek Communist Party, had a robust following among left-wingers but, curiously, had suddenly become the voice of the Greek crisis for the overseas media because of her ability to offer impassioned sound bites in fluent English. In terms of the referendum, she told an American TV station it was "a fake referendum" and the question posed by it about austerity was not "a question for a reasonable nation like Greece".

She added: "The question is (for Greeks), 'Do you want to die, or do you want to be killed?'" This comment flashed around the world and came briefly to sum up the difficult position Greeks found themselves in during the crisis, with no apparent options.

Kanelli also famously commented on the nitpicking over Greece's fiscal failures: "We are not a company, we are a country." And she also quipped that Greece was nothing but an "EU experiment". When she was told by Jon Snow during a live interview for Channel 4 news that the world regarded Greece as a shambles and that Greeks had failed on basic things like collecting taxes, she replied: "No-one can pay the taxes now in Greece. Many people have had their wages cut by 50 per cent."

With Greece just weeks away from bankruptcy if further austerity was not implemented, Papandreou's referendum bid failed and he stepped down as Pasok leader. He sealed a deal with the opposition party, Nea Dimokratia (New Democracy), to form an interim coalition government, which also included the far-right party LAOS (Popular Orthodox Rally). Lucas Papademos, former European Central Bank vice-president, was appointed head of the new coalition government, tasked with overseeing the latest 130 billion euro bailout, a tough budget for 2012 and a privatisation drive.

While many Greeks saw these events as the country's last chance to avoid leaving the eurozone, or what popularly became known as the 'Grexit', for thousands of others involved with anti-austerity groups this acceptance of a "technocrat economist" represented the dismantling of democracy. By the end of the year, an angry mood had intensified. The rejection of ruthless austerity measures – as many Greek workers were plunged into unprecedented poverty, with a steady rise in unemployment, suicides and mental illness – created a robust nationalist movement, often directed at perceived German domination of the country.

In a sinister development from this, it offered an opportunity for the violent, far-right party Golden Dawn to seize the advantage and rise slowly in popularity, a circumstance which would become one of the most feared political developments during the Greek crisis.

17

Don't worry, Santa will fix everything

ONE Saturday there was a knock at the front door. It was Marina and Andreas. Marina was loaded up with things in baskets and myriad plastic bags hooked over her wrist. I was very afraid though when I saw the big pointed red hat of what appeared to be a papier maché Santa Claus.

"Good morning, I've brought some Christmas things. I will just sort them out, yes?" she said.

With her usual proprietorial charm that we had fully accepted now, she barged passed us. I assumed she was taking them to the *apothiki* to leave until Christmas. Andreas stayed on the doorstep because his feet were muddy and he handed us a bag of sweet oranges from his trees. We stood outside, talking and leaning on the wrought-iron railing on the top steps, while Zina and Wallace snuffled about, much easier companions these days since their breakout. Andreas was still mystified about how they escaped and every now and then he would wander around the property, checking the fences and shaking his head.

Andreas was talking about the upcoming olive harvest and how he would need help with it, but he couldn't afford to pay the gang of local olive harvesters he usually used. Like everyone else in Greece, Andreas had suffered wage cuts and the food supply company he worked for had been struggling because some of the businesses they dealt with couldn't pay their bills. He would have to strike a compromise for the harvest, and instead of paying the local guys for their work, he would offer them half the olive oil yield in lieu of payment.

While we chatted outside, we forgot all about Marina. Suddenly I became aware of furious scurrying and hammering going on behind us.

"What's happening inside, Andreas?"

He rolled his eyes. "Marina has just decorated your place for Christmas."

"What?"

We turned around and the living room, which had looked atmospheric and Greek, now resembled Santa's Grotto at a John Lewis store. The big red Santa was on the dining table and tinsel was strung up over the fireplace, with Christmas lights, candle stands and a dozen statues of Father Christmas striking various festive poses.

"Here," said Marina, pushing two festive woollen socks towards me. "For Christmas Day."

"But Marina, it's only November. Too early for Christmas, surely?" I pleaded.

Andreas shook his head. "I agree, Margarita, but Marina loves Christmas, you have no idea."

Oh yes I did! The living room — lit up and pulsating, lacking only a sound system for Christmas carols — told me so.

"This old place looks better now, don't you think?" said Marina, hands on hips like the presenter of a TV home makeover show.

One of the things we liked about being in Greece at Christmas was the lack of commercialism and houses lit up like Blackpool seafront. It was a quiet, reflective time instead. But now we had the whole Christmas fizz inside the house. We laughed over it all later and slowly began to dismantle the effects, leaving some of Marina's festive tat in place and hiding the rest in the *apothiki*, hoping she wouldn't notice. Days later she returned, bustling around the house saying: "Now it's time for the rugs."

She came out of the *apothiki* with an armful of hand-woven rugs in bright colours, which had been in her family for a few generations. She spread them out on the tiled floors in each of the rooms and we agreed they made the place seem cosier. The only drawback was that before long they became hairy rugs, covered in white Wallace fur that resisted all attempts to remove with the couple's ancient vacuum cleaner.

We were also given quick instructions about the open fire, which seemed odd when the temperature during the day in November was often in the mid to high 20s, though the evenings were beginning to feel chilly. Andreas had left a huge stack of olive logs under the house from the previous harvest and we were told to use as much as we wanted.

The open fireplace was the best feature of the house, but it had a peculiar design addition for pumping warm air out the front of the chimney breast through two holes with metal doors. Marina's father had the fire specially designed, with a pump in the bottom drawing air under the grate, where it was warmed and forced out through the two tiny doorways just above the mantelpiece. We scoffed at the idea we'd need these curious heat portals, but we didn't know that by mid-winter, with cruel winds strafing the house from the Taygetos, we'd be clinging to them for dear life.

Even before we'd checked out the ancient, massive boiler under the house, which looked like it had been clawed off a Mississippi paddle steamer, we knew we wouldn't be relying on central heating, with the price of heating oil having soared to 1.5 euros a litre. As it was an old, lumbering system, it was going to chew through money. And it did, at something like 50 euros a week, with the heating running just one hour in the morning and one hour at night.

It was more pleasant to have fragrant olive wood logs burning in the grate, spitting out jets of bubbling oil, fanning the flames massively. By the end of November, we had the fire burning every night, with a miniature rattan chair parked either side of it, that had once belonged to the children. Marina would find charming excuses to knock at our door so we would have to invite her in for a warm-up. Her ancient wood-burning *soba* in their *spitaki,* she said, took ages to pump out any heat, but I suspected she just had a passion for the old fireplace and that it brought back happy family memories.

Many times she knocked at the door in the evening and offered us winter vegetables from the garden – crispy giant cabbages and broccoli – or homemade cakes. Each time, I would see her dark eyes flickering with pleasure towards the crackling fire and I couldn't help but invite her in. While Jim fussed over the olive logs, Marina and I would sit on either side of the fire, practically in it, our clothes sprinkled with ash, while we sipped red wine.

"*Ti les,* Margarita? *Eimaste san dio Stahtopoutes,*" she once said. (What do you say, Margarita? We're like a couple of Cinderellas). Her eyes sparkled with glee, or maybe it was from too much heat and wine. A few months of this and I thought we'd both start to look more like Cinderella's wizened stepmother.

Sometimes Andreas would join us at the fireside while he watched the TV news, and the regular nail-biting political dramas over austerity.

Before Christmas, we told them we would definitely stay for the next summer, as Jim had been signed up finally for another season with Apollo Adventures.

Marina touched her heart, the way Greeks do in gratitude, and it made us feel good at least knowing the rent money would help them through another difficult time. Marina was still lucky to have her job in the public sector, despite staffing cuts, but like many employees she had not been paid for many months. This was a common occurrence with government jobs, where many departments were waiting for funds directed from the EU bailouts.

"Why do you go to work every day if you're not paid?" I asked her.

"If we don't go in we might get sacked." It was hard to notice the difference, as far as her income was concerned. "We want to keep our jobs in case the situation improves. *Ti na kanoume?* What can we do?"

Andreas was delighted we were staying, but also slightly mystified.

"*Paidia,* are you sure you want to stay another summer, when we don't know what troubles are ahead?"

"Yes, Andreas, we are sure. We may never get a chance to have this kind of long adventure again," I said.

Andreas nodded thoughtfully. "Ach, maybe things won't be so bad after all. And we are okay here, aren't we?" It was something Andreas often said, as if their property here was magically separated from the brutal world outside.

"If it doesn't all go to plan, at least we'll have plenty to write about one day," I added.

"Did you hear that, Marina?" he said, and translated everything into Greek.

"Bravo, *paidia!* Stupid euro people they don't tell *us* how to live," she announced boldly in English, and we all laughed.

But our staying on in the house clearly wouldn't solve all the couple's money worries. In late December, when Adonis returned from university for the holidays, he knocked on our door to wish us a merry Christmas. He looked sad and when we asked how things were going he said he had surrendered his car number plates to the tax office because the family couldn't afford the road tax, insurance and the MOT any more, which was a common occurrence now.

The car had been his pride and joy, and was to be mothballed in the space under the house for the near future. Studying medicine at Athens University, he was already making plans to move abroad for specialist studies when he graduated, perhaps even to Britain.

There was certain irony in the fact that while Greeks were scrambling to flee the country, we were choosing to stay, like the last few passengers on the Titanic, taking small comfort from the dance band still heroically playing while the ship went down, glad for those who had managed to get away, but not anxious to follow them, because that's the way we felt about the place.

Adonis's car being left under the house underlined a subtle shift in our relationship with Andreas and Marina. As the winter months progressed, our lives were increasingly over-lapping as the couple sought to shore themselves up against the crisis. They began to visit the property nearly every day now, sleeping over at the *spitaki* now and then. Even the animals were drawn more to the big house.

One afternoon, before the couple arrived at the property for their usual nightly chores, we opened our front door to find Zina sleeping on the mat and all the chickens sitting on the front steps outside. The kittens were also there, screeching loudly to be fed.

Although we were fond of the family, there were times when, inevitably, our British sense of privacy held sway and we occasionally felt that instead of renting the house, we had adopted the family and all the animals as well. Sometimes we felt the line was overstepped, but often with amusing results.

One night at 10 o'clock the buzzer on the intercom went off in the house, announcing someone at the front gates.

I answered and a gruff voice said: "Open up – we've got the truckload of onions here."

"We don't want onions!" I shouted back, especially not a truckload of them.

"We can't hang about here all night. Open the gates and we'll load them under the house."

"We don't want your onions under the house," I snapped back and hung up.

"Cheeky buggers!" I said to Jim.

"Who was it?"

"Some hawker selling onions. Honestly, they can be so pushy."

"Not at this time of night, surely?"

The buzzer went again. Same thing. This time the man asked for Andreas.

"He's not here. But I'm sure he hasn't ordered onions," I said, slamming the intercom phone back on its hook.

Ten minutes later, there was a commotion outside. I could hear the big gate being rolled back and a clamour of men shouting at each other.

"What the hell!" Jim said, opening the front door and staring down at the garden, where a truck was backing in. We could hear Andreas's voice too, so we went down to investigate.

"I didn't know you were here so late," I said.

"Marina and I decide to stay over tonight," he said, his eyes flickering towards two men, who were unfastening the back flap of the truck.

"What? For onions? I told the man on the intercom we didn't want onions. I was sure you hadn't ordered them."

Andreas burst out laughing and waved his arm around, windmill-style.

"Margarita, it's not onions, it's roof tiles for the *spitaki*. We will get the roof repaired soon. You got your onions, *kremidia*, muddled up with the roof tiles, *keramidia*. Ha, ha!"

It was true. It was yet another set of similar Greek words I constantly mixed up, with embarrassing results, and now here were the men unloading heavy pantiles and stacking them under the house.

Why hadn't Andreas told us the men were expected? It was one of the maddening things about Greeks that they are not good at filling you in on anything. They won't tell you a certain thing is happening until the minute it does. It's a seat-of-the-pants philosophy that probably got them into financial trouble to start with.

By the end of winter we had become so used to seeing the couple regularly that it seemed odd when they weren't around. I began to look forward to Marina's evening 'deliveries', opening the door to find her standing outside with an arty basket over her arm like Bo Peep. The vegetable offerings were always welcome but they started to arrive in eccentric pairings with other things, as if gathered by a supermarket shelf-stacker with dyslexia.

"Hello, Margarita. I've brought you broccoli and floor cleaner," she announced one day in her best English. Other times she offered cabbages with firelighters, cucumbers with oven gloves. Occasionally they had a spark of logic: spring onions and mouthwash. One day she gave me a beribboned basket.

"Here, I have bring you axe," she said in English.

"What?" Then I recalled what Andreas had said about her ability to slaughter chickens. Did she want *us* to try it now?

I took the basket from her and peered gravely at the white tea towel on top, which seemed a funny accompaniment to an axe. Underneath, however, I found over a dozen eggs from the *kotetsi*, with their typically crazy shapes.

"Eggs!" I said, laughing with relief.

"That's what I said, Margarita, axe." Then she frowned slightly. "Aspro's last axe."

It no longer seemed funny. Poor little Aspro. But one day in the future, when we had finally returned to Scotland, I knew I would miss this kind of crazy Greek behaviour.

18

There's something about Greece

I N the next few weeks, I contacted several Australian publications with Papa Lambros's story. In the end, one of the popular dailies in Sydney, owned by Rupert Murdoch, was keen for a feature angled on the Greek crisis. I called the *papas* and told him my news. He seemed very pleased and I arranged to be at his next Sunday service, so that I could take photos of him.

During the service, he cut an impressive figure in a formal robe of gold and red, and with his confident Greek and mellifluous delivery, it was hard to see the smiling Aussie guy behind the formality of Byzantine rituals and the clouds of incense swirling about him. He had become seriously Greek and I felt a slight shiver of anxiety about the story when I thought of what we had discussed: a Greek priest with modern worries and opinions, with a plan to return to Australia perhaps. How would all this be received, particularly within the church? Yet, it was too good a story not to proceed with.

After the service, and before he'd changed back into his black robe, I managed to get some photos of him standing in front of the ornate *iconostasis*, with its images of Christ and the saints, and the results were stunning.

Afterwards, we went across the road to a seafront café, where I had a few more questions for him before wrapping up the interview. While we sat and talked, people stopped at the table every few minutes to say hello, or to quickly discuss church matters. It was easy to see how highly regarded he was in this corner of Kalamata.

I decided to ask him again if he was still happy about the crisis angle to the story and he was, agreeing it was too important an issue to ignore. He was also generous in not wanting to see the story before I emailed it to the section editor I had dealt with on the Sydney paper, and I guessed he was just far too busy with two jobs to deal with it.

"Don't worry. I trust your judgement," he said.

The story ran on a Saturday in the feature section of the Sydney paper. I was sent a link to the piece but it didn't go online until Sunday morning, Greek time. While nothing in the story had been changed, the headline and layout weren't what I was expecting. They made me feel uneasy. They were somewhat sensationalist, as I had come to expect from a Murdoch paper. But freelancers have little say in the editing and display of their stories.

I thought the headline 'A Greek Tragedy' was a bit clichéd. The subhead read: "A priest is torn between his congregation and a better life for his family", which was at least true. For me, what was most troubling about the full-page layout was the use of one of the photos I'd sent of the *papas,* standing before the ornamental *iconostasis.* In order to make a slightly more mischievous point, I imagined, his figure had been etched from the background and superimposed across the corner of another picture of people wildly demonstrating in Syntagma Square during the crisis, with someone holding up a Greek flag. The image had turned a gentle, though candid, servant of God into a radical. I hadn't seen this coming at all.

Yet, because the story itself was sympathetic, and timely, I thought Papa Lambros would be still be pleased with the results. How wrong I was.

The next day, Jim and I went to the church to give him a print-out of the story, as he wouldn't have had a chance to see it yet. The service was long and intricate. It started at 7am, which was usual, but was now spinning out to 10.30. Even though we hadn't been there from the very beginning,

I began to feel the intensity of it. My nerves were slightly on edge again. At the end of the service, we waited until most of the congregation had drifted away and we took Papa Lambros aside. He looked tired and strained.

"I've seen the story," he said, quickly, anticipating what we were about to say.

"Already?" I said.

I glanced at Jim and saw an eyebrow flicker with surprise.

"A relative in Australia got the paper and scanned the piece into his computer late last night and emailed it to me, and my phone hasn't stopped ringing. Everyone's talking about it," he said, in a soft but weary voice.

Judging by the way he looked, I imagined the comments hadn't been congratulatory. What I hadn't counted on was how many people in the Greek community in Australia would get wind of the story so quickly, sharing it everywhere, including the Aussie/Greek community in Kalamata. I started feeling more anxious. He sensed it.

"It was a good story, Margarita, and truthful. I thought it was important to say all those things, but I'm just as surprised as you are about the reaction, some of it a bit critical, I admit. I honestly didn't expect it."

Some of the congregation interrupted, calling him over to a café by the seafront, which was their Sunday ritual after the service. Papa Lambros told us to come as well and it was difficult to refuse. We all sat at the same table. Once the others realised I was the one who had written 'that Aussie feature', the atmosphere turned icy. No-one bothered to speak to me at least, or criticise the story, but their dark looks said it all.

Papa Lambros sat beside me. He silently drank his coffee and looked thoughtful. The Last Supper must have felt less tense than this gathering. While the churchgoers were chatting amongst themselves, I leaned towards Papa Lambros to tell him I was sorry if the story was now causing him grief.

He tapped me gently on the arm, lowering his voice so that only Jim and I could hear. "It's not your fault. I agreed to do the article and I'm not sorry. But it's difficult for everyone else, especially family and friends. They have strict ideas about how a Greek priest should behave and what they should share outside the Orthodox community. Even still, I'm surprised at all the fuss." He lapsed into silence again, tugging lightly at his beard.

Finally, I mentioned the photo, and how inappropriate it was.

"I'm sorry for the way the paper cut your image in with the photo of the demonstrators."

"Yes, that was pretty unexpected. I reckon it made me look like a bit of a revolutionary *papas*," he said, with a fleeting smile. "But it wasn't your idea, I imagine."

"No, of course not, Pater," I said, wondering, not for the first time, what Bishop Chrisostomos might think about all of this. On a darker note, I worried that Papa Lambros's position in the church might now be jeopardised.

Papa Lambros left the café soon after and I watched him cross the road, calm and dignified in his long black robe, yet there was just a hint in his deportment of the august saints on the walls of his church, with their kindly but overburdened faces. He was unlike the sunny Aussie guy I had met that Monday evening in church.

As we drove back to Paleohora, I felt pretty miserable.

"Well, Jimbo, that story was a bit of a disaster, wasn't it?"

He nodded sagely.

"I've now probably offended the Greek Orthodox Church – and even God himself."

"Only those two? Couldn't you have aimed any higher?" he said, with a cheeky grin.

"Very funny," I said, smiling, staring out the window for a while as the Mani coastline came into view with its small sheltered coves and dazzling water.

"The fact is, my stocks will be pretty low now in Kalamata."

His eyes flickered towards me for a moment. "I agree, Margarita. Your stocks will be so damned low, when you walk around the city people will shout after you, 'Sell, sell, sell!'"

Jim has a great knack for seeing the funny side of anything, as I do too normally. I laughed this time and my mood went up a gear, but by the time we got home I was feeling low again. Jim went off to have a siesta, tired from the early start that morning. I lay down as well, but couldn't sleep. Wallace was on the bottom of the bed, engaged in the compulsive obsessive paw-licking that he does when he's anxious, as if he had picked up on my mood. I decided the two of us needed a walk.

We set off for the olive groves on the other side of a shallow gorge near the house. The trees were drooping heavily with fruit, just weeks from the olive harvest. A soft light was filtering through them. I found a quiet spot overlooking the gulf, where a very old olive tree with a thick, gnarled trunk had fallen, and was left like a park bench. I sat down and thought about the day's events. I was rattled by the antipathy the story had generated.

I'd had a long journalistic career, with many interviews under my belt. People had always opened up to me easily and it had made for some insightful interviews. I believed I had a good sense of what people should reveal about themselves, and what they might later regret. I like to think I had saved a few people in my time from publishing embarrassing truths about themselves in an era of journalism that was more genteel than it is today.

But I had missed something with the *papas*. I had lost my concentration, for some reason. Perhaps I was slightly in awe of him. Because of this, I failed to save him from expressing candid thoughts he would later regret about the state of the priesthood in crisis-torn Greece.

But that wasn't the whole story. I hadn't just failed to tap the brakes on some of Papa Lambros's narrative, I had failed to get to grips with Greek culture as well. I had stepped over the line badly, the way many foreigners do in this country, even with the best of intentions.

I was reminded of the Ayios Yiorgos celebration in spring when I tried to take pictures of Papa Nektarios and the other village men and he had not been pleased. I should have been paying attention then. Bells were ringing – and they weren't the silver ones tinkling on the church censer. I began to feel as if I had learnt nothing at all in the past two years in Greece. But then, who had?

These were extraordinary times we were all living through. The crisis had stretched everyone to the very limits of endurance. We were all tagged by this fiscal foul-up that had its roots apparently everywhere: in past wars, colonialism, dynastic politics, global banking, EU-bumbling, greed, jack-booted quick fixes, and in the Greek character, too. Many educated Greeks will tell you that the crisis, most of all, had heightened their sense of not having made the grade in some way. That it harked back to old ideas of inadequacy and conflict.

The Nobel Prize-winning Greek poet George Seferis wrote with great emotion about the "tragic predicament" of Greece. In his poem *In the Manner of G.S.*, there's a line that is famously loaded and heart-wrenching:

"Opou kai na taxidepso, i Ellada me pligonei."

"Wherever I travel, Greece wounds me."

In one sentence, he encapsulated a complex set of feelings about being a native of this country. On one level it is about the painful nostalgia that Greeks feel when they are far from their homeland. But there are other layers to this poem.

As one Athenian writer and academic explained to me: "It relates to the contrast and contradictions that the poet perceives around him when travelling through Greece. It is the irreconcilable contradiction between the old and the new, the glorious past and inglorious present."

The poem was written in the mid-1930s and captures the sense of turmoil and melancholy that Greeks felt in the inter-war years, particularly after the events of the Greco-Turkish war from 1919 to 1922, culminating in the destruction of Smyrna (where Seferis was born) and the slaughter of thousands of Greeks in an area of Asia Minor they had populated for 3,000 years.

In the poem, Seferis also expressed his disappointment over what Greece had become, a place that was floundering, a place that people were constantly shipping out of, not unlike the crisis-torn Greece of modern times. "Greece is travelling and we don't know anything," he wrote.

Seferis's words had particular resonance for me that Sunday and as I left the olive grove with Wallace, my melancholy seemed to have intensified. When I got back to the house, Jim, who had just wakened from his siesta, quickly noticed it.

"You're taking this incident far too hard," he said, rubbing his sleepy eyes. "Papa Lambros knew what he was doing when he spoke to you. He's an intelligent guy. How were you to know that other people would gripe about the feature? What's their problem?"

"I feel sorry for him really."

"I do as well. He's putting out a call for help and no-one's listening. Everyone has a dark story in crisis-torn Greece. No-one should be surprised when someone breaks ranks and cries out. They should be grateful."

Yet no-one likes the messenger, I thought.

We were sitting on the front balcony in the warm winter sun, admiring the view.

"You know, Jimbo. I was thinking today that maybe it's time for us to go back to Scotland. Things will only get a lot worse here, what with more austerity on the way. What happened today... well, it just makes me question why we're here."

Jim gave me an uncomprehending look. "Go back? In the middle of a Scottish winter? Are you kidding? And scrape ice off the windscreen every morning and do a few more deathly pirouettes along the driveway? No way!" he said, referring to the Arctic winter before we left Scotland in 2010, when Jim broke his wrist performing an impromptu ice folly on his way from the car. "You've had a bad day, haven't you? I never thought I'd hear you say you were tired of Greece."

"I'm not tired of it. I'm just thinking our timing has been lousy."

"But I remember at Christmas you told Andreas we wanted to stay another summer and that we might not get another chance to have this kind of adventure in life."

"Yes, I remember I did say that."

"So what's changed?"

"I don't know. Maybe I wasn't thinking clearly then, too delirious about the idea of staying another summer," I said, biting my lower lip.

Jim was quiet for a time, then he pulled his chair up beside me, reached over and playfully stroked my hair.

"Look, Margarita, you must forget what happened today. It's not our fight. Let's wait until the summer and see how my second season at Apollo goes. On the strength of this year's bookings, it will undoubtedly be my last summer with them, and then we'll have to go back to the UK in the winter, whether we want to or not."

I sighed. "I guess you're right. Why hurry the inevitable?"

A week or so later, I called Papa Lambros on his mobile to see how he was. He told me everything was fine, yet I knew it wasn't. I could hear a fine current of anxiety in his voice, even when he was trying to put a light spin on things.

"At least no-one's in any doubt there's a real problem in Greece now, in the priesthood anyway. But my main problem is whether I should stay in Greece or go back to Australia. One good thing that's come from the story is that a few friends there have offered support if I choose to go back."

I imagined that hadn't made his dilemma any easier and I sensed he was being pulled in many directions. I wanted to ask if any of his interview comments had filtered up to the church hierarchy yet, but thought better of it.

"Come back to the church sometime for the service, you and Jim. It would be nice to see you both," he said.

"Thanks, I appreciate that."

Nothing would have given me more joy, but I knew I couldn't go back for a while. The Aussie-Greek element of the congregation, at least, would probably want to throw me on a barbecue with a few other raw prawns.

I decided also not to call Papa Lambros for a while. I couldn't bear to hear the struggle in his voice or the thought that yet again in his incredible life, God was testing him. Testing all of us.

And I was beginning to accept that Greece is one of those places where nothing is ever going to fit into a straightforward template. All the greatest thoughts and ideas of life had erupted here. Its accomplishments have been grand, just like its failures. It is not a place of easy but dull predictability.

19

Athens, 1970s

ONE March afternoon at the Halandri apartment, while Nikos was out with Pericles visiting a relative, Deirdre came into my room.

"We must talk," she said, pulling up a chair at the window, where I was sitting, reading. She looked strained and I sensed some bad news.

"I'm thinking of leaving Nikos...finally. I should have done it years ago."

Well, that's the end of my job then, I thought, closing my book. Deirdre explained she was planning a trip back to England in a few weeks and would take Pericles, telling Nikos it was just a short holiday to see her mother, much like she'd done in previous years.

"Then I won't come back – unless he makes some kind of gesture to save the marriage," she said.

"What gesture?"

"I don't know. If he gets a job, pulls himself together, stops drinking and hanging out in ouzeries, or borrows some money from his family to get a proper house. Don't be fooled – the family have money and land. They can spare something to help."

"How long will you give him to make the gesture?" I asked.

"Not long, and I doubt he'll come up with anything, so basically I probably won't be back."

"You won't want me to stay on then?"

"Don't worry, you can stay a while yet. I'll keep paying you, just in case I do return. But you are welcome to come back with me if you want. I'll pay your plane fare to the UK, but after that you're on your own. I'll write you a great reference, don't worry."

It was a generous offer, in its way, but it didn't hold any appeal.

"I don't really want to go back yet."

"You'd rather stay *here*, in Greece, under *this* regime?" she said, pulling a face like a lemon harvest.

"I guess so."

"Suit yourself, but I'm afraid I've been here far too long. I don't want Perry to be brought up with all this political crap."

"Nikos will be devastated, losing you both," I said.

"He will miss Perry, I know that, but it's got to be done. You don't know the half of it. I can't take his black moods. He just doesn't try to do anything with his life. It's frustrating. He used to be such a vital, clever man... and a great journalist."

"It's not really his fault, is it?"

"Lots of people have suffered under this dictatorship. They haven't all gone to pieces."

Yes, and they weren't all married to the unsympathetic Deirdre, I thought. I felt sorry for Nikos. Maybe he was simply depressed and probably drank heavily to cover it. I didn't think he deserved what was about to happen to him.

"He won't let you take Perry out of Greece if he suspects it's for more than a few weeks, will he?" I asked.

"No, absolutely not!"

"Well?"

"So, he's not to suspect anything. I have a plan."

Deirdre explained it, and how it would involve me, unfortunately. She didn't want Nikos to have any inkling she might not be coming back, but she wanted to take as many of her things, and Perry's, as she could. She would hide a big suitcase under my bed and pack things away, bit by bit, while Nikos was out or asleep. She would get one of her friends to take her to the airport early in the morning on the day of the flight. She knew he hated getting up early after his long boozy nights and this way he wouldn't see the size of the suitcase and guess at her plans.

So I'd be in the middle of the whole thing, as Rory had once predicted. I'd have a job at first but if Nikos found out I'd helped Deirdre to leave, it wouldn't last long. Nikos had a dark side, I knew that. There had been a lot of drinking over Christmas with his *ouzeri* pals, a lot of fights between him and Deirdre.

Yet I could never bring myself to dislike Nikos. Despite his faults, he was smart, and funny too, and many times when Deirdre was out teaching he told me stories about his job on the Athens paper and the assignments. It was all fascinating stuff. Nikos wasn't just the one who suggested I write a book, I think he may have steered my vague dreams of journalism towards something more realistic. In an odd way, I probably owed him a lot.

"Is this okay with you?" Deirdre said, with a piercing look that implied I didn't have much choice.

"I'll go along with the plan, if you want, but I won't feel comfortable with it. I'll feel like I'm betraying Nikos. I work for him too."

"Yes, darling, but he doesn't pay your salary, does he?" she snapped.

A moment later she softened, leaning over and tapping me lightly on the knee.

"Look, don't feel too bad about things. One day you'll be far away from Greece and you won't give a second thought to any of this."

How wrong she was. But I'd certainly think about poor little Perry trapped in this hellish family set-up. And I, too, was tangled in it for now.

I could have left the job. There were many similar positions around Athens but, strangely, I couldn't be bothered. I was settled here. So I agreed to Deirdre's big suitcase under my bed and hoped she'd see sense and come back soon after her trip to England.

I agreed not to breathe a word of the plan to Perry, in case he innocently gave some clue to Nikos. I also promised to say very little about Deirdre's 'holiday', after she left, to the couple's gossipy landlord, who had an apartment on the top floor of the building.

It was Nikos who had christened him *Kyrios Vatrahos*, Mr Frog, because he had bulbous eyes and an oily sheen to his skin, and had a habit of bounding into view when you least expected it.

"If the Frog gets any notion that I'm not coming back he'll make trouble," said Deirdre. "He's a cunning old bastard. Watch him!"

"He'll find out eventually," I said.

"Let's worry when 'eventually' comes," said Deirdre, showing that after years in Athens she had picked up the national sport of living in the minute.

Deirdre left with Perry in early April, without arousing Nikos's suspicion. Despite missing the boy, Nikos seemed happier, more relaxed. I even saw him laugh occasionally.

But all that stopped when he got a letter from Deirdre to say she wouldn't be back for a while. She was giving Nikos time to sort himself out, as she had explained it to me. Nikos was mad with rage. He ramped up his drinking sessions and slept even longer during the day.

I feared he would eventually fall apart, but at least he never bothered me, so I had more free time and was able to indulge my interest in visiting ancient sites.

During those weeks I received a letter from Rory, telling me about his exploits in London, sharing a flat with Canadian students, working in a bar, enjoying his bohemian lifestyle.

"We'll catch up in London one day. I've got plenty to tell you," he said. It sounded enticing, but even then I thought

London was a long way off. Athens still held me in thrall, and life in Halandri was as good as it could be, under the circumstances. That was until the arrival of Nikos's wizened-faced, embittered old mother, all the way from Crete, to take charge of his household.

20

Slipping into Hades

ONE February morning, we stayed in bed later than normal because it was too cold to get up. Finally we understood the sting of winter on the Road of the Olive Orchards. *Odos Elaionon,* two beautiful Greek words that rolled off the tongue, with the same ease as the icy wind now peeling off the snow-capped Taygetos mountains. It raked its way through the big gaps under balcony doors and ill-fitting windows.

I don't think we had ever felt this cold in our lives and press reports in Greece said this was the coldest winter here since 1918, with temperatures dropping overnight to around minus 5 to minus 10. We could only afford the central heating for a short time, twice a day, but in the evening we piled olive logs on to the fireplace until our cache was nearly depleted. During the day we huddled in the study, with our one electric heater, and it was almost bearable, enough to be able to work at least.

During that long, cold winter, I was able to keep writing my book about our first year in the Mani, while Jim sat on the bed reading, waiting for his turn on the computer, with Wallace curled up beside him for warmth.

We had a few storms in the winter, some that lasted all night, with dozens of white forks of lightning jabbing at the Messinian peninsula opposite. One night, when a bad storm was brewing, we went to the *spitaki* to let Zina off her chain, thinking we were doing her a favour, so she could hide somewhere on the property if she wanted. It turned out to be a big mistake. She woke us in the early hours of the morning with ferocious howling. Tired of the night's pyrotechnics, she had finally snapped and decided to mount a protest session. She climbed on to the top of the *fournos* and from there to the old tiled roof above the *spitaki* kitchen, to bark and curse at the sky.

We went down to see what all the noise was about and saw her big wolf-like shadow, head thrown back, accentuated against the illuminated sky, like something out of a Hammer horror movie. Eventually, we coaxed her down with a packet of biscuits and let her follow us up to the house. We knew the routine by now – and the bathtub beckoned.

But on that particular February morning we had no urge to get up until I heard the phone ringing at 10. I got up, padding over the freezing tiled floor to the phone by the front door. It was Foteini. The message was simple: Eftihia's mother Pelagia had died two days earlier in Kalamata Hospital and Eftihia wanted us to go to the funeral at 3pm that day in the village. We were distressed by this news. Pelagia was one of the loveliest women we had met in the village and it was unexpected. We had seen her a few weeks earlier and she seemed fine.

I had no idea how to prepare for a Greek funeral and rang my Australian friend Geraldine. She would know the protocol, having been to enough funerals during her several decades in the southern Peloponnese. She told me exactly what would be expected and what we should say to the family, and gave me firm instructions.

"Whatever you do, don't confuse the word for 'condolences' with 'congratulations', as I have done in the past, because the two words sound very similar. That would be a disaster," she warned.

The word for 'condolences' is *sillipitiria*. 'Congratulations' is *singharitiria*. Given my history of Greek language dysfunction, I was only able to avoid the latter word by focusing on the 'sing' part of it, something you should never do at a Greek funeral.

"Don't worry, everything will be fine. By the way, you're very privileged to be invited to this funeral by Pelagia's daughter. The mother must have been very fond of you both," she said. The statement made me feel unbearably sad, as if we had somehow only discovered the depth of the friendship now that it was all too late, as is often the case in life.

A funeral is a desultory experience in any culture, but in Greece it is much more raw and sombre. There is no attempt to soften the blow of death and protect the bereaved from feeling their worst, or to hide heartache behind a veil of western-style self-restraint. The rituals of death are impressive and strong here, but also cathartic.

At 3pm, a lone bell chimed every few seconds from the main village church dedicated to the *Theotokos*, Virgin Mary. It was a melancholy sound. We stood outside the church with a few other villagers in the tiny *plateia* that was bordered on one side by the Kali Kardia *kafeneio*. The wind felt raw as we waited until the hearse drew up at the church door.

From the church, the village road winds up towards the shop and on past Eftihia's house and then to the graveyard. A noise filtered down to the church – the sound of a procession shuffling slowly down the incline – and then the first black-clad mourners came into view, advancing in lines. All the while, the bell tolled.

Leonidas, one of the most gentle of village farmers, and an elder of the church, was at the head of the procession, holding a large cross aloft. Behind him came three priests in black robes and stovepipe hats, one with a long black veil over his hat, which lent a slightly biblical air to the proceedings. Then in a broad line were Eftihia, Yiorgos and their family and, behind them, the lines of villagers. As they came closer, my eyes locked for a moment with Eftihia's and I inhaled sharply. I had never seen her look so desolate.

How would she bear this loss, I wondered? Pelagia had been her life, her other half. I used to jokingly call them bookends – but that was exactly what they were like. They were always together and you could never imagine one without the other. She wouldn't survive this, I felt sure.

The lines of mourners stopped for a few moments while Yiorgos and several others carried the coffin into the church. Many of the villagers remained outside for the service because there wasn't much space in the church. They came and went, the way people do in Greece, but Jim and I were resolved to go inside and last the duration of the service to show our respect for this gentle soul.

While Jim stayed on the right, with the men, I squeezed along the aisle to where Foteini was standing, looking more formal than I'd ever seen her, in a black jacket and skirt, a simple cross at her neck. She looked tired but when I drew close, she took my hand and pulled it up under her arm, as if for support, and kept it there for most of the service. It made me think fondly of other times I'd seen Foteini in church and some of my more spirited exchanges with her that had earned the women's section a lashing of incense from Papa Nektarios's censer.

Despite Foteini's comforting touch there was no escape from the powerful funeral liturgy, the sonority of the chanting, the villagers huddled together like a flock of mournful blackbirds in this small church, where the sombre eyes of saints looked down on us all. This Orthodox service seemed to have been constructed to heighten the sense of drama and loss. And there was no escape from the sight of the coffin at the front of the church, left open during the service, and the appearance of Pelagia's thick dark hair springing above the rim as if even in death it couldn't be tamed.

When we finally walked outside again, to a cold afternoon laden with soaky rain, I felt overwhelmed by what we had just experienced. We walked up to the cemetery, behind the family and most of the villagers. We waited outside the perimeter wall of the graveyard while the family filed in first and lowered the coffin themselves into the depths of a heavy marble tomb, over which a lid of marble would be placed. Later the family lined up outside the graveyard for the congregation to file past and shake each of them by the hand and offer a '*sillipitiria*'.

When I reached Eftihia, I embraced her tightly.

"So Foteini rang you then, Margarita," she said. "I told her to, but I wasn't sure if she'd done it or not. You know what I mean."

I managed a thin smile. Sometimes telephones and Foteini didn't mix well.

"Come and see me sometime," she said, with a tremble of her lips, and turned quickly towards the next person in the line.

As one of the much-loved matriarchs of this village, we knew Pelagia's death was a bitter loss to Megali Mantineia and its traditional way of life. This death in particular, coming in a bitterly cold February, also heightened the villagers' sense of gloom about everything that was happening in Greece.

This month would turn out to be one of the worst in the crisis so far, if that was possible. It would scupper every last grain of hope.

"A disorderly default will plunge our country into a catastrophic adventure. It will create conditions of uncontrolled economic chaos and social explosion."

Those were the chilling words of Lucas Papademos, interim leader of the coalition government, uttered in the week starting February 6, 2012, when Greece came the closest it had ever been to a 'Grexit' from the eurozone.

In February, the coalition government was debating the terms of the second major rescue package for Greece, worth

130 billion euros. This was crucial as the country had up until March 20 to repay 14 billion euros of maturing debt or else it would probably default.

The Troika – the IMF, EU and European Central Bank – were demanding yet more punishing measures and it was met with bitter resistance by a population already impoverished by three years of crisis. Many of the coalition MPs were also vehemently opposed to the terms and many later resigned from Parliament over the issue.

There were to be more job losses, cuts to salaries and to another swathe of pensions, as well as a 22 per cent cut to the minimum wage. Eurostat, a European statistics agency, revealed that poverty in Greece was now affecting a third of the country.

During this week in February, ahead of a Sunday vote in Parliament, there were general strikes and protests. As one Athens protest placard read: "We choose to be free. Keep your money."

We watched TV reports all week until late into the night as party leaders and MPs bitterly debated the new measures. The words "overnight thriller" appeared most evenings on the banner subtitles on news bulletins. There were endless discussions and shouting matches between heads in boxes. We now felt we were in the vortex of one of the most gruelling and testing periods of Greek history, and it was compulsive viewing, night after night.

Evangelos Venizelos, Finance Minister and Pasok leader in the coalition, weighed into the debate with an impassioned plea for austerity, for the "eurozone medicine", as it was called. He said: "The choice we face is one of sacrifice, and even greater sacrifice, on a scale that cannot be compared."

As the debate in Parliament became more divisive and protracted, frustration also increased throughout the EU. Most European leaders insisted Greece should remain in the eurozone because it would be a disaster for Europe if it didn't.

Jean-Claude Juncker, head of the Euro Group, said: "We cannot kick Greece out anyway... If we force them so much that they resign, we would still be forced to support Greece and would have to invest unimaginable sums."

However, it was Hannes Swoboda, Austrian MP and leader of the European Parliament's Progressive Alliance of Socialists and Democrats, who condemned the EU's handling of Greece. During a visit to Athens in February, he said: "The way things are being done by Brussels and the IMF, and especially by Germany, is not acceptable for us, because they are acting like a dictatorship from the outside. They want to dictate conditions that are not helpful."

Even after the Greek coalition government voted finally on the Sunday night in favour of the new measures, public anger spilled over to the next week, when the Troika announced the second bailout funds wouldn't be handed over until the Greek government supplied details of how a huge funding gap of 325 million euros would be closed. It did nothing but inflame Greek hatred of the Troika, and particularly Germany.

Angry headlines and leader columns followed in most of the daily papers. Finally, Yiorgos Karatzaferis, leader of the smaller party in the coalition, the populist right-wing LAOS party, spoke for millions of Greeks when he denounced German interference, with a nationalistic soundbite that would become an anthem of the anti-austerity movement. He said: "Greece cannot live outside of the EU but it can live without the German boot."

He also railed against the vote for austerity, saying it would plunge the country into deeper poverty and take away "its last trace of national sovereignty".

The Sunday of voting in Parliament sparked some of the most vicious street battles Greece had seen during the crisis, as protesters fought with police, hurling firebombs and torching more than 40 buildings in the centre of Athens.

Pictures on TV showed scenes of devastation, with fires burning all night, like the worst kind of war zone.

During this vicious rioting, it seemed as if the country was teetering close to anarchy, and the recurring fear that these events could spark some kind of military takeover seemed much less improbable to many Greeks.

The respected *Kathimerini* broadsheet described the street battles in Athens as "catastrophic chaos" in its Monday headline. In a stirring column piece, Nikos Konstandaras said: "What is lost in the flames may be greater than the incomes that will be reduced, greater than percentages of wages and pensions, greater than deposits lost and hopes abandoned. What is at greatest risk is our identity, our civilisation. If we cannot stay in the eurozone, if we find ourselves on Europe's edge, we will be defeated, humiliated and alone."

Konstandaras also railed against the pantheon of politicians debating the new bailout loan: "On Sunday we again saw our politicians skirmishing in Parliament, as if they still had the luxury of division and false narratives, as if they could keep looking for external threats when that which is killing us is the plague within our walls. Again we saw the popular rage which feeds off the indifference of our leaders ... Our incompetent state does to citizens what Europe does to Greece – it condemns them to deprivation and insecurity and then sits back and watches them flounder..."

As I watched the rioting on the Sunday night on TV, and footage of the fires around areas of the city I had once known so well, it was impossible not to think of how 'innocent' Athens had seemed, even under a dictatorship, when I first stepped off that bus from London and walked along streets that were now burning.

I thought of Nikos Papadakis saying to me once: "Welcome to the home of democracy." For Nikos, what was inimical about the dictatorship years was the illusion of harmony and control that the Colonels tried to foster, in contrast to the oppression and violence going on underneath that foreigners, at least, didn't see much of.

If I were talking to Nikos now, I think he'd probably say he approved of the demonstrations and would have hurled a piece of marble paving stone at the riot police, along with the other 'indignants'. He would have loved to see Greeks venting their anger openly and passionately. He never got the chance to do that all those years ago, and all his fury was turned inwards.

@@@@@

The big table in front of the *spitaki* was set for an afternoon feast. The old *fournos,* with its ill-fitting metal door, belched thick smoke as trays of lamb sprinkled with fresh rosemary sprigs and lemony potatoes sizzled inside, sending delicious aromas wafting through the olive trees.

On Easter Sunday in mid-April, Andreas and Marina had organised the traditional family feast at the Paleohora property, inviting their family and friends. It was a joyous day, with everyone squeezing around the big table, where trays of meat were set in the middle, surrounded by bowls of salad, boiled *horta* and plates of feta in thick slabs sprinkled with herbs and olive oil.

Although it was a chilly day, the sky was an indelible blue and cloudless. *Ilios me dontia*, as the Greeks describe this kind of day, "Sun with teeth".

Everyone had *kefi*, high spirits. The couple's two children were chattering excitedly, meeting up with cousins they hadn't seen for a while. Lunch was a long, languid affair and when it was finished someone rigged up a sound system to a radio station playing popular Greek music. When a favourite song came on, everyone got up to dance the *Kalamatiano.* A long chain of people, holding hands, threaded its way through the olive trees, scattering cats, chickens and two crazy dogs. That scene stays in my memory as one of the sweetest in our Greek odyssey.

Later, everyone found their own corner to sit a while and chatter. Marina had invited one of her close friends, Myrto, an attractive woman who was a teacher at a Kalamata primary school. She had studied overseas, had fluent English and asked us what we thought about the crisis and, mostly, what kind of image Greece was projecting overseas.

"Newspapers are describing us as lazy and frightened of work. What do you think?"

"That's clearly not true," said Jim with great conviction. "These stories are beat-ups, as we say in English. Greeks are among the hardest working people in Europe. Millions of tourists who come here every year know that. I think most people in the western world are on your side."

She looked neither pleased, nor grateful, and paused to light up a cigarette, inhaling deeply. "But for how long will they be on our side? The Troika say we are not doing enough to tackle things like tax evasion and corruption."

The others had grown silent, apart from Andreas, who suddenly leapt into the discussion. "Yes, the Troika moans at us becows they say we don't make changes fast in the government, and with taxes ... but they want us to change centuries of customs and business in a few months. We cannot do it! Impossible! And for what? We won't see any of the money, *paidia*. It's not for peoples like us. Our lives get worse now," said Andreas, looking flushed.

Myrto was smoking nervously now. "Greeks are deeply ashamed of the crisis and what austerity is doing to us. Look, have you been to Nestor's Palace, near Pylos?"

It seemed an odd question, but in fact we had. In its day it had been the grand two-storey Mycenaean palace of King Nestor on the west coast of the Peloponnese, and an influential stronghold. In Homer's *Iliad*, it is said that here, Telemachus came to ask Nestor about his father Odysseus, who was serving as an envoy in Troy during the Trojan War. The palace is now a ruin that only hints at greatness.

"The palace had a sewerage system," said Myrto. "Imagine that, over 3,000 years ago? The Greeks invented plumbing and sewerage systems even before the Romans thought of it."

She must have seen our bemused looks, but I did remember that one of the few preserved items in the palace ruin was a magnificent stone bathtub, with channels for waste water.

"Okay, I know what you're thinking. Why worry about sewerage systems when we built the Parthenon. But you see, we were amazing people in ancient times. So clever, so innovative. And look at us now," said Myrto.

It was a common lament from many educated Greeks that while they had the legacy of the Ancient Greeks, the vitality and integrity of their civilisation had been lost. It dovetailed with the thoughts of other writers and thinkers through the years about the ways in which Greece could never quite cut it now on the European stage, and that was even before the economic crisis. It was sad to hear such an accomplished young woman feeling this negative about her own country and its prospects, and everyone lapsed into thoughtful silence, except for Marina.

"No more talk about the crisis, *paidia*. It's Easter. Let's have the *glika* now."

She went into the kitchen and brought out a large plate of *galaktoboureko*, custard pie, and cut it into fat slices. Apart from the youngsters, no-one seemed very hungry now.

There was something about that day, about the air and the light, that seemed sharp, almost metallic. I started to feel a migraine coming on, which was not a common occurrence for me. It wasn't a painful migraine but one that manifested itself with dazzling lights in one eye, an aura, which always makes me feel oddly disconnected from the real world.

I got up, with the intention of going back to the house for a while, but as I did, the ground began to shudder slightly. Then I heard that strange other-worldly noise, like a moan and a jet of wind, and everyone looked around anxiously. Their chairs were rattling and a few smaller things were shaken off the big table. Wind chimes hanging from the olive tree branches played a discordant tune.

It was an earth tremor, but one of the strongest yet at 5.5 on the Richter scale, we discovered later, with its epicentre right in the Messinian Gulf.

As soon as the tremor ended, we looked at each other grimly, waiting for another to follow – but fortunately it never came. Oddly enough, my migraine 'lights' started to fade straight afterwards and I felt much better. The others began to chatter excitedly about how funny it was that the tremor struck just as we were discussing the crisis.

"Not funny, *paidia*," said Andreas, standing up theatrically and waving a fork in the air with a cube of custard pie wedged on the end of it. "It is a sign of what is to come peeeerhaps in this country. Things will get much worse. We will be forced out of the euro and chaos will break out on the streets, no money, no food. Greece will be *halia*, a mess."

"I know that word *halia* now," said Jim to me, with a grim smile.

I was reminded of the first tremor we'd experienced in the house while working in the study. It was strong enough to ping my icon of the venerable Ayios Theologos (St John the Theologian) off the wall, where it dropped into the wastepaper basket below.

"Don't you think it's odd," I said, continuing in Andreas's apocalyptic vein, "that the Book of Revelation, predicting how the world might possibly end, was written by Ayios Theologos, in a cave in Greece, of all places, after he was expelled from the Holy Land. He could have gone to any country in the Mediterranean to write it, but he chose the island of Patmos. Spooky, don't you think?"

Everyone looked serious for a moment.

"Yes, very spooky," said Myrto. "But the Theologos probably wasn't predicting the end of the world – more specifically the end of Greece."

21

Cantering in the sky

I PARKED the car outside Foteini's *ktima* just as she was arriving at the front gates, leading Riko on a long rope.

"*Yeia sou, koritsara mou,*" she shouted. That was her favourite nickname for me, 'my girl'.

The donkey stood patiently as she undid the padlock on the gate. He was bulging either side with plastic bags filled with *horta,* their handles hooked over the pommel of the saddle. Foteini had been out collecting the spring greens that grow everywhere at this time of year.

Spring comes suddenly in Greece, bursting out almost overnight with swathes of herbs and bright wildflowers covering the hillsides, as if they can't wait a minute longer. The almond trees herald the season and blossom early, filling the air with a sweet, almost cloying aroma, like a blast from Papa Nektarios's wayward censer.

Despite a darkening sky that threatened a heavy down-pour, Foteini had plenty of *kefi* that day and was singing a tune, her eyes crinkling with mirth, but my attention was drawn to her feet. They looked odd, an old welly boot on one foot and on the other a bizarre makeshift contraption, an old flat shoe bound up in a thick piece of plastic.

"Why are you wearing that?" I asked her, smiling.

"Come in for coffee, Margarita, and I'll tell you."

"I can't stay long. I've been a while in the village already and there's a storm coming."

But I knew I would stay longer than intended. That was the way it was at Foteini's *ktima*. But she always made me laugh, and laughter had been in short supply for everyone in those months.

The day had started off on a very different note. I had been to see Eftihia in Megali Mantineia. It was now several weeks since her mother had died and I had promised to visit her. But when I stepped into the kitchen and looked at Pelagia's old chair by the fireplace I knew this wasn't going to be an easy get-together.

Eftihia was dressed completely in black and had gone into a more formal mourning than a lot of Greeks do nowadays. She would wear black for a long time and at least until the year's anniversary of her mother's death, and would not go to any social event or gathering, apart from church events. This kitchen would be her world for the next 12 months.

She made coffee and we sat at the dining table. Eftihia had deep dark shadows under her eyes. It was obvious she wasn't coping well with her loss. For over an hour she told me the story of her mother's sudden illness, how a chest cold had suddenly developed into pneumonia, as Pelagia also had other medical conditions to deal with. It meant she had to go into hospital.

"I am burning up inside about what happened to my mother in the hospital," Eftihia said at one point. "She shouldn't have been there. They treated her for the pneumonia but it was difficult for us to make her comfortable. I think she had a terrible time of it."

Eftihia felt her mother had been let down slightly by the system, though I couldn't grasp all the details. Although Kalamata Hospital was new, and had a good reputation, at least for the calibre of its doctors, during the crisis there were shortages of drugs, equipment and nurses.

"My mother told me many times in the past that if she was about to die she wanted to be here, at home, and I let her down. Ach! I can't get these thoughts out of my head!" she said, rubbing her forehead as if trying to expunge the memories.

"I have been able to help so many other people in the village with their illnesses, but I couldn't help my own mother at the end," she said, wiping a big solid hand over her cheeks that were wet with tears.

I sat quietly and listened. I couldn't find the right words to console her, let alone in a difficult language like Greek. Even if I had managed it, I don't think it would have made things any better for her. I understood the closeness of Eftihia and her mother, a bond that is more typical in Greek society, where family members share houses, bedrooms, every detail of their lives, sometimes forever. And like this family, they do it with good grace.

I surrendered to her story as much as I could, frequently losing the threads of it, as she spoke fast in her anxiety. I felt that at least I could perform a role here, much like the wedding guest in Coleridge's dramatic poem, the *Rhyme of the Ancient Mariner*. At least Eftihia was getting the whole thing off her chest, and I hoped it might help her. She only stopped now and then to make me several more cups of Greek coffee and ply me with biscuits.

When I said goodbye on the terrace, Eftihia hugged me and I was reminded of the last time we had seen Pelagia here, laughing with Eftihia over one of Yiorgos's jokes. I walked quickly up the steep incline to the car, where I sat for quite a while, feeling heavy-hearted, not sure I wanted to go home yet, as Jim was in Kalamata for the day.

That's when I decided to visit Foteini, as I knew she'd be hurt if I didn't, and I needed to shrug off some difficult thoughts about my own mother in the last weeks of her life when we had returned to Scotland, in 2000. We had been close like Pelagia and Eftihia and there had been regrets and guilt, too, after she died. I never quite believed the old adage that time lessens grief, rather it just pushes it further into our subconscious mind, where it cunningly waits for any chance to re-emerge.

All gloomy thoughts were scuppered, however, as I stood before Foteini in the *ktima,* examining her bizarre footwear. The improvised shoe was a piece of thick plastic stitched along the top with some kind of twine, the edges of it sticking up the way and scalloped. It looked like a Cornish pasty. I laughed gratefully at the madness of it all, and the thought of Foteini brazenly plodding along the road like some Shakespearean eccentric. Malvolio in *Twelfth Night* came to mind, with his yellow cross-gartered stockings.

I was used to seeing Foteini's odd *ktima* couture: the mannish layers, the clashing patterns, plaid with paisley, and the trousers that had split their bums and were patched up with child-like giant stitches using the wrong-coloured thread. But the shoe was even more extreme.

"Why are you wearing that thing?" I asked her, with the hectoring but jokey familiarity that had developed between us.

"Ach, the other boot has holes and I had to go out and collect my *horta* in the fields. This will do for now," she said.

While we stood there discussing shoes, there was a great crack of thunder in the sky over Mt Kalathio.

"Let's go, Margarita. The rain's coming."

She bolted over to one of the olive trees, where she always tied Riko, in front of the big feta tin for his water.

"Stay here a moment," she said, and raced off down the stone steps towards the old shed, returning with a huge sheet of scuffed plastic, the same provenance as the boot, I imagined. Just when I thought she was about to fashion a bit more footwear before the rain set in, she draped the lot over the donkey, clipping two edges together under his chin. Riko stood still, a vision of stoicism. I had never seen a beast more compliant than this one, whether he was having a massive bundle of olive branches strapped to his sides – or being dressed in rainwear for a Paris catwalk.

There was always a delightful Mad Hatter's quality about Foteini's farm and that afternoon I wondered how crazy it might get. I also pondered what else she could do with plastic sheeting that no-one had thought of yet. I laughed again at the thought of it as I trundled down the path towards her shed. My laughter stalled though when I contemplated coffee in the rain, under the mulberry and fig trees that usually buzzed with fat hornets. Big spots of rain were beginning to fall as I moved the plastic table under the trees.

"*Panayia mou!* We're not sitting out here in the rain. Come in to the *kaliva*."

She hurried into the cramped gloom of the shed and suddenly the coffee break didn't seem like such a great idea. In all the time we'd known Foteini we'd never been properly inside this small wooden structure, with its jumble of objects and dusty corners. She set a tiny stool down for me to sit on, something fashioned apparently by one of the Seven Dwarfs, and a small upturned barrel became a coffee table. On the wall behind the door was an incongruous heavy chest of drawers. She pulled out the middle one, which was deep, filled with screw-top jars that stored things she needed for the Greek coffee, and much else besides.

"This keeps the mice out of my things," she said, pulling a face. "I've got mice everywhere here."

She put the jars on the top and started spooning coffee and sugar into the blackened *briki,* along with some water. The *petrogazi*, two-ring cooker, was an old thing, set on a benchtop, with a huge gas bottle on the floor underneath. The rings on the cooker were blackened and crusted with age. I'd seen her use it many times, but always from the doorway, looking in. Mostly the cooker worked first time, on other occasions it refused to sputter into life. This was one of those days.

Foteini turned on the gas from the bottle first and then the knob for the ring, trying to ignite it with a lighter – but nothing happened. It was obviously blocked. She cursed and tried again and again, firing the lighter. At one point, she went outside to see why Riko was suddenly braying, and left the gas knob in the 'on' position. I had a nervy vision of the ring suddenly unblocking itself while she was away and the gas hissing out. When she did come back, I asked her meekly if she should give the whole endeavour a rest, for fear she'd blow us up. She gave me a strange sideways look.

"Ach, Margarita! This *kalivaki* (little shed) could do with being blown up. It's an old, worm-eaten pile of shit now!" or words to that effect, I thought. I was still struggling with her rural accent and the strange way she chopped the ends off words.

She started firing off the lighter again, stopping now and then to wipe the ring with a bit of rag. I could feel my forehead beading with sweat. I held my breath, looked away and promised God there were five things I'd definitely do if I walked out of the shed in one piece that day. Strangling Foteini was high on the list.

Finally, the gas ring ignited with a bang that rattled the ill-fitting window on the wall above the cooker. Foteini hardly flinched and I guessed it was a common event. Flames licked up around her leathery fingers, but she seemed not to feel them. She hovered over the briki and sang in a surprisingly sweet voice as the coffee mixture hissed and roiled up to the top of the briki. When it was ready, she brought it to the upturned barrel. It smelt good and strong. She rattled about in the drawer again and pulled out a jar of small honey biscuits.

"Why don't you get a cat here for the mice? I can bring you a kitten from our house in Paleohora," I said.

"I don't want another cat. I had one. Skinny thing. It got squashed on the road. Useless!" she said, matter of fact, showing the rural Maniot tendency to treat goats like small beloved children, but dogs and cats like pests.

As we sat drinking our coffee, we heard thunder roll around in the Taygetos. Rain started to drum loudly on the rickety, corrugated-iron roof of the shed. It was deafening but rhythmic, like a Riverdance climax. It was so loud in the end, we couldn't talk. There was nothing else for me to do but check out the shed interior.

This was a shed to the max. Not your bijou hobby shed so beloved of the British, with curtains, electricity, running water and an Ikea sofa bed for sleepovers. This one was messy, with sacks and boxes with indeterminate contents sitting on the earthen floor and farming tools leaning over dusty corners. On one side of the shed was a single bed with a dusty cover over it. When the rain eased, I asked her what the shed had been built for.

"My husband and I used to come here in the summer to look after the animals and in the winter during the olive harvest."

The land originally belonged to her grandfather, who came from Altomira, high in the Taygetos mountains. Many of the villagers had moved down from the mountains by the middle of last century to seek an easier life in hill settlements like Megali Mantineia, or to work in Kalamata. But many others continued the ritual of living in Altomira in summer, in their old stone houses, and then transporting their families and all their animals down to lower areas in the winter to escape the harsh climate.

Foteini's family had done this for decades, bringing their 100 goats, and mules and donkeys, down on the old Biliova *kalderimi*, one of the longest cobbled donkey tracks in rural Mani. The journey led through a string of villages and eventually to Megali Mantineia, which took at least a day and which for the young Foteini was a glorious adventure.

The family stayed at the house the grandfather had built on the edge of the *ktima,* though the old place is now a wreck. In the 1980s, when the family, including Foteini's brother, tired of this yearly trek, they left their house in Altomira for good and moved to a permanent house in the village, where Foteini still lives.

She talked a lot about those mountain days and her family. She rarely talked about her husband. It was the kind of day, I thought, for candour.

"What was your husband like?" I asked.

She contemplated her mismatched feet a moment. "A good man. We had a good life. Hard too." There was little emotion in her face.

"But no children. That's a pity."

She frowned and looked away. I could see she didn't want to talk about it and I couldn't pursue it further, but I knew her husband had a son from a previous marriage, although she never spoke about him much either.

Foteini had been in her 40s when she married, which was late for a Greek. It was a pairing arranged by a relative, but I found it hard to figure what she might have gained from it. I had touched on the subject with other villagers when Foteini was mentioned, but no-one ever had an opinion about the husband, or perhaps they were being discreet.

It was revealing to me, however, that one day while in the village graveyard after a *mnimosino,* memorial service, I happened to pass by the grave of Foteini's husband. Greek graves are hugely decorated, with a small glass and marble cabinet fixed to the head of the grave, usually containing a photo and small mementoes. This one was dusty and bare, apart from a small, unlit oil burner.

We lapsed into silence again as another powerful attack of rain hit the shed roof. Foteini sat with her big meaty hands wrapped around the small white coffee cup, as if to warm them, yet I couldn't imagine the heat breaching those asbestos fingers.

"This is cosy, Margarita, isn't it?"

Cosy wasn't the word I had in mind, but I felt amused by the comment and wished I'd had my camera with me that day. I felt like a hillbilly from the Appalachian Mountains and suddenly had the urge to play bluegrass on a battered banjo, guzzle home-made sage brew and occasionally shake my fist at the sky.

Not for the first time during our Mani adventure did I mull over my friendship with Foteini, which was so odd as to be almost beyond analysis. We had so little in common it was scary, and yet I had always been fond of her and fascinated by her life, by the duality of her behaviour and her appearance, and the fact that she could live like a hillbilly and yet turn up in church looking as scrubbed as any of the other Greek village woman.

My fascination with Foteini was complex. To have a window into her life, into her soul, was a gift, something I would never have achieved without coming to the Mani. In all my life, despite many trips to different parts of Greece, I had never met anyone like Foteini. She was unique.

However, to get a sense of that you had to work through a kind of pain barrier: sitting in sheds in the rain; boiling under mulberry trees in summer among critters; clawing olives down from trees all day during olive harvest season; and eating *myzithra*, the cheese so loved by the rural people of the southern Peloponnese but which we loathed with an intensity that would have curdled milk. I suspect it was not a friendship that any other Greek villager could fathom – and certainly not the expats.

One day, on a visit to the village to see some other Greek friends, I got into conversation with one of the British expats with a holiday house there. Cynthia asked me very directly:

"Why do you spend so much time with Foteini? She's mad, you know."

I was taken aback. "I think you mean eccentric, surely?" It was kinder at least.

"No, she's quite mad!" said Cynthia with confidence, despite never having spoken to Foteini, as she had no Greek, let alone giving her a Rorschach inkblot test for crazy behaviour.

"In what way mad?" I asked her.

Cynthia bristled. "Well, she has very odd ideas, I hear; she's very insular, rude. She thinks every piece of land hereabouts is hers for the taking."

I smiled to myself, thinking that what Cynthia was describing sounded like some of the expats in the village.

The reference to the land concerned one English expat who had bought an old derelict house to renovate, and some adjoining land, where Foteini once grazed her goats. As the property had belonged to a relative who had given her permission to use it, she innocently thought she had lifetime grazing rights. But, of course, the new owner thought differently. Foteini was one of the farmers who hadn't quite come to terms perhaps with the way in which their village life was changing forever.

While Foteini and I sat together in the shed, with thunder still grumbling in the distance, the conversation turned to Pelagia.

"When I die," she said, "I want my soul to fly around the place like a bird. That will do for me. I don't want to be stuck away in the dark somewhere."

It was a strange thought – Foteini, strafing the sky in diverting layers. I told her I saw her more as a figure flitting about on a mythical Pegasus horse, or perhaps an airborne Riko. I described the scene in detail for her, as it was the kind of stormy, confined day when you can give your imagination free rein. But I had underestimated her commonsense.

She gave me an odd look. "Margarita *mou*, donkeys don't fly. And I don't know who or what this Pegasus is."

Okay, she'd only had a village education. I tried to make it easier.

"Just imagine then that you're riding Riko home loaded up with good things, except that instead of being on the road you're up in the air, galloping above Mt Kalathio, wearing your big straw hat, and em.... your boots ... but not that one," I said, pointing to the plastic pasty.

"Don't be so ridiculous!" she said, slapping her thigh. "You don't need boots in heaven!"

It could have been her epitaph – or one of them, anyway.

22

Kalimera and g'day!

IN a village *kafeneio* on the island of Kythera, where we went for a short excursion in May, I overheard two guys having a conversation in broad and loud Australian. I couldn't help but swivel round to listen.

"Hey, Shane. Why haven't you been round to see us since you've been back?"

"Mate, I've been flat out like a lizard drinking!" They both laughed, enjoying a daft Aussie moment.

I laughed as well. I hadn't heard that expression for years, but Kythera was a long way from Sydney – or was it?

Kythera lies off the southern tip of the right-hand Laconian Peninsula in the southern Peloponnese. It is called "Little Australia" because some of the 20,000 or so islanders who left during the 1950s and 60s in the mass migration programs to Australia have returned, or at least their descendants have. Many come back regularly for holidays, or to holiday homes that were once ancestral ruins, but some Kytherians have moved back for good.

There are an estimated 100,000 people in Australia – mainly in New South Wales – of Kytherian descent, which is why many of the current population of Kythera (around 3,000) refer to Australia conversely as "Big Kythera".

It's just one of the many things that make this one of the most charming and unique of the Greek islands and because of its location, on the way to nowhere in particular. It has a slight time warp feel about it, except for the Aussie repartee. Throughout our week there, we picked out strong Aussie accents wherever we went, or at least Aussie-accented Greek.

The idea of visiting Kythera had been a last-minute decision, a holiday within an odyssey, and a chance to see a bit more of the southern Peloponnese, now the weather was warm again. Jim had also been told in the winter that while his contract with Apollo Adventures would be renewed for the summer there were few bookings so far, and nothing until the end of May. Again it illustrated the point that tourists were nervous about coming to Greece, especially after the scenes of rioting in February that were flashed around the world.

The trip to Kythera was an easy hop by boat from the fishing village of Gytheio, at the head of the Laconian Gulf. We were lucky to find a studio apartment in the north-east of the island that would take a dog, as there were few tourists around in early May. The studio was on the ground floor of one block in the complex, which was opposite the owners' (a mother and daughter) own flat, across a skinny garden. It showed the peculiarity of Greeks and the fact they like everyone to be close. Or maybe the owners just wanted to keep a gimlet eye on our 'pesky' terrier.

Kythera — the island where Aphrodite, goddess of love, was born, rising from the sea on her scallop shell — seems like a sleepy backwater, but it once had an important commercial position on the busy sea route between the Ionian and Aegean seas, and was a strong link from the mainland to Crete. It was mainly the Minoan settlers (3,000BC to 1,200BC) who originally saw its potential as a trading centre and the island thrived, even though during its history it was invaded around 80 times.

In the 10th century the Saracens from Crete invaded, causing much destruction of the place, and later the island was occupied by the Venetians. Kythera was offered protection in the 12th century by the Eudaimonias family, from Monemvasia, and became a refuge for Byzantine nobles and artisans, which possibly explains why there are many important Byzantine churches on this island with notable frescos.

Kythera continued to have a certain cachet in the Mediterranean until the Corinth Canal, in the north of the Peloponnese, was opened in 1893, which lessened the island's importance as a trade link. After the Second World War, the islanders began to move away in search of better opportunities, mostly to Australia.

It was during one of the island's most brutal of invasions in the 16th century that some of the more unique sites became 'ghost towns', like the spooky Byzantine town of Palio Hora, once called St Dimitrios, which we had earmarked for an early visit, as we planned to write some travel articles when we returned to the Mani.

Palio Hora was built by Monemvasians (from the famous monolithic rock settlement in Laconia) in the 12th century and later became the island's capital. It was built down a craggy peak with a castle at the top, with the intention of it resembling a small Monemvasia or Mystras, the deserted hillside city near Sparta that became the last bastion of the Byzantine empire. Some of the frescos in Palio Hora's churches are said to have also been painted by leading artists from these two places.

The town is also situated on the edge of a 300ft-deep ravine, for extra fortification, which later became known as the Kakia Langada, the Bad Ravine, because of the pirate raids from the coast in 1537 by the "black menace" Hayreddin Barbarossa, the Turkish admiral of the fleet. He invaded Palio Hora and went on a killing and looting spree – but not before many of the terrified village women had thrown their children into the ravine and then followed them, rather than face the prospect of being raped or sold into slavery. The town has been deserted since this time.

On the day we visited, despite a blue sky and warm sun, there was a cool, querulous wind stalking the edges of the Bad Ravine. It was easy to understand why many islanders say this place is haunted and that at night you can hear the anguished cries of mothers and children. There was no-one else about that day and no evidence of any other visitors for a while, as all the paths were overgrown with gorse and wildflowers, obscuring in parts the treacherous, narrow pathway along the edge of the ravine, with a sheer drop below.

Yet everywhere we turned we found remarkable Byzantine churches and ruined houses rambling up the overgrown hills, and even small buildings set into the side of the ravine, their small, shutterless windows like lifeless eyes gazing down on the abyss. The churches were all locked. This is a vexation all over Greece, but most of Kythera's churches were locked after of a spate of thefts in the 1990s. Finding a key holder on this island can be an adventure in itself, as we were to discover before leaving.

Palio Hora was one of the strangest and most atmospheric 'ghost towns' we had visited during our stay in the Peloponnese and ranks alongside Vathia, famous for its clutch of stone towers, and other deserted hill villages in the Mani. But this place had its own ghastly souvenir awaiting us.

Wallace had been tramping happily beside us on his lead during our visit, through the long grasses and along the ravine edges, without complaint, happy to be exploring. When we returned to the car, I lifted him on to the back seat to attach his harness to the seatbelt jack, his usual travel device, to stop him pinballing around the car. That's when I noticed he had polka-dot legs. On closer examination, it turned out to be dozens of ticks.

I called Jim over and we stood looking at Wallace, wondering what to do.

I had put Wallace's Scalibor collar on a few days earlier (which we did every spring, mainly for noxious sand flies) but I guessed it couldn't have kicked in yet. I had his small medical bag in the car boot and gave him a dose of neck drops for fleas and ticks, hoping that would help in the coming days. But what to do for now? I had a handy tick-removal gadget that I had brought from Scotland, with a small plastic hook like a crochet needle, but with a thin slit in the middle that caught the tick around the neck, and I had become adept at twisting them off.

I tried to remove a few of the ticks in the car, but for every few I could see, there were others burrowing their way through his thick fur and around his feet – and Wallace goes mad when you touch his paws.

"Poor little guy," said Jim. "This is a tick infestation."

While I worked away in vain, I suddenly thought of the problem of taking Wallace back to the apartment.

"The owners will freak out if they see Wallace like this," I said to Jim, wiping beads of sweat from my forehead. If only I had thought to start all of Wallace's treatments earlier.

"We could take him to the beach near the apartments and let him paddle about. It might loosen a few," said Jim.

"I don't know, these buggers are already Velcroed in."

"Who would have thought a tranquil site like Palio Hora would be covered in critters?"

"Curse of the Byzantines, Jim."

"Let's go to that beach anyway and see if we can sort him out there. No-one will hear his screams … okay, I was joking!"

It wasn't that far from the truth. We drove to the car park beside the empty beach. We planned to sit at the end of the beach but there was a strong wind blowing in from the sea, so we stayed in the car, positioning ourselves at either end of the back seat for the 'procedure', with Wallace in the middle.

We had to use his muzzle because Wallace isn't a good patient at any time, which was why his Kalamatan vet Angelos jokingly referred to Wallace as 'Killer Machine'. He constantly squirms and snaps – and that's just Angelos, trying to calm Wallace down!

The muzzle, a small plastic cage, made him look like a miniature Hannibal Lecter. Not that Wallace had ever bitten anyone in 11 years, except for one man – a bad-tempered plumber in Scotland, whom I had my doubts about anyway. One day when Wallace and I were in the kitchen with him, the man pulled out a tool from his kit bag far too hastily and headed towards a leaking tap. Wallace didn't like the cut of his ratchet and went for him, biting him on the bum, though he inflicted no damage, as the man was wearing thick denims. The plumber never came back, and I thought that was no bad thing.

I started work on the ticks and every time I yanked one out, I flung it out the door, on to the car park. Once I had removed a dozen or so ticks from his legs I started on his paws, the part I had been dreading. The hysterics began as I gently parted his claws to reveal clusters of ticks in the soft skin between. I pulled out a few but couldn't get much further, with all the insane yapping and squirming going on, even with Jim holding Wallace down. All I seemed to have achieved was forced migration of the foot ticks back up to the legs. I was exhausted with the torture session.

"I can't do this any more. I feel like Doctor Mengele."

"I know," said Jim "and sooner or later we're going to attract a crowd of passers-by probably wondering what the hell's going on in the car. The dogs are already curious."

It was true. The tick-removal had attracted the attention of two skinny strays, who might have thought I was flinging treats out the door. But with the strong wind blowing I was also sure more of the ticks were flying back inside the car than were heading out. It all seemed a bit hopeless.

"I think we'd be safer sorting this problem out at the studio," I said.

Jim agreed. We drove back to the parking area beside the apartments, hoping no-one was around, but Dimitra, the daughter, was in the garden, pruning some young oleander bushes that had been ripped in the sudden wind.

"Now we're stuck. When we walk past her she's bound to see the ticks, especially on Wallace's legs," I said.

Dimitra seemed a rather particular kind of woman and I felt sure she wouldn't want ticks inside the apartment. And neither did I. The studio was pretty smart for its price, with blue-and-white striped curtains and matching scatter cushions. It was lucky she'd accepted the dog to start with.

"Maybe we should drive away again and wait until she's finished gardening," Jim said.

I turned round and looked at Wallace.

"The wee guy looks traumatised. I think we should try to get back inside."

There was no other way in, apart from the path leading off the edge of the car park. We sat in the car, staring at the studio block. Jim had a familiar glassy look in his eyes.

"What would the Spartans have done, Jim?" I said at last.

This had been the daft opening line on one of our more audacious feats while in the Mani, when we smuggled Wallace into Ancient Messene, an important archaeological site near Kalamata. We had arrived with Wallace, thinking that as it was an open kind of site the dog wouldn't be a problem, but we were refused entry.

That's when Jim decided to take his inspiration from the Spartans, who tried every sneaky tactic to infiltrate Ancient Messene and seize control. Spartan soldiers had famously dressed on one occasion as women and hid knives under their skirts. We had hidden Wallace in our backpack, with the lure of chicken sandwiches.

In our minds, Dimitra was just another kind of site attendant, but we didn't have the rucksack now, and there were no chicken sandwiches.

"I've got an idea," said Jim, getting out of the car, opening the hatchback and raking about in the boot. Then he leaned over the back seat into the car and lowered his voice.

"Okay, listen up. We'll put Wallace in my beach bag and cover him with a towel. Dimitra won't think to ask about him. Compared to Ancient Messene, this will be a snip," said Jim confidently, checking his watch, as men do with these daft military-style follies. I started to giggle.

"Sssh, Margarita! This is no time for levity," he said.

Jim put Wallace in his rather garish beach bag and covered him up. Wallace was tired and didn't seem to object. Jim hooked the bag handles over one shoulder, keeping Wallace pinned in the bag with his bent arm.

Dimitra got up when she saw us approaching.

"*Yeia sas*," she said. "Have you had a nice day?"

We told her we'd been to Palio Hora for a few hours and then to the nearby beach for a swim.

"What? In this wind?" she said.

"Yes," I said, with a mock shiver.

She narrowed her eyes at the beach bag. "Where's the dog?"

At the mention of 'dog', Jim's Spartan manoeuvre was busted. Wallace's head popped out of the bag and the sight of Dimitra holding a set of secateurs made him twitchy.

"What's the dog doing in there?" Dimitra asked, looking at us oddly.

"Ah, well... he's a bit tired and cold. We put him in the bag. He's an old guy now," Jim said.

"He swam in the sea as well?" Dimitra asked. Double madness. What are *xenoi* like, her expression seemed to say.

"Yes, he swam, so we'd better get him inside."

Wallace had other ideas and started squirming energetically, wanting out. Jim pushed him back in and covered him with the towel again, hoping Dimitra hadn't got a proper look at the polka-dot legs. She was glaring all the same, squeezing the handles on the secateurs in quick succession. Wallace growled softly.

"You know, I meant to tell you both yesterday about Palio Hora. It's very overgrown. No-one has been there for months. It's infested with snakes and ticks at this time of year," she said.

"Really?" said Jim, giving me a warning look. "Can't say we saw anything like that. Lucky for us."

"Have a nice afternoon," I trilled as we shuffled to the front door of the studio. I glanced back at Dimitra, her hands on her hips, eyes narrowed. Oh, she knew all right! She knew what we were up to. Once inside the studio, Jim tipped Wallace out of the beach bag.

"Okay, let's not panic. I don't think she saw the ticks," he said.

"She looked suspicious though. She'll probably check the room tomorrow. We'll probably be asked to leave now."

Jim looked around the studio pensively.

"Yes, I guess we've broken the rules here."

"What rules? About ticks?"

"Interior design rules, Margarita. Putting polka dots and stripes together. Unforgiveable!"

@@@@@

We spent the next few days touring the island and occasionally having a laugh at yet another fix Wallace had got us in to, though it wasn't his fault this time. As it turned out, the tick problem was a fizzer. In the morning, when we checked Wallace in his bed, we found him tick-free, with a few dozen dead ones scattered around his bedding. The collar and drops had obviously kicked in quicker than expected and our manic tick-removal session had been a waste of time. Nothing Spartan about us. We were tick-busters with anxiety issues, obviously. However, ticks weren't to be our only frustration on this island.

We had planned to see some of the historic churches on Kythera, partly for the travel articles we were hoping to write. Before we left the Mani we emailed the director of the Byzantine Museum at Livadi, in the south, to ask if she could

221

organise a key holder to unlock one or two of the more interesting churches with well-preserved frescos.

Phaedra, the director, was as left field as you can imagine for a Byzantine museum boss when we visited her at the island museum. Okay she wasn't compelled to dress like a Byzantine saint, but when she introduced herself, I was surprised by her long bleached hair, vertiginous heels and plunging cleavage. I hadn't seen a ravine like that since Palio Hora. Jim arched his eyebrows at me when she bent towards her desk to pick up a chirping mobile phone.

We asked her about our church visit. She wrinkled her nose, saying it was hard to locate key holders at "short notice", and apparently forgetting our initial email. We pressed her a bit more and finally she came up with the unusual church of Ayios Dimitrios, which had been on our wish list and was only about 20 minutes' drive from Livadi.

It is actually four churches set under one roof, with a wealth of frescos dating from the 12th century. It doesn't get better than that, except for the name of the village where the church was located — Pourko. It sounded more like a Russian lap-dancing club.

Phaedra dug out the number of the key holder, a man called Babis, and rang him. There was no response.

"I will try again, but I see you have some Greek," she said to me. "Maybe you can call him tonight and arrange to meet at the church."

She wrote down his number. "If you have problems, get in touch with me. But I think this is easiest."

But this is Greece. Nothing is ever easy here.

That night I called Babis on his landline. A woman answered, telling me she was his mother. When I told her what I wanted she gave me the number of the local kafeneio.

"He's there when he's not here."

I called the *kafeneio* and asked for Babis. While I waited for him, I could hear the gabble of men fuelled on strong spirits, the blare of a TV, the clack of the board game *tavli*. Finally, someone picked up the phone.

"Babis here. What is it?" His voice was rough, like sandpaper on wood.

I explained that we wanted to see Ayios Dimitrios and asked if we could meet at the church around 1pm the next day, if he was free. He agreed, reluctantly, I thought, but I put that to the back of my mind. Phaedra had already scratched out a few instructions and I had a map of sorts.

"How will I get in touch with you if there's a problem? Do you have a mobile?" I asked him.

He laughed. "No mobile. Leave a message at home. My mother will find me." Greek homing pigeons flew unbidden into my mind.

The next day we set off for Pourko. According to our instructions, we were to turn off the main road where a signpost indicated the church of Ayios Dimitrios up a narrow road. The trouble was, there were no further directions and at one point the road split, without telling us where in God's name we were going.

We took the right fork, for no reason, and then drove about, stopping to ask directions from locals. This meant getting in and out of the car, darting into front gardens and up driveways, into a lemon orchard at one point, wherever I could find a local, usually an old woman, to get some directions. In between the abysmal tally of lefts and rights, I heard several life stories and gripes about the economic crisis.

Greek roads are bad, the road signs bewildering, but Greeks have proved to be worse than the Irish when it comes to giving directions. You simply need a brain that's wired backwards, or stop and have a glass of Guinness somewhere. Just when we were about to give up the search because it seemed hopeless, we spied a strange conglomeration of church domes bunched together, which I fancied looked like a flattened version of the Sydney Opera House. The domes were in a fold of land way in the distance.

We drove in haste, the car wheels spitting gravel along the dirt road, and we punched the air when we finally saw the sign for Ayios Dimitrios. We got out of the car, expecting to see an open door and Babis waiting for us – but the place was deserted. It was 1.30pm by now. Surely he would have waited? I called Phaedra and explained our difficulties in finding the church and that Babis was missing. Had he made contact? I asked.

"No. Babis will have probably gone home, thinking you weren't going to show up."

"He didn't wait very long."

"Call his home," she said with a sigh.

I did. His mother answered the phone as usual but this time she spoke in a shouty voice, as if she'd grown tired of this perpetual search for Babis.

"Try the *kafeneio*."

We were suddenly back where we'd started. Jim rolled his eyes. I decided to call Phaedra one more time.

"Don't you have a master key?" I asked her, wondering why I hadn't thought of this before.

She laughed. "Do you know how many churches we have in Kythera? The museum would resemble a locksmiths. The master keys are not here. They are in Athens for safekeeping. But my dear, the next time you are in Kythera, I will personally get the key from Babis and drive you to the church of Ayios Dimitrios. Enjoy the rest of your stay," she said, ending the call quickly.

I was exasperated with the whole thing. It was one of the vexatious charms of many Greeks that they would never do a certain thing until they absolutely had to, a philosophy that had probably got them into their fiscal pickle to start with.

And I now understood why the majority of Kytherians, with a propensity for losing their way, and each other possibly, finally left for Australia.

Perhaps the whole island, if not the country, had become unhinged that week in 2012, as it was the General Election on the Sunday, with a lot riding on the results. The Troika had threatened that if the Greeks didn't vote for a pro-austerity party, willing to carry out vital economic reforms, then the funds from the second bailout package, finalised earlier that year, wouldn't be released.

The favourite to win the election was now the charismatic Alexis Tsipras, the young leader of the new radical left-wing party Syriza, which was running on a strong anti-austerity ticket. He had threatened to rip up the agreement on austerity on the second bailout if he gained power, which was an enticing pledge for crisis-weary Greeks.

In the village of Potamos on polling day we had coffee in the main square and watched people troop off to vote, each clutching a thick sheaf of candidates' flyers that had been handed out all morning. I helped an elegant elderly woman at the next table in a *kafeneio* to retrieve her pile of flyers after a sudden gust of wind sent them into the air like confetti.

She sighed when they were all back in her hands and told me in English: "I have come back here to my home town to vote, but for the first time in my life I don't know who to vote for. I want to vote for New Democracy but I am tired of austerity. I have lost nearly half my pension in the austerity cuts. I like the sound of this young man Tsipras, but I don't want to live under a left-wing government. Is he going to go around and take our houses away?"

The day after voting we toured the rest of the island. We stopped at a small *kafeneio* in a picturesque fishing village, with caiques moored nearby and wonderful sea views. The owner was a young Aussie Greek called Nasos. We got chatting about the island and told him about our saga in trying to find the church of Ayios Dimitrios. He laughed.

"You should have called a taxi, folks. They can sort everything."

225

I asked him how he thought life here compared with living in Australia.

He rolled his eyes. "Jeez, are you kidding? There's not a day goes by when I don't think I must have a few kangaroos loose in my top paddock to still be living in Kythera, especially in the middle of a crisis. Nothing is ever straightforward or easy here, as you've discovered. But, hey, this is where my roots are. This is home. The rest of the stuff can go disappear up a goanna's bum." He gave a raucous Aussie laugh.

The woman in the *kafeneio* on polling day was right to feel her vote was useless. The results of the May election threw the country yet again into a tailspin. New Democracy, led by Antonis Samaras, which the Troika hoped would gain a clear majority and continue the fiscal reforms, managed just 18.8 per cent of the vote, followed by Syriza on 16.8 per cent and Pasok with 13.8 per cent.

But it was an astounding result for Syriza, which had only polled 4 per cent three years earlier, and Greeks predicted it was the party to watch. That proved to be the case when, in 2015, it finally won a general election.

However, the fact that Greeks had voted mainly in this 2012 election for smaller anti-austerity parties hinted at a change in outlook for Greeks. It was a clear rejection of Troika interference and of mainstream Greek politics that had been dominated by political dynasties for decades. Neither of the highest polling parties (New Democracy or Syriza) in this election were able to form a coalition with the other parties and fresh elections were called for June.

A caretaker government was scrambled together, with once again an interim head selected. This time there was irony in the choice of leader, High Court judge Panayiotis

Pikramenos, whose surname in Greek means 'embittered'. You couldn't have made this up if you tried, and the irony was not lost on leader writers in the daily papers.

The darkest side of these elections, however, was the rise of the extreme right-wing party *Chrisi Avyi*, Golden Dawn, which won 6.9 per cent of the votes (gaining 18 of the 300 seats in parliament) on an anti-austerity, anti-migrant ticket. And they would win more seats in the June elections, when Samaras was finally be voted into power with a small majority.

This was the start of a different kind of crisis in Greek life, as Golden Dawn set its own agenda, with a campaign of brutality against migrants, particularly in Athens and Piraeus. The rise of this fascist party would blight Greece for the next few years and give Greeks yet another reason to be ashamed of the direction their country was taking.

After the May elections, however, there were more threats by Germany in particular that the wrong vote in June against austerity would force Greece out of the eurozone, which would push the European economy into a crisis not seen since the 1930s. *The Times* newspaper summed it up with a splash headline in May saying: "Greece on the brink of collapse."

The day the story ran in *The Times* we were down at the *spitaki* in Paleohora, watching Andreas unpacking a box of new chickens and two roosters, one russet, the other white. The other chickens had long gone, including our favourite Aspro, all dispatched from their earthly patch and taken back to Kalamata for the two mothers to cook up. We watched the tiny chickens rolling about the yard like tumbleweed.

"The kitchens will grow nicely, *paidia*," said Marina, never having quite got the word 'chicken' under control. We all laughed, but the high spirits didn't last long. Jim told Andreas about *The Times* headline.

"They said that? We are on the brink of collapse?"

We nodded.

"Did you hear that, Marina?" And of course he told her.

"Stupid world!" said Marina, picking up a hoe and heading towards the garden.

Andreas shook his head and stared at the olive trees, as he seemed to do regularly now.

"Ach, last year was bad enough. Now this. But we are all right though. We are still alive. Our children are still at university. Money is not plentiful but we have the vegetable garden and the chickens. Peeerhaps we will survive."

The couple, however, had both lost money through the austerity cuts and their mothers also had cuts to their pensions. Marina was now owed nearly a year's wages, and at Andreas's work, men were being laid off. How they were surviving, we had no idea. I think that was probably the month where I understood the whole philosophy of Greeks 'living in the moment'. To have thought about the future too much would have been catastrophic.

23
Touching heaven

"*PO, po, po!* Did you hear that, Marina? Margarita is getting her wish. She is going to stay in a monastery."

Andreas smiled at Jim and made a claw of his hand, twisting it back and forth beside his head.

"Crazy woman, eh, Dimitri? But don't worry about it becows I take you out in Kalamata and we have good time. I knows places," said Andreas, winking.

"What places, Andrea?" chirped Marina, as she put a plate of freshly washed figs on the table.

We all fell silent, however, gorging on figs, followed by glasses of cold water. After that, the conversation turned back to monasteries and fantasies about nights of liberation.

"Don't worry, Marina. This is boys' business now," said Andreas, giving Jim a nudge.

A month or so earlier, I had conceived the plan of going on a short retreat to a monastery with my Australian writer friend Geraldine, with whom Jim and I had spent many convivial lunches in Kalamata. She was keen on the project and I knew I would be glad of her company and her fluent language skills. We both had slightly different expectations for this jaunt but what we did have in common as writers was the desire to witness this rarefied way of life, still shrouded in centuries of Orthodox mystery, before it disappeared altogether.

Dimiova is situated on the high north-western slopes of the Taygetos Mountains, in the Mani peninsula, east of Kalamata. It is still a working monastery but with only two elderly nuns left. Geraldine suggested there was probably a protocol for organising a retreat, so with this in mind I turned to Andreas. His late father had had a long association with Kalamata's cathedral, the *Ipapanti tou Sotiros*. Andreas agreed we would need "clearance" from the head of the church of Messinia, Bishop Chrisostomos, the same bishop who Papa Lambros had mentioned. It revived feelings of anxiety over the *papas* and his candid story. I hoped Andreas wouldn't be giving the bishop too many particulars of the would-be pilgrims.

Andreas said he would make the request for us but it would take a few weeks for a response. If we were lucky we might make it to the monastery for the August week that celebrates the feast of the Assumption of the Virgin Mary. Andreas wasn't a religious man and only went to church on the most holy days. The monastery idea had made him doubt my sanity, but he wasn't the only one.

"You're not going all religious on me now, Margarita?" Jim asked one day when I was talking, perhaps too enthusiastically, about the retreat.

"Don't be silly. Andreas has been winding you up, hasn't he?"

He laughed. "No. I just wondered what was behind your Dimiova quest, that's all."

"Jimbo, you know what's behind it, just an interest in a working monastery, and something to write about, for a freelance piece perhaps. And I don't think you can get to grips with Greek culture if you don't look at the religion as well. That's all it's about."

"Are you sure?"

"Of course I'm sure. Do you think I'm going to leave you and join the order? Ah, that's probably it, isn't it?" I chortled.

"I take your point about the culture and all that, but you seem to be taking more than a passing interest in religious subjects these days."

"Oooh! That must be a scary idea! Would it be more acceptable if I went and swam naked with piranha fish in the Amazon, or signed up for a course in advanced pole dancing?"

"You're being silly now, Margarita," he said, with a frown.

"I know, but this isn't a serious discussion, surely?"

Jim was far from amused now. He got up and went off to fetch Wallace's lead to take him for a walk. That's when I realised that we frequently did the same things without knowing it: we each took Wallace for a walk when we needed solitude. From the balcony, I saw them both leave the property and walk slowly towards the olive groves.

Jim is normally an easy-going, tolerant guy and I couldn't understand why he was so nettled by this monastery retreat, unless he thought I really was going bonkers. I wouldn't be the only person in Greece in those days to 'break my chain', as our landlords would say.

I wasn't crazy yet, but I had felt some challenges on a personal level during the previous nine months. I felt dispirited by the depth of the economic crisis, by Pelagia's death and particularly the fall-out from the Papa Lambros story. It had made me fear that our 'big, fat odyssey' wasn't the great adventure it had started out as two-and-a-half years earlier, when we were more carefree.

Maybe I just needed to take some time out and get back some of the faith that I had lost along the way.

Jim never questioned the monastery visit again, but I knew that on some level it still bothered him.

@@@@@

On a blistering hot day, we were sitting with the couple at the *spitaki* table when Andreas told me the visit to Dimiova had finally been approved. But before we could go, Geraldine and I had to introduce ourselves to the priest who took the services at the monastery and looked after its ecclesiastical well-being. We were to meet Papa Sotiris (meaning Saviour) at one of his other parish churches in the lower Taygetos the following Sunday. We were to explain to him what our aims were, and it sounded curiously like a job interview.

Jim offered to take us to the church and it was over an hour's drive from Paleohora to the village of Eliohori. We parked the car and then walked up a narrow, shadeless road on a tortuous incline towards the church of Ayios Ioannis, the Theologos. It seemed the creator of the Book of Revelation was making another fateful appearance in my life.

Although it was only 9am, the heat was already intense and the towering outline of the Taygetos mountains ahead of us seemed to make the hike seem more vertiginous. By the time we reached the church, we were grateful for its cool confines, even though it was already packed with villagers, as this was the feast day of Mary Magdalene and there were tables set in the forecourt for a *yiorti* later.

The service was long, but concluded with a burst of chanting, the squeal of impatient village children and the smell of goat roasting on a spit outside in preparation for the day's feast, to which the three of us were invited. While Jim ducked outside to find a spare lunch table, Geraldine and I hung back until the church was empty, and introduced ourselves to Papa Sotiris.

He was a genial young priest and he seemed delighted (and a little intrigued) by our request to visit Dimiova, and was happy to agree to it. Although we had hoped for August 15, he said the visit would take place a few days earlier because there would be too many people at the monastery on the Feast of the Assumption. He also wanted to impart the 'rules'. Geraldine flinched at the word and gave me a despondent look.

We would have to be at the monastery at 7am sharp for the start of the liturgy. The clothing rules were predictable: sensible, dark clothing, long skirts, no bare arms. We were told the nuns led a simple, strict life and would be adhering to a semi-fast in the lead-up to August 15. There would also be no talking at the monastery. No talking? Papa Sotiris told us talking wasn't forbidden but the nuns didn't like to talk unless they had to, especially at this devout time of the year.

"We were hoping to write about the monastery, but how will we be able to glean anything about the nuns' lives if we can't talk to them?" asked Geraldine.

We were simply to find that out for ourselves, Papa Sotiris seemed to indicate, rather mysteriously. Then came the final disappointment. We would not be allowed to stay overnight. The *papas* told us the monastery was basic, with no facilities for guests, but we could stay as long as we liked during the day.

Later on, over roast goat, Greek salad and local wine, the three of us discussed this change in arrangements.

"Well," said Geraldine, laughing. "If the monastery's as basic as Papa Sotiris says, maybe he's doing us a favour. I don't imagine that walking down dark corridors at midnight to find a toilet will be much fun." I agreed.

However, Jim was laughing merrily as he poured devout measures of wine into our glasses.

"You girls have been in such a hurry to deprive yourselves. But you never know, if you charm the nuns on the day they may change their minds. So take your toothbrushes and em... a torch, for toilet visits, just in case."

"I knew you'd be happy with this turn of events," I said, giving him a slightly dark look. He didn't reply.

"I don't think I'm too distraught about it really," said Geraldine, holding her glass aloft. "*Yeia mas*, good health!"

@@@@@

I invited Geraldine to stay the night before at our Paleohora house, so we could leave at 6am sharp on the Friday morning.

We left suitably dressed, as if we were going to a funeral and Geraldine had the added accessory of a black broad-brimmed hat that made her look rather like she was setting off for Cheltenham racecourse.

As I drove our little Fiat along the coastal road, the sky was turning pearly grey over the Taygetos. The air was cool and fresh and it belied what would be another scorching day. The drive towards Dimiova passed through a string of villages, the houses still shuttered at this time of day. Beyond Eliohori, the ascent though the lower mountains was full of hairpin bends. Stretches of road were covered in scree and the occasional boulder from recent landslides in unseasonable weather, and the Fiat struggled over some of it.

When Dimiova finally came into view, tucked into a wooded mountain slope of fir and pine trees, it was bigger than expected. The outer walls and monastery buildings were white and the tiled, domed roof of the main church was poking up from the inner courtyard like a jaunty hat. I was anxious to get there and bumped the Fiat up the last steep stretch of dirt road to the front gates.

A morning service had just begun in the monastery church of the Dormition of the *Panayia* (Virgin Mary). A bell tolled and the sound of the liturgy was spine-tingling in this lonely mountain location. At the door of the church we were met by the Abbess, Sister Kiriaki (meaning Sunday), whom we were relieved to find did indeed talk, though not volubly.

But she had rather charmingly forgotten why we were there, or what to do with us. She looked a little tired but at least the cold drinks and *loukoumi* (Turkish delight) and fruit we offered as gifts were met with a smile. The large water-melon was given an especially warm appraisal. She ushered us into the church, where Papa Sotiris was taking the service. We were placed next to Sister Christina, the other nun here.

Kiriaki left the church, returning with offerings of her own, a *komboskini,* prayer rope, comprised of thick knotted wool interspersed with small beads (like a Catholic rosary), which she gave to Geraldine to hold during the service, and to me she gave some *filakta*, tiny embroidered pouches filled with lavender and other herbs. The service was particularly devotional, despite only a handful of people and one chanter. It had an extra layer of drama, when several long segments of chanting were accompanied by Kiriaki energetically striking a wooden hammer against a piece of wood, the *talanto*, which I had never seen in a Greek church before.

The church is a lovely example of early 17th century design, with well-preserved frescos painted in 1663 by the monk Damaskinos. The main focus of this church, however, is the much revered icon of the Virgin Mary and Child (*Panayia Dimiovitissa*), which is claimed to have miraculous powers, as are many icons in Greece dedicated to the *Panayia*. The icon is best known for the curious mark on the *Panayia's* right cheek, which is said to be a bloodstain, and there is curious story as to how it got there.

Papa Sotiris later explained the icon was believed to have been damaged by a blow from a knife or axe during the struggles of the Iconoclastic period of Greek history (8th and 9th centuries AD), when many icons were defaced or even burnt. The icon, he said, had been brought here for safe keeping some time in the 8th century, when a former monastery building had been on this site, and during a violent skirmish between the defenders of the icon and interlopers, the image of the *Panayia* was struck, and blood sprang from her face, and the signs of it remain today.

During the 15th century, Dimiova was set on fire by the Turks and rebuilt a century later, only to be attacked by them again in 1770. However, it survived and became a meeting place for some of the great revolutionary leaders in the Greek War of Independence against the Turks in 1821.

After the service, Papa Sotiris invited us, and several other parishioners, to assemble in one of the old dining rooms for morning coffee. We sat around a long wooden table, with the *papas* at its head. Despite the no-talking rule, Kiriaki was in good conversational form.

In her mid-60s, she told us she had lived in Dimiova all her life, brought here as a two-year-old orphan. Her story was not unusual in Kalamata. After the Second World War, there was a curious tradition in the city, where war orphans and poor children were left under a certain plane tree near the Ipapanti Cathedral for kind Kalamatans to 'adopt'. An orphan housed in this way was known as a 'plane child' (*platanopoulo*). When no-one adopted Kiriaki, she was given to Dimiova monastery. She has known no other life but this.

It's a fairly regimented existence, with a 5.30am start for prayers, a simple breakfast (they only eat twice a day) and then work in the fields and gardens, and tending the monastery's sheep and goats. They retire at around 8pm, depending on the season. The winters here, said Papa Sotiris, are bitterly cold and dark, with very simple accommodation and heating. They have no TV, no computers and only one radio, tuned into an Orthodox religious station.

"The nuns are allowed to speak if they want to, but most of the time they find it more peaceful not to. They are like two canaries in a cage. It's a lovely cage, though and they don't want to fly away to the outside world," said the *papas,* with a disarming smile.

Kiriaki illustrated this notion rather more dramatically by adding: "I would rather stab myself in the heart than leave Dimiova."

Geraldine and I exchanged amused glances at this emotional flourish. For the two nuns, I imagined it must be lonely at times on this mountainside, yet once it would have been quite the opposite. When Kiriaki was a child there were a few dozen nuns in residence and earlier in its history, as a refuge for monks, it was capable of housing up to 100 people. Over the years, though, as the older nuns have died, the numbers have not been replaced.

The monastery isn't a locked cage by any means and the two nuns make regular visits to Kalamata. Yet generally, the outside world is kept at arm's length. Talking is negotiable after all, but TV and computers are not.

"The internet is the devil!" said Kiriaki, in another passionate outburst.

The nuns don't allow computers at Dimiova and Kiriaki told us an amusing story of one guest who stayed the night a few years ago (when it was permissible) and brought a laptop computer, and insisted on using it. It wasn't clear why, as there is no wi-fi here and visitors are expected to surf the spiritual plane instead. However, when the nuns asked the guest not to use her computer, she refused. To head off any further transgressions, the feisty Kiriaki got a screwdriver and completely removed the electric wall socket in the room, where the computer had been plugged in, so it couldn't be switched on.

"Wasn't that dangerous?" I asked her.

"No," she said with a mischievous smile. "I had the protection of the *Panayia*."

Many people visit the monastery to pray to the miraculous icon, and in this region there are many stories about its powers. Kiriaki related one tale with great affection.

"A lovely young couple came here one year and told us they were praying to the *Panayia* because they had been unable to have children. They were given a blessing by the priest with holy oil and then they left. A year later they came back here again to pray. This time they told us it was in thanks because by then the wife was pregnant. I will always remember this particular couple and how happy they were."

The miracle that needs to befall the monastery at the moment, sadly, is funding. The buildings and the church, which were partially damaged in the 1986 earthquake, are in constant need of maintenance and restoration.

Over a simple lunch that day of black lentils with onions and sturdy village bread, Kiriaki told us the monastery was suffering from a lack of funds because of the economic cutbacks. With restoration work on some Byzantine churches in rural areas being scaled back, the future of monasteries like Dimiova was more in doubt than ever.

Later in the afternoon, we sat with Kiriaki and Christina (the older of the pair) in the broad passageway, with its long bench seats that led from the open wooden doors, where a cool afternoon breeze was gusting in from the valley below. Normally at this time of day the pair would be having a siesta, and yet they said they didn't want to sleep. We raised the issue again of staying the night. and when Papa Sotiris later joined us in the passageway there was a discussion between them all.

But Papa Sotiris again told us it was out of the question. In the past, monasteries were obliged to house pilgrims, but times have changed. While the trio were chatting, I turned to Geraldine and said softly: "I think Jim's cooking a curry tonight and that might be a good compensation for not having a sleep-over. What do you think?"

"Okay, I'm in on that. I'll buy the wine," she replied.

We chuckled over it, but at the same time I couldn't help but feel it would have been a spartan but interesting night at the monastery. While Papa Sotiris returned to the main building, the two nuns seemed eager to please and were suddenly pinging with conversation, as if they'd each had a double espresso.

It was their turn to ask us questions. What were we doing in the southern Peloponnese? Did we have family here? Children? Geraldine was delighted to talk about her children and grandchildren, and she got nods of approval. When it was my turn and I told them I had no children, they both gave me looks of abject sympathy, because to be without children in Greek society is a lamentable occurrence. To make me feel better, they offered words of consolation about how health and happiness were the main thing, and children a bonus.

Geraldine winked at me discreetly from her opposite bench, thinking I would be finding the conversation intrusive. After 30 years of living in a rural village in Messinia, she admitted she had a slightly harsh view about Greeks.

"They don't do discretion or sensitivity, I'm afraid," she once told me.

I didn't find the talk intrusive and I simply told the nuns I'd had a career that had taken up my life, and children simply hadn't happened, which was half the truth anyway. In the late afternoon a couple of other women from nearby villages arrived at the monastery ahead of the *esperinos* evening service. They sat on the bench beside Geraldine, chatting to Christina. Kiriaki left for a moment and came back holding a black prayer rope, and sat beside me, pushing it into my hands. She bent close to my ear and whispered.

"You know that problem you talked about earlier, about not having children. Maybe the *Panayia* will help you. Pray to her and she will answer your prayers," she said, smiling warmly.

When she went to the dining room to fix cool drinks for the new visitors, I beckoned Geraldine over to my bench and showed her the *komboskini* and related what Kiriaki had said.

"You see that," said Geraldine, pointing to a small medallion on the chain of knots. "It shows the Virgin and child. Very appropriate. She is definitely hoping the *Panayia* will grant you the wish of a pregnancy."

I chuckled. "Well that *would* be a miracle, wouldn't it, in my 50s? I don't look young enough to be a child-bearer. Not today, anyway, after the early start."

"But she obviously thinks you are. And you just never know," said Geraldine, with a wink.

Towards early evening, we decided it was time to think about the drive back home, but first we planned another stroll around the monastery. Geraldine was keen to see some old photos in a small sitting room off the courtyard, while I walked up to the first floor of the old dormitory wing with its wide, airy balcony. There was a row of small doors. In the past, these would have been the nuns' rooms. I wondered how basic they really were. I had to admit it was a long walk back down the stairs, across the courtyard to the toilet block. But for one night? Hardly a problem.

I leaned on the balcony railing and turned my attention to the view down the valley. The afternoon breeze was now sweetly loaded with the aroma of fir, rosemary and lavender. There was hardly a sound, apart from the murmur of the two nuns below, and a tinkle of goat bells in nearby fields. In this peaceful eyrie, all the care and anxiety of the outside world had quietly drained away. I felt a sense of repose and something bordering on joyous emptiness. There was no space for any kind of thought at that moment, let alone a discordant one. It was enough just to be here.

A church bell broke my reverie. The *esperinos* would soon be starting and I made my way down there. Geraldine and I had planned to go into the church one last time to place a healthy donation in the box marked 'building restoration fund'. We strolled about the icons as the bell tolled above us. I gazed again at the shy-eyed *Panayia* with the strange gash of blood. I offered a small prayer — though it wasn't for babies, I regret to say.

At the front entrance, we prepared to leave, kissing the nuns goodbye, and Kiriaki gave the prayer rope that I still had in my hand, a knowing look. Papa Sotiris wished us a safe journey home.

240

Once outside, and well out of earshot from the main door, Geraldine and I looked at each other and burst into happy laughter, as if it were a belated reaction to what had been a long, formidable day. I had no regrets now about not staying the night. I felt that I had found the thing I was most looking for here.

But Geraldine was chortling over something specific.

"Greeks – God love 'em," she said.

"What do you mean?"

"One of the village women sitting beside me at the front door said, when she saw me put my black hat on, 'You know, if I wore a hat like that in my village, people would throw eggs at me'."

We burst into gales of laughter and scurried quickly down the path towards the car.

"Greeks just speak their minds, I'm afraid," Geraldine said.

"The nuns were entertaining though," I said and we discussed Kiriaki's hopes for my fertility.

"You know, you could extend the notion of a baby and think of it as another creation. Maybe you've got a book inside you that needs to come out. I would pray for that," said Geraldine.

I liked that idea and in fact I had finished writing the book about our first year in the Mani. I hadn't told Geraldine yet. Writer's superstition, I guess, wanting to wait until I received a firm publishing offer.

As we drove back down the mountain road, we talked about our day and what had made the greatest impression. For me, it was meeting the two nuns, though Geraldine slightly mocked the canary in the cage analogy.

"The truth is they don't know any other life," she said.

I agreed, but here were two people uncomplaining about a life pared down to the bone. It's not how everyone would want to live, but the nuns' simple life had a way of cutting

241

through all our modern worries, like that church bell tolling on a deserted mountainside at 7am.

When we arrived back home, Jim hugged me warmly at the front door.

"Good to have you back, Margarita!"

He turned to Geraldine, who was clutching two bottles of wine, bought on the way back from the monastery.

"Was it worth it in the end, girls?" he asked us, with a hint of laughter in his green eyes.

"Absolutely! But it's nice to be home," I said.

"I'll agree with that," said Geraldine, "and it's not even my home. I'm dying for the curry, by the way, Jimbo. It's been a long day on one plate of lentils."

24

The curse of Medusa

MEDUSA was the mythological minx with venomous snakes for a hair-do, and a petulant disposition to match. Her furious eyes were said to inspire fear and disgust in the beholder. She could even turn a man to stone with one look. Bad temper notwithstanding, this is a gift most women would still find invaluable. But what might she do to a Jack Russell terrier?

In late August, we went down to Sandova beach one morning early, before the Greek holiday crowds arrived because Greeks and dogs on a beach don't mix. We took Wallace as a treat because he'd seemed a bit off-colour for a few days and we'd all had a bad night's sleep, with the heat and mosquitoes and another strong earth tremor.

It was a glorious morning, the sky indelibly blue, the sea flat and clear, and Wallace was suddenly frisky. He has loved the water since he was a puppy, swimming in the summer streams of rural Scotland. He is an athletic swimmer, with great stamina. We also had a small cork surfboard to amuse him. When he tired of swimming he'd climb aboard and we would pull him along. Some of the Greeks on the shoreline watched us and were gently amused by Wallace's antics. No-one complained – until Medusa arrived with her two children.

I named her Medusa because of her big hair – black and curly, big enough to hide vipers and the odd power tool. She wore a brief bikini and had a tribal clutch of bangles on her wrists. The family all spoke Greek and English with a bit of a twang and I guessed they might be Greek Americans on holiday. We were in the water when she arrived, Wallace on his board and Jim pulling him around in lazy circles. I could see Medusa's eyes flashing towards us and the sight of a dog in the water made the kids fizzy.

"Trouble at two o'clock," I shouted at Jim because we know that Wallace and kids don't always get along.

"It's not that late surely? We just got here."

"Not the time, Jimbo! I'm fixing the co-ordinates of possible disaster."

As we got out of the water, the two kids made a dash for Wallace, wanting to pat him, but he was having none of it. He launched into a round of screamy barking and grabbed his surfboard in his mouth and ran up the beach with it, which the kids thought was the introduction to a game. Off they went in hot pursuit, screaming with excitement. Medusa was not amused.

She eyeballed the scene and bellowed to the kids to get their 'asses' back here, and her hair was writhing with intent to commit a serious offence. Jim ran up the beach to collect Wallace and when all the miscreants had returned, Medusa approached us.

"Can you please control your dog. And please do not take it into the water again. It's against the law," she ordered us.

"No it's not," said Jim.

"I think you'll find it is."

Jim looked at me. I shrugged. We'd never heard it was illegal, but then laws in Greece can be bendy things.

"Keep your dog out of the water. He will make it dirty," she said, pulling a face like milk on the turn.

Wallace gave Medusa a squinty, dark look. Clearly, he didn't like her tone.

"Do you think a dog in the water is filthier than that," I said, pointing to an overflowing plastic bag filled with rubbish, dumped on the beach nearby.

"I agree that is dirty also. But dogs in the water? Very bad, please keep it out."

244

Jim scooped Wallace up and we huddled under our umbrella, watching Medusa as she put on a strange purple Esther Williams swim cap with rubber flowers. To keep the vipers dry, I wondered? Wallace kept his gimlet eyes on her as she dived into the water, doing a fast, commendable freestyle several yards from the shore. The kids were left to amuse themselves in the shallows.

"Let's go," said Jim. "This wasn't such a great idea after all."

We started packing up and forgot about Wallace for a bit, until we looked up and were horrified to see him in the sea, paddling like mad out towards Medusa. It was impressive how quickly he was gaining on her. For an older dog, he was amazingly fast. We'd never seen Wallace do anything like this before, but I feared what he might do when he reached her. He'd either climb aboard, thinking she was an exotic surfboard, or he'd eat her. Either way we were in trouble.

I thought of putting my flippers on and swimming after him, but I'd never be able to close the gap. Medusa was ploughing on, oblivious to the Jack Russell in her wake. The kids were watching and near-hysterical with mirth. And the Greeks on the beach were beginning to laugh as well at the woman and dog race, as if it were an impromptu summer event.

"We have to do something, Jimbo, or this will end in tears," I said.

"Are you thinking what I'm thinking?" he asked, with a wink.

"Yes, Jimbo, I am."

"Okay, let's go for it."

We both cupped our hands around our mouths and yelled: "CHICKEN!"

The magic word.

Wallace's eyes flickered towards us at the first 'Chicken!' but he kept going. The kids joined in as well, screaming the word over and over. Finally, Wallace's head swivelled round with interest and he gave up the race, paddling towards the beach for a possible treat, with Medusa freestyling into the distance. We gathered him up quickly, waved goodbye to the spectators and fled.

Wallace lay on the back seat of the car on the way home, looking exhausted. It hardly seemed surprising, given his swimming efforts, but I began to think that maybe it wasn't a good idea taking him to the beach again, not in summer anyway.

A few days after the beach outing, Wallace started vomiting a few times a day, for no apparent reason. In 38/40 degrees of heat we worried that he would become dehydrated, so we called our Kalamatan vet Angelos. He told us to bring him straight to the surgery.

We had always taken Wallace to Angelos in our years in the Mani. He was a genial soul with a big personality and large brown eyes. He had studied and worked in America and England and spoke perfect English. He was always amused by Wallace's eccentric behaviour, but when we told him he'd been swimming, he shook his head.

"Wallace is a dog, not a fish, riiiight!" he said, showing his tendency to always exaggerate the word, which we found comical.

We spared him the details of Wallace's race with Medusa but he thought that Wallace had probably swallowed some sea water and had a bad reaction to it. Or that maybe he had picked up some object on the beach and swallowed it. Angelos gave us some anti-vomiting tablets and antibiotics, in case of a bacterial infection. We had to find inventive ways of hiding them in Wallace's food because he won't take tablets, and yet he wasn't eating very much. Consequently, during the following week he wasn't much better. He had virtually stopped eating and drinking water and was suffering from terrible diarrhoea.

Andreas and Marina often asked us how Wallace was getting on. Andreas was particularly concerned since he had become quite fond of him. I tried to make the descriptions of his explosions from both ends less graphic because I felt they had enough to worry about with Greece going down the pan.

Most worrying of all was the sudden appearance of blood in everything. We called Angelos again and he told us to come right back to the surgery for some blood tests.

Wallace is never a good patient. He squirms like a hooked barracuda, and even with his muzzle on, it took three of us to hold him steady enough for his blood test. Later Angelos needed to take a sample from Wallace's bottom in case he had parasites.

"Oh, good luck," I told him, pulling a face.

Wallace put on a typically hysterical turn and within seconds Angelos's forehead was glistening with sweat from all the effort.

"Recently I had my hand right inside a Rottweiler's mouth for an examination and it was much easier than examining Wallace's bottom, you know. Riiight?" We all laughed and images of Wallace on the back seat of the car in Kythera came unbidden to my mind.

After the tests, we waited in the front office for the printouts from a computer analysis of the blood sample, while people came and went, buying medical supplies, dog food, or just calling by to shoot the breeze. Angelos was a popular character in this part of the city, like a Greek Pied Piper attracting all the animal lovers from the nearby myriad apartment blocks, which in a country not known for its love of domestic animals was pretty amazing. Finally, the printouts were ready and he showed us the results.

"This is really curious because everything looks fine. All the organs are working fine. Don't get me wrong, that's good news for Wallace, but I would have expected the tests to show *something*, some abnormality, considering his symptoms," he said, wrinkling his brow.

He decided to change the treatment slightly, and put Wallace on daily injections to calm down his stomach and stop the bleeding, which meant a week of taking Wallace in every day for the jabs and occasionally for a fluid drip in the hot weather.

After a few days of the new treatment Wallace was holding things in at both ends and seemed more lively. The minute the treatment stopped, however, he started vomiting again and became quiet and lethargic. We began to worry it was something more serious that had not shown up in the tests.

In the early hours one morning, Wallace woke me, jumping on to the bed beside me. He sat motionless, his head bowed down. He looked like he was in grave discomfort. I put my arms around him and he slumped against me. I felt helpless because I couldn't do anything to make him feel better, but at least he lay down eventually and fell into a doze of sorts. This was one of the worst health problems Wallace had suffered, apart from a health scare in our first year in Greece when Angelos had to remove some suspect lumps from his back, which later turned out to be benign.

Wallace had been healthy and strong from his puppy years, possibly because of the cooked chicken his breeder Brigit fed to all her puppies. Yet not all her cuisine choices were to Wallace's liking. She also gave her Jack Russells, as a treat, dried pigs' ears. In her kitchen there was always a scattering of them around the dogs' bowls.

As I lay awake that night, I smiled to myself when I remembered the little 'starter pack' she lovingly gave to all the new owners of her puppies. It was like a canine Christmas stocking filled with goodies: soft toys, dental chews and, of course, a pig's ear. But Wallace wouldn't have anything to do with the ear. He hid it down the side of our sofa and it was discovered months later by the local vicar of our Scottish village, who had come round for a cup of tea and a discussion about Jim and me joining a few church groups, as we were new arrivals. When he plunged his hand down the side of the sofa to retrieve a dropped pen, he pulled out the somewhat embalmed-looking ear. He tossed it on to the floor in disgust, as if he were having a tea break with Fred and Rosemary West – and never returned to the house again.

After I replayed a few of Wallace's other misdemeanours, I shed a few tears as well and prayed that he'd survive this ordeal. I even thought fervently of the lovely icon of the *Panayia* at Dimiova and her supposed miraculous gifts, and wondered if she could work some magic for us now.

Wallace had been such a big part of our lives for 12 years, especially as we had bought him not long after moving back to Scotland from Australia. They had been joyful and occasionally turbulent years and Wallace was a link back to them. He was also a dear friend and I was on a mission now to make sure he survived.

The next day we were back in Angelos's surgery. He had been sure the injections would sort Wallace's problem, but now he was very concerned for him and wanted to do X-rays, to rule out the possibility that he had a foreign object inside his stomach. Wallace was tranquillised first to keep him still on the X-ray table.

When we saw the results there didn't seem to be anything trapped inside and everything else seemed fine, including his heart, which on the X-ray looked like it could fit in the palm of my hand. Such a tiny thing for such an energetic, 'big-hearted' dog. However, Angelos was worried about some irregular shadows at the start of Wallace's small intestine.

"It could just be trapped air, or something else. I can't tell absolutely what is going on here. I can't rule out that it isn't something serious. It could be an ulcer, or even a tumour."

I felt my bottom lip twitch and even Angelos's big soulful eyes looked serious for the first time.

"Listen, Margarita, I don't think it's going to be that, on the evidence I have so far, but I can't rule it out either."

But the X-ray procedure for Wallace wasn't over yet. There were some other anomalies on the X-ray and it wasn't clear if they were flaws in the film itself or something to do with Wallace's condition.

"I'm afraid we need to take these again. I have to make absolutely sure this is nothing serious. We'll get Wallace back on the table while he's still a bit tranquillised."

We went back into the X-ray room and this time Jim and I were co-opted into assisting, as Angelos had no other help that day. It proved to be an experience you could only ever have in Greece.

Jim and I needed to hold Wallace steady on his back under the X-ray beam, while Angelos operated the controls next door. We were both given lead-lined aprons to wear, which weighed a ton in the summer heat. We had to stand at both ends of the X-ray table, each clutching an end of Wallace's anatomy. Jim had the front legs, I had the back. But drowsy Wallace was having none of that and started wriggling about.

"We must keep him still for the X-ray," said Angelos, coming back into the room to help us.

Keep him still? Was he kidding? Our attempts to quieten him were feeble. We were like two ham-fisted new parents with a hyperactive child. Angelos couldn't wait any longer.

"ENOUGH, Wallace!" he boomed. The windows in the room rattled. Wallace's eyes swivelled towards Angelos, then towards us, and he lay still as a rock. In other circumstances it might even have been funny.

"That's the way to do it," said Angelos, smiling. "Get tough, riiight!"

The second X-rays proved the first film was slightly flawed but there was still a shadow on Wallace's small intestine. Angelos warned us that if Wallace kept on vomiting and didn't respond to any more treatments, we would have to go to a specialist animal hospital in Athens so he could have an endoscopy, where a small flexible tube with a camera is passed into the stomach. Vet practices in Greece cannot afford this equipment, and so much else that is taken for granted in British practices. As with many human conditions as well, more complex investigations had to be done in Athens.

"This will be a lot of trouble for you both and it will be expensive, but you need to have this investigation done if we are to know finally what's causing Wallace's illness," he said, with a note of urgency in his voice.

I prayed we wouldn't have all the drama of a drive to Athens in high summer and a hotel stay overnight, maybe even for a few nights. I had been back to Athens several times since the 1970s and had always loved it, but now it was a place that even Greeks had the jitters about. There were no-go areas in the city, where supporters of the far right-wing party Golden Dawn were attacking migrants, and in retaliation, one of the party's city offices had been firebombed. In general, there was tension all over the city centre, with people out of work, food queues, food banks, boarded-up shops, and the sight of ordinary people raking in rubbish bins for food.

It was not a place we wanted to visit right now – even for a medical emergency.

25

Athens, 1970s

A CAULDRON-sized pot was bubbling at the back of the stove, stirred by a gaunt figure dressed all in black, with a scarf swathed about her head. Nikos's mother had arrived to take charge of the apartment now that the *xeni* wife had fled. Life on Lemonias Street would never be the same again.

The mixture inside the pot was supposed to be *horta*, the staple dish of rural Greek communities, a mixture of tasty spring greens and herbs, boiled, and then doused in olive oil and lemon juice. Thekla's version, however, had an industrial sheen and a powerful odour, and from the moment she moved in, there was always a sticky mass of it brewing on the stove, or something worse.

Thekla was in her 70s, tall and skinny, with a long face and deep-set black eyes. She was born in a mountain village in Crete and moved down to Herakleion when she married Nikos's father, who ran a small business in the town. Despite that, it seemed that Thekla never relinquished her mountain ways. She was scary.

Old Greek women are a breed apart. From my experience they are mostly good-hearted, stoical, hospitable, but also shrewish, flinty and vengeful when need be. Nobody's fool. They have withstood wars, famine, earthquakes, Greek men and village plumbing. Like the Parthenon, they are solid emblems of survival. They are national treasures. Unfortunately, Thekla wasn't one of them.

Nikos must have taken after his father because on the face of it he seemed nothing like the puritanical Thekla.

252

When she first arrived, carrying a small suitcase and a plastic bag filled with spiky, wild artichokes, he introduced me, explaining I was the poor hapless nanny left, just as he was, in the lurch by the *"malakismeni"*, appalling, Deirdre. He was trying to illicit some sympathy for my plight and smooth the way, but it made no difference. I was foreign, single – and an interloper.

To Thekla's conservative mind, a single woman who lives alone with another woman's husband, especially when it's her own son, is a *poutana,* prostitute, a word I heard Thekla mutter regularly under her breath when I was near. Nikos swore he had never asked his mother to come to Athens. It was her idea. My biggest fear was that she was never going to leave.

From the beginning she never spoke to me, apart from regularly cursing like a sailor behind my back. Meal times, when Nikos wasn't in the house, were a thing of torment. She sat silently at the table, eating and staring at me as if I were about to do a wicked thing like slip hemlock into her food. If I'd had hemlock I would have taken it myself.

The menu never varied much. If she wasn't cooking *horta,* it was other village staples: giant beans, small beans, black-eyed peas, lentils. In no time at all my guts were roaring like the Meltemi wind.

Like Nikos, I spent less and less time in the apartment and took to wandering around Athens more than ever. In a month I had seen every museum in the city and every ruin – even ones that hadn't been unearthed yet. I also took bus trips out of the city to other archaeological sites. But all the while, I prayed that Deirdre would see sense and come back, so that Nikos's mother could end her tour of duty.

Deirdre phoned me once at the apartment.

"Thekla," was all I had to say.

"That bloody old harridan? In my house? How dare he bring her there! She'll be plotting my downfall, you can be sure." Finally, I could see how Nikos's mind might be working.

Thekla's glacial stare wasn't just a thing of meal times, it tracked me everywhere. Perhaps in her twisted mind she blamed me for the mess of her son's marriage. One thing she did achieve, however, was to wind up the prejudices of the landlord upstairs.

The Frog had taken to watching me as well from the windows of his top-floor apartment, with the same dark assessment, no doubt, as Thekla: a loose, foreign woman. When I arrived or left the building, I could sense his fat fingers angling the slats of the shutters in my direction. Then one day he pounced from his lily pad.

I had been studying Greek in my room, sitting across the single bed, my back against the wall. The Frog walked straight in, no knock, no announcement. Thekla must have opened the front door for him. He seemed agitated.

"Pack your things and go – and don't come back. We don't allow foreign girls to live alone with Greek men in this building," he told me in Greek.

I was too stunned to speak.

"Did you understand me?" he shouted.

"Yes, but I don't live alone with Nikos," I stammered. "His mother is here, and Deirdre will return soon."

He sneered. "Return? Pah! Deirdre has flown."

"Wait for Nikos. He will explain."

"No! You will leave now!" he boomed.

I didn't get a chance to respond. He lunged at me, grabbing my feet, trying to pull me off the bed. As it was small with casters on the legs, and he was strong for a pond hopper, the bed started to roll away from the wall into the middle of the room, with me still on it, a textbook in my hands. It was like a scene from an innovative dance performance.

I don't know what mischief the Frog had in mind but I didn't wait to find out. I leapt off the bed and told him to leave the apartment, which he did, after a whispered conversation with Thekla that I didn't catch.

I packed quickly, stuffing my few belongings into my rucksack. I didn't know where I was going to go, but I had to get out of here because if the Frog suddenly decided in a mad moment to call the police, I'd be in trouble, especially if they sussed out my working arrangement here, with no work permit, and my residency permit also due for renewal. But the bottom line was that the Frog would depict me to the authorities as a foreign troublemaker with a few banned books in my possession. Nikos would be labelled a layabout boozer and adulterer. We would be going down, big style, with or without a few bars of Zorba the Greek.

When I walked out the front door, Thekla was sitting on a wicker chair on the front balcony, staring. Her face was hard and stony. Mount Rushmore in a headscarf. She had got me finally. I threw my door key on to her lap and said in my best Greek: "*Dropei sou!* Shame on you!" And added in English: "You miserable old hag."

I walked down the road towards the bus stop, never looking back, tears in my eyes.

So that was how my job with Nikos and Deirdre ended, and my glorious Athens adventure. Rory had been right all along. How naïve and foolish I had been.

I met up with Nikos in Athens a few days later, after I had sorted out some temporary accommodation. We met in one of his regular basement haunts and drank ouzo. He chain-smoked and seemed agitated. When I told him the whole story he was furious.

"I am sorry this has happened, and for my mother's part in it. But she's a villager. She has old ideas and she saw you as a threat. It's really Deirdre's fault, the witch. She hired you and then dropped you in this *skata*, shit, pardon my saying it." He slapped his hand down hard on the table, attracting a few odd glances from neighbouring imbibers.

"But look, Deirdre might never come back, so you're as well to leave while you can, without trouble," he added.

Nikos put his hand in his jacket pocket and pulled out an envelope. "Here, take this."

It was the wages he owed me and an extra month's pay as well, which I didn't want to take, but what the hell. The money would be useful. I told him I planned to have a few weeks' holiday and enjoy the summer, exploring a few islands before I left for Britain.

"I know you don't want to leave, but I think it's the wisest thing. It's the wrong time to be here. This regime could go on for years, though some of my countrymen seem to think life has been better under a dictatorship. *Hondromalakes!* Mega-wankers!"

I listened to him sound off about the regime while I sipped my ouzo. It was strong and I enjoyed the sensation of numbness that washed over me, dulling the aggravations of the past few weeks. When we left the ouzerie, he bear-hugged me goodbye on the street.

"You're a good kid and I liked your company a lot. I feel bad about what happened but I hope some of your time in Athens has been useful. Not too dramatic."

"The drama's fine. It will be something to write about one day, definitely."

"Yes, of course, the book!" he said, suddenly remembering our Aliens Bureau ruse. He laughed loudly until it veered into a smoker's cough and I noticed under the street lighting that he looked slightly haggard, as if the events of the last few months, and living on boiled weeds and beans, was slowly gassing him from the inside. I knew the feeling well.

"I expect you to write that book and to send me a signed copy one day. Don't forget," he said, winking.

"You take care now," I said, which seemed ironic coming from someone without a home, or a job, floating like a gypsy round troubled Greece – and I was barely into my twenties.

I did finally make it back to Britain and shared a flat in London with some Aussie girls and found some temporary work. During short winter days, however, I thought constantly of the Greek sun, of favourite haunts around Athens. I longed to go back one day when the Colonels had been routed and see more of the country, but I had already made plans to study in England and it would be a while until I saw Greece again. I compensated though with newly-acquired Greek friends in London. And there was Rory. We had spirited chats whenever we met, about our time in Athens, about experiencing the 'dark side of the city'.

Despite Nikos's prediction that the dictatorship would be hard to shift, it ended the following year, in July 1974. By the end of 1973 there had been a slight cooling of military rule, which gave students in particular more freedom than they had had in years and, ironically, it had given them the freedom to decry the dictatorship.

In November, students at Athens Polytechnic held a lock-in strike and set up a radio station to broadcast their anti-dictatorship messages. Around 1,000 other Athenian students joined the activities, and protested outside, many carrying placards calling for Americans to get out of Greece.

With no signs of the protest abating, the military tightened its grip once more and sent out a tank early on November 17. It crashed through the front gates of the building, killing 23 people and injuring hundreds. A few days later Colonel Papadopoulos was ousted as leader, but it was the events in Cyprus in the summer of 1974, following a coup on the island and the Turkish invasion that followed, that finally led to the fall of the military dictatorship.

26

Athens, 2012

WE were driving on the motorway when the mobile rang. It was Angelos the vet. "You have to be at the hospital by two, riiight! The doctor's name is Athanasios Mavros. He is expecting you."

"Okay, don't worry. We're still on the outskirts of Kalamata, but we've got plenty of time," I replied.

"Only Kalamata?" he said, with a nervy catch to his voice. "I thought you would be nearer to Athens."

"Don't worry, we'll make it okay. We've got four hours to get there."

The Attiki Hospital for Animals, south-east of Athens, is a busy private hospital with a good reputation, and we knew Angelos had pushed Wallace's case to get an endoscopy at short notice, so he was anxious we didn't miss the appointment.

I looked at Wallace on the back seat. His ears had pricked up while I was talking on the phone and then his head slumped back on to the seat again. We'd been told not to give him any water before his procedure and he was already looking hot and exhausted in temperatures around 35 degrees. There was still a long way to go to the hospital.

Since our last visit to Angelos for the X-rays, Wallace had started to vomit blood again and the only choice was the endoscopy and a scan at the Athens hospital, so we could find out what was causing his illness. The hospital was in an area we knew nothing about, on a long busy road in what looked like an industrial area. The building was small at the front, but once you were inside it was a Tardis, with a long corridor down the centre of the building, with treatment rooms running off it.

Although the staff were expecting us, and were friendly, I felt nervous when we checked in at the reception desk and Wallace was jittering about. Dr Mavros was late, despite all the anxiety about us being on time.

While we waited, we saw Athenians, mostly young people, coming in with their dogs and cats, showing the kind of affection we hadn't expected in a country not known for its tolerance of domestic animals. It was heart-warming to see, especially during Greece in crisis, when everyone was financially stretched.

One teenager sat and talked quietly to his golden retriever, while on a chair opposite a studious-looking guy had a small fluffy white dog on his lap, attached to a drip. He stroked the dog and kissed its head several times. In front of the dog, the man had squeezed in his laptop computer, the lid open. It was a quaint scene, the lapdog and laptop side by side, while the young man tapped away at his keyboard, sending emails. We started to feel more confident about the hospital visit, and we knew Angelos had done the right thing for Wallace. The rest was in the laptop of the Gods.

Dr Mavros turned up, looking rushed and apologetic. He took us into a treatment room, where he looked at Angelos's copious notes – one set in Greek, one in English, along with X-rays and all the other tests. He had a quick examination of Wallace and explained he would need an ultra-sound scan and we would get the results later that evening. If they were inconclusive, Wallace would need an endoscopy the next day.

A young nurse took Wallace into a room at the back of the building and put him into a small cage alongside several others in a row. A young cat next door was wearing a 'lampshade' collar. Wallace normally detests cats and yet here, with everything levelled by illness, he couldn't care less.

Wallace looked small and nervous and we felt a pang of anxiety for him.

Later, Dr Mavros asked me to sign a disclaimer for the general anaesthetic the next day, if an endoscopy was needed. He was a sensitive guy and shrugged apologetically.

"We have to ask you to sign it. It's a formality, I am sorry. And Wallace is an old dog. There is a risk," he said.

I signed the paper, but for the first time I realised it was true. Though he has always seemed like a hyperactive puppy in our minds, Wallace was old now and he might not pull through. Dr Mavros tapped me affectionately on the shoulder. "We will look after Wallace, do not fear."

There were no hotels near the animal hospital, so we booked a room for the night in a large chain hotel in the popular coastal town of Glyfada, on the Saronic Gulf. This stretch of coastline on the Attica Peninsula, from here to Cape Sounion, is known as the Athens Riviera because of its beaches, marinas and seafront properties, and historically it has been a magnet for Greece's rich and famous.

It was once a popular hangout for Jackie Onassis during her ill-starred relationship with shipping magnate Aristotle Onassis. Glyfada had always been affluent, with a slew of upmarket stores and restaurants, but now there were signs of the crisis, with some shops boarded-up and a few beggars huddled on the pavements.

Later that evening, Dr Mavros phoned us at the hotel to say the scan had shown nothing unusual. This was good news, but the endoscopy would be more revealing, he said. It was scheduled for 3pm the next day, so we had plenty of time to kill. It wasn't far to drive into Athens and we were more confident now in tackling the city centre, but I had something else in mind to do, something I should have done years earlier.

The route we picked from Glyfada to Halandri went through the centre of the city. When we drove past Syntagma Square it was hard to reconcile the devastating TV scenes of the city burning, that we had seen in February, with what we saw that day. Now it was almost empty. August is the month when most Athenians decamp to the islands, mainly, for their summer holidays.

Even still, this wasn't the Syntagma Square I knew in the 1970s, with its outdoor cafes and perpetual buzz of life, a popular meeting place and the heart of Athens. The elegant cafés had gone. The edges of the square were scruffy and desperate. Migrants were milling about, selling faux Chanel bags and cheap watches. On one pavement we saw a young woman sitting on the ground, holding a big piece of cardboard with the word '*pinao*' scrawled in large letters. "I'm hungry".

Despite living in Halandri for nearly a year in the 1970s, while working for Nikos and Deirdre, the place now seemed alien to me. I didn't recognise any of it when we got to its outskirts. It had become a huge sprawling suburb with the usual kind of Euro-bland shops you see in other mainland cities, apartment buildings and a modern metro station. I began to think this wasn't a good idea, coming back to look at Odos Lemonias after all this time.

I couldn't have found it without the sat nav to guide us through amorphous streets. Even when our arrival in Odos Lemonias was announced, I felt a sense of dislocation. It was still a quiet, leafy street, with low-rise apartments and a few old houses, yet we could have been in any well-heeled suburb in Athens. Nothing seemed familiar, until we drew up at the old apartment block which I knew from its unusual L-shaped layout.

It had undergone a makeover of sorts, with new shutters and a plastering job. It had survived at least. Young trees were planted along the pavement and I smiled when I noticed at least two fledgling lemon trees. The main front balcony of the flat had a cluster of pot plants. It was quiet, just like the last time I'd seen it, with Thekla sitting on her wicker chair after she betrayed me.

"So, I take it none of the people you knew then are living here now?" Jim asked.

I shook my head.

"Why don't you knock on the door? If there's someone in you'll get a glimpse of the flat from the front door at least, for old time's sake."

"It's siesta time. No-one will want a knock at the door. And anyway, I'm not sure I want to see *inside* the place."

"But we've come all this way."

A glimpse back to the 1970s. The idea now seemed scary. I felt like Orpheus descending into Hades to rescue his beloved Eurydice, with the one stipulation from the god of the Underworld that he couldn't look back at his wife as they made their way out – or else she'd be stuck in hell forever. Perhaps no-one should look back. At least Orpheus was clear what his mission was. I couldn't say the same for myself, or why it had taken me all this time to revisit the street.

My eyes scanned the front of the building and I smiled when I saw a shutter on the upper floor creak open just a bit, and a shadowy face peer out. Could a decrepit Mr Frog still be in residence? What I'd like to say to him now!

"Did you keep in touch with the couple you worked for?" asked Jim.

"Yes, for a while," I said, lapsing into silence.

Jim rubbed his eyes with fatigue. I knew he was thinking that of all the places to kill time, why had we come here? I had told him most of the Athens story in bits and pieces in the time we had known each other. I knew he had forgotten most of it, so on the way here, I retold it quickly. But I hadn't got to the ending yet.

"Let's go down the street and see if the old bakery's still there. I must see that at least," I said.

We drove to the end of the street, where the bakery had once been. Now there was a place called the Artemisia Café, with an awning at the front and chairs and tables on the pavement. I laughed, thinking of how it would have been more appropriate to have called it the Dionysus Café, given the ancient connection with the suburb and the bad boy of Greek gods, as Nikos had informed me once.

"Might as well have some lunch while we're here," I said, though with the heat and the worry over Wallace, I wasn't particularly hungry.

While Jim sat outside I went inside and ordered a couple of frappés and cheese pies. The place was fresh and modern. The young woman behind the counter was pleasant and chatty.

"Did this used to be an *artopoleion*, years ago?" I asked her.

"Yes it was, from the fifties to the nineties. How do you know that?"

"I used to live in this street, in the seventies."

She gave me a wide-eyed stare. "Really! You were here that long ago?"

I felt old. "I'm afraid so."

She shook her head. "Well, I wasn't even born then."

Now I felt ancient.

"See the picture up there," she said, turning and pointing to an old black and white photo in a frame on the wall behind the till. Even before she explained it to me I knew exactly what it was: the inside of the old *artopoleion*.

I was thrilled to see that such a thing had survived the decades. The woman reached up and unhooked the photo, wiping the dust off the glass and pushing it towards me. The picture was grainy but full of atmosphere. It was just as I remembered it: the big gaping mouth of the *fournos*, the trays along the counter, plucked from the searing heat, and an old woman in black, serving.

"It's a great photo. I remember it looked like that."

She nodded. "My father bought this place in 1993 and turned it into a café, but he kept some of the old pictures that were hanging up. The *fournos* was taken out and sold, which was sad. It used to be about there," she said, pointing to an area further inside the café. There were a few tables and chairs and a sign on the wall told patrons there was free wi-fi. At just about the spot where the *fournos* used to stand, a young man was tapping away on his laptop, oblivious to the warm currents of history swirling around him.

Despite all of that, I was able to look at the place she indicated where the *fournos* had been and scenes came back unbidden. The shop had seemed cavernous in those days, hot and full of mouth-watering aromas. It had been a functional place that beamed with life. I smiled when I remembered the joke Nikos played on me, teaching me the word for 'penis' instead of 'bread' and how the assembled women had laughed.

How vivid those scenes were to me, as if there were months between that incident and now, instead of decades. How close the past was to us when we allowed ourselves to see it.

Jim and I ate our lunch outside. It was still very hot, but there was a small breeze toying with dried leaves along the dusty pavement.

"I feel guilty sitting here, having a kind of city break, while poor Wallace is in hospital," I said.

"I know what you mean," said Jim, finishing his cheese pie quickly. "He'll be having his endoscopy now, so we should head back to the hospital soon."

We were both silent a moment, thinking of Wallace and the health torment he'd faced this summer.

"Before we go, tell me what happened to the couple, Nikos and Deirdre. Did the wife come back?" asked Jim.

"Yes, she did, after six months in England." Then I explained the rest of the story.

I had already left Athens by the time Deirdre came back. I had written to Nikos when I arrived in London giving him my address. He never wrote back and I didn't expect it really. It was Deirdre who wrote to me later on. She was very contrite about my expulsion from the apartment. She told me she had gone back to Athens reluctantly, mainly because she hated the English weather.

Deirdre talked Nikos into getting a larger apartment in the centre of Athens and planned to start up her own English language *frontistirio*, college. Nikos remained jobless, however, and kept to his old nocturnal habits.

Two years after I left Athens, I received a final letter from Deirdre after a long interval. It brought the sad news that Nikos had died suddenly of a massive heart attack. He was just 39 years old. Deirdre was matter of fact, saying Nikos had ruined his health with smoking and boozing in late-night ouzeries. I didn't fall for that. I was sure Nikos had died of a broken heart, his spirit crushed in the mess of political upheaval and hopelessness that was Greece in the 1960s and 70s, and from his loveless marriage.

I shed a few tears when I heard about Nikos for the dismal waste of a life. Nikos had been a huge character in his way, a kind of Greek *mangas*, the almost untranslatable word for a confident, likeable scoundrel who lives on his wits, so immortalised in the *rebetika* blues songs of the last century.

It had been my good fortune to have known Nikos at the threshold of my adult life. He left an impression that has stayed with me. He was simply unique. Once, when he was having a strop about Greek politics, I had asked him if, despite the regime and what had happened to him, he still loved Greece. He had been trying to eat a plate of his mother's oleaginous bean stew. He slammed his fork down and shook his head as if I'd just asked the most ridiculous question.

"Yes, desperately!" he said. "I love this country, like my own life. That's why it kills me to see what's become of it. Why in God's name must everything that's rotten in the world have to happen here, to Greece, to our people? That's what I don't understand!"

Years later, I can still feel the resonance of those words.

Outside the Artemisia Café, I looked at my watch. It was getting late. "So that's how the story ended, Jimbo."

Jim looked thoughtful. "That's not the way I thought it would pan out. I thought Nikos would get his act together in the end. Poor guy."

"We should go now," I said, sensing that a melancholy had descended on the street.

"You know something, Margarita," said Jim, his lovely green eyes searching my face inquisitively. "I know how much you love Greece, even though I met you later on and wasn't able to share all the incredible times you had here. But hearing this story…it occurs to me that part of your yearning towards Greece might have been a bid to recover lost youth. It was such an exciting, edgy time. I can quite understand …," he trailed off.

I could see how he arrived at that thought, and it had struck me a few times. How well I remembered that first flush of independence and the future stretching out ahead of me, like the bulk of a tantalising novel still to be read.

Finally, I shook my head. "Oh, no. I'm not going to let you get away with that one, Jimbo! We're all looking to recover our youth. You can do better than that."

"Okay. Let's try this then. What happened with Rory? You haven't said."

I smiled and looked away for a moment. "Nothing happened. Rory was working in London. I met up with him a few times, not in hamburger joints though. I think he was over that. We had a lot to talk about and at least he was able to laugh about the attack in Athens, even though he still had a small scar on his forehead. 'The Greek souvenir'. In the end he went back to Canada to study, and apart from a few letters over the coming months, we didn't keep in touch. We were just too different."

"But you liked him a lot."

"Oh sure! He was very attractive, but there was nothing in it. Nothing!"

"Really?"

I didn't answer. Jim smiled.

"*Po, po, po*, Margarita! You're doing that Greek thing … for 'no comment', flicking your eyebrows up and tutting."

"I didn't tut!"

"You did. Good God, you're turning Greek on me! But you didn't answer the question," he gently probed.

"Even if there had been something between us, it was a long while ago. It's history."

"Ancient history!" said Jim, with a smirk. "Okay, let's go and see how the wee man's getting on in hospital."

As we got up, I turned and stood for a moment, looking at the bakery and along Lemonias Street. I felt myself being tugged back to those strange, crazy days. Then a figure appeared at the door of the café. It was the young boy who had been using the wi-fi. He walked on to the street in a gust of energy, yammering loudly into his mobile phone, and that illusive thread to the past dissolved. I knew I would never see this street again. Maybe I didn't need to now.

I thought of Rory again, though, with a smile. If he knew I was back, living in Greece, in another scary period of its history, he would have shaken his head and lectured me. But then we never did agree on anything to do with Greece.

@@@@@

"We have found something," said Dr Mavros, when we walked back into the hospital in the late afternoon. He must have seen us on the CCTV cameras, driving into the car park, and he was at the reception desk before the front door closed automatically behind us with a hiss of air. His promptness alarmed me.

"We did the endoscopy and Wallace has come through it okay, but we discovered...." he said, stopping a moment, as if trying to gather up the right words in English. I was expecting to hear the worst.

"Wallace has an ulcer in his stomach and another one in the beginning of the small intestine."

Jim and I looked at each other. We were hugely relieved it wasn't a tumour of any kind. The ulcers were serious enough though and I began to understand how much pain Wallace must have been in at times, and that this had been the source of the bleeding. Poor Wallace.

Yet if ever there was a dog ripe for ulcers it would be Wallace, who had always been an anxious little soul. If Wallace was human he'd be driven, thin, nervous, probably a chain-smoker who slept four hours a night. But smart and funny with it. Bill Gates meets Billy Crystal, maybe.

Dr Mavros explained the ulcers could be treated. That was the good part. The bad part was that the treatment would be difficult for a dog like Wallace, who was oversensitive about being handled and especially having anything popped into his mouth, like tablets. Easy maybe if his appetite returned, impossible if it didn't, as we couldn't hide the tablets in anything. The treatment also meant giving him a syrup to control his stomach acid, three times a day, every eight hours. I felt light-headed, wondering how on earth we'd manage that. And the Hannibal Lecter muzzle would, for once, be useless.

We were told he was still weak from the anaesthetic but we could pick him up first thing in the morning. When we got back to the hotel, Angelos called to say he was relieved that the endoscopy had not found anything more serious. It still wasn't clear what had caused the ulcers. Apart from stress, it could have been a number of things and, of course, the swim in the sea the day he chased Medusa could have aggravated a much smaller condition, or worse still, could even have caused it. The Curse of Medusa. I didn't doubt it.

"When you're back in Kalamata come to see me and we'll discuss the treatment," he said.

"Ah, the treatment!" I laughed nervously. "Wallace taking syrup, orally."

Angelos was philosophical. "I know it will be difficult, but you love Wallace, riiight? You will find a way."

The next morning, we drove back to the hospital. Dr Mavros appeared through the double doors, carrying Wallace under his arm, a wriggling fluffy bundle. His excitement at seeing us was immense but he couldn't leave without scooting off to see everyone else in the waiting room – the big golden retriever was also checking out and the small laptop dog as well, now off his drip. A good outcome for everyone.

I don't think many people in the waiting room had ever seen a Jack Russell before, not one like Wallace anyway, and everyone wanted to pat him on the head. Who says Greeks don't love domestic animals? They probably invented them. They invented everything else!

27

Even Odysseus went home in the end

WALLACE'S treatment proved as difficult as we had expected. The syrup was the worst. We had to find various ways to get him to swallow it, which was a weary task at 1am, his last dose of the day.

At first we improvised, filling a plastic syringe with the liquid and coaxing him to open his mouth a bit so we could squirt the contents inside. Most of the time he just shook his head and we ended up wearing it. We were constantly on the phone to Angelos, like anxious first-time parents, asking advice. We had spent so much time liaising with the vet that he quickly became a good friend, someone you could turn to at any time for help. It had proved to be a lifesaver for two foreigners in Greece.

After a while, Wallace began to sit patiently and let us rub the syrup on his front teeth, not well pleased but perhaps something instinctive kicked in and he realised he was not going to survive this problem without our help. His appetite slowly returned but there were still odd days when he was sick and other days when he seemed tired and listless, and we never stopped worrying about him.

The good news for Wallace was that Angelos recommended he only eat fresh boiled chicken and rice. Was he kidding? A perpetual diet of chicken. Wallace had just won the lottery. Wallace has always been a picky eater but now there were to be no more struggles at meal times. By October, he was almost his old self, with a few more grey hairs around his eyes.

We had always been prepared to return to the UK, if Wallace hadn't improved or became sick again, because we feared the hot climate in Greece might not be helping. However, it wasn't Wallace's illness that finally forced us leave, or even the Greek crisis, or the fact that Jim was told by Apollo Adventures his services wouldn't be needed in 2013 due to lack of bookings and cost-cutting by the company. In the autumn, Jim's sister contacted him to say their father, now in his late 80s, had suffered chest pains and tests showed some serious blockages in the arteries around his heart. Further tests would be needed, possibly a heart bypass.

This was something we couldn't ignore and we decided it was time to go back, finally. It would be painful leaving Greece after three incredible years – the most intriguing and sometimes difficult of our whole lives.

"*Paidia*," said Andreas, when we told him the news. "You can't leave, just when we are all getting to know each others." His grammar was still a thing of comical beauty. "But I understand, and you are leaving Greece at the right time. Everything sliding into a mess now. *Xalia einai*," he added, his big brown eyes looking mournful.

In early November, three weeks before we left, we saw Adonis and Iphigenia, home again from university because of a teachers' strike. We had lunch at the big table near the *spitaki* on a warm day. I looked around the yard and thought how much I would miss these convivial get-togethers, and the surroundings: the trees with their fat purple olives ready for harvest again, the orange trees with their sweet, ripening fruit, and the pomegranates, red and rosy, drooping like premature Christmas decorations on their boughs, much like Marina's kind of festive folly.

The only thing that spoilt the ambience was a volley of gunfire now and then from Orestes next door, keeping birds out of his precious almond trees that were hanging heavy with nut pods. I knew I wouldn't miss him at all, or his wife for that matter, with whom I had only ever had one bizarre conversation.

Later, while Andreas and Marina were working in their garden behind the *spitaki,* Adonis lingered a while at the table.

"I wanted to finally tell you about the night the dogs escaped. I couldn't tell you at the time. My father would be furious, especially with Zina. That afternoon, I had a long siesta in the *spitaki.* I slept like the dead. When I woke up my parents and sister had gone. No-one there, not even the dogs. I should have chained Zina before I left but because I didn't see the dogs, I forgot all about them, but they must have been somewhere on the property, playing about," he said with a shoulder shrug.

"I got dressed and I was in a hurry to go out and see my friends I have not seen for months. I left through the small door in the big gate rather than use the padlocked gate – it was easier. But when I got down to the bar, I could not remember if I locked the small gate or not. My father is always worried about security, so I had to come back up the hill again. I found the gate half-open, which was strange, but I thought I must have left it like this, and then I locked it this time. Again, I did not look for the dogs. I was selfish, wanting to get to the bar again. After I heard about the dogs I imagined that Zina and Wallace must have gone through the small gate in the time I went down and came back up. I didn't say anything because my father was very angry once when Zina got out. She caused a lot of trouble. *Po, po, po!*"

He stopped and looked uncomfortable.

"It's all right, we know about that incident," I said.

"You do?"

We nodded.

"Sorry if I caused anxiety. But I don't know how else the dogs would get out. And also, I am not sure how they got the gate to open."

"I know," I said. "Zina opened it. She did a similar thing once, up in the house one stormy night, when she was hiding in our bathtub."

"In your bathtub? She does that?" He suddenly looked a lot like a young Andreas, with his wide brown eyes and a light windmill gesture of his arm.

"Yes, it's a long story, but she can do it, she can work a door handle with her paw. The small gate opens out the way, so it was easy. But once she was outside she obviously couldn't shut it again. That would be incredible. That's why you found it partly open."

Adonis laughed, and so did we. It was quite funny, really. No wonder Zina was always on a chain, the old Houdini dog that she was.

"At least we found out eventually. It's been bothering us all this time," I added.

"And my father. He drives us crazy trying to understand how did Zina and Wallace get out that night. He goes round and round the place looking for holes in fences. But don't tell him, okay. Our secret," said Adonis.

So finally the mystery was solved, more or less. Except we still had no idea what the dogs got up to while they were out that night.

In November, there were many things to do, but we made time for a farewell meal with friends from Megali Mantineia. Despite having lived in Paleohora for a year-and-a-half, we remained closer to our original village friends. We got together at Chrysanthi's taverna, where we had spent so many nights, sitting with locals, watching crazy Turkish soaps, and where Yiorgos liked to twiddle his big moustache and say, "Greece has no maaaaney!", and make everyone laugh. And he was still saying it.

He was there that night with Eftihia, who had come out on a rare social outing as her mother had not been dead a year yet. I felt Pelagia's absence keenly on that occasion as I knew others did as well. Foteini was there and Leonidas, the gentle farmer who had sorted a few issues out for us in our first year in the village. There were other local farmers and their families and we shared plates of *mezedes* and jugs of wine on a long table. Greek music was playing and later on some people danced, some sang and others told stories about some of our mad exploits together.

Before we left, we were given small presents, mostly bottles of the local, bright green fruity olive oil, which we knew we'd have some trouble cramming into the packed Fiat car, but it was simply too good not to take with us. Each of the villagers kissed us goodbye and wished us safe journey, *kalo taxidi*. Eftihia bear-hugged me and whispered in my ear: "You come back, Margarita. You know you're one of us now."

It was possibly the nicest thing anyone had said. After three years of living in the Mani and struggling to make sense of the culture and the language, it was praise indeed to be *Maniates* (Maniots) at last. Finally, Foteini stepped forward and hugged us both.

"Ach, Margarita, I'm suffering, really I am, to know you're both going finally. But you'll come by the *ktima* one more time, won't you?"

Of course we would, I told her, but I knew it wasn't going to be the easiest of farewells.

In the following days I found time to call other people we had met to say goodbye. One of them was Papa Lambros. I had been thinking about him a lot and finally I plucked up the courage to call him on his mobile. He sounded pleased to hear from me and his sunny Aussie accent was very welcome. I asked him how everything had finally panned out. It was nearly a year since the story had been published in the Australian newspaper.

"Well … in a way it turned out for the best. The story caused a bit of a storm to start with, as you know, but it made us, as a family, sit down and talk about what we wanted from

274

our lives and how we could move forward in this crisis. And for now, we've decided to stay in Kalamata, at least until all the kids leave school. We will survive the crisis, just like everyone else."

I felt overjoyed at this news. It seemed like exactly the right approach.

"So, no need to feel bad about anything, Margarita," he added. "I had a lot of thinking to do. When I first saw that interview in the paper, I admit, I was shocked. I kept thinking to myself, 'Where is the spiritual stuff? Where are my thoughts about God? I'm sure we talked more about that'. But later, I realised I hadn't talked enough about that. Of course I hadn't. I was preoccupied with practical things, with the crisis. That was my oversight. I am sorry for that."

"Don't take it badly, Pater. Your love of God was always there, always implied."

He then told me that for him, the saddest outcome of the crisis was that many Greeks, rather than turning to God, were losing track of their spirituality in the struggle to survive.

His words made me think of a wonderful woman I had met in the village of Mystras, near Sparta, named after the glorious Byzantine city, build on a nearby hillside, with churches and monasteries still surviving in good condition, and some of the most famous frescos in Greece. Maria is a traditional icon painter who had created a small icon for me of Ayios Theologos. I reckoned that if the saint fell off a wall and into my wastepaper basket during an earth tremor, maybe he was trying to tell me it was time for a new icon, if not a new life.

Maria painted a small icon of the old saint with his characteristic crinkled forehead as he held a piece of the scriptures, written in Greek. It was an icon full of light and vibrancy. From the moment I saw the finished work I knew it was something very special and would always be a symbolic link with this part of the world. Despite her great talent,

Maria told me candidly that during the crisis her business had suffered. "When people don't have enough money for bread, they don't want to buy icons."

Papa Lambros offered blessings for our trip back to Britain and I was sorry there was no time to meet up with him before we left. Knowing him had been one of the defining moments of my three years in Greece. If my controversial newspaper feature had caused him to think about the nature of his life, the incident had had the same effect on me.

When I told him I was sad to be leaving Greece, he just laughed softly, as I knew he would. He didn't have to say anything. I knew he would understand that for some of us, the migrant kids who criss-crossed the globe in the wake of restless parents, there is never an easy road to finding out just where we really ought to be.

⊚⊚⊚⊚⊚

In the last half of 2012, there was bickering between the Troika and the Greek government, led by Antonis Samaras, over the progress of austerity cuts and fiscal reforms. The cuts were demanded by the Troika before it would release the next tranche of money from the second bailout, which had been agreed to earlier in the year. It seemed the same problem kept repeating itself over and over again.

It wasn't until late in November that the Troika finally unlocked the funds to Greece, worth 44 billion euros. It also agreed to a series of measures to make Greece's debt more manageable within a decade. Already Greece had received around 150 billion euros in rescue loans, out of the total of 240 billion, the biggest financial bailout in history.

While some Greek commentators called this latest agreement on austerity the last chance for the country to escape the crisis, others thought differently and described it as a "slow death for Greece". In the coming months there were strikes, demonstrations and a spate of vicious attacks on migrants. A prosecution was begun against at least one Golden Dawn MP for an attack the previous year, during a heated debate on Greek TV, on two left-wing female MPs, one of whom was the charismatic Liana Kanelli, who had spoken up for Greece during the height of the crisis.

Greece wasn't about to die, but the coming months would bring a slow, bitter realisation that the road ahead was going to change the country for ever. As one Greek had told me when I asked him if he thought the country was in better shape than it had been in 2010: "I don't know if the crisis is easing, but I know that Greeks used to be happier."

28

Adio, Foteini

"SO, you're finally leaving, *koritsara mou*," said Foteini, sitting on an upturned bucket, and looking at me with a mournful expression, squeezing her big hands together. "I'm suffering, just thinking about it."

Foteini never thought this day would come, and neither did I. While we sat at the plastic table under the fruit trees, I distracted myself with the view and realised, yet again, that location was everything here: the Taygetos mountains looming over us, the deep brown cave halfway up, where Foteini once told us she used to take her goats on hot summer days from Altomira; the small hill on the way up to the village of Ano Verga, with its brooding Trikitsova Castle.

I would miss this small piece of paradise, if not the ramshackle *ktima* itself.

Before we were ready to leave, Jim went out to the car for something we had planned as a kind of farewell present. He walked back into the *ktima* holding a large cardboard box, and Foteini's eyes lit up when she saw it. It had never been easy giving her gifts. She usually gave everything away, especially foodstuff, for reasons I never really understood. Cakes, biscuits, bread and much more had been redistributed to passing friends in cars.

Jim put the box on the ground and opened it. We crowded around and peered in. At the bottom, crouching on a folded-up newspaper, was the one-eyed cat, Cyclops.

Foteini turned and looked at me in disbelief. "Ach, that devil!" she said, looking down and aiming the side of her hand at him. "*Tha fas xilo, re!*" You'll eat wood, mate. Or, otherwise, 'you're bloody doomed!' Suddenly her anxiety over us leaving had been displaced for a moment.

Foteini had come across Cyclops many times at our first house in Megali Mantineia. He had a habit of sitting outside the front glass door, watching us and winding up Wallace. Whenever Foteini called by, the cat seemed to conspire to trip her up and send her down the front steps.

"Why do you think I'll be wanting this thing?" she said, looking down at his raggedy face.

"Because you need a cat to keep away the mice, remember, and Cyclops needs a home now. We don't want to leave him at the Paleohora house. Too many cats there already. So we are giving him to you. He's not a bad type really. He's old. So I am asking you to please look after him."

This, I thought, would be a real test of our friendship. She gave me a feisty look and then glanced down at the cat.

"Ach, what a face! It's enough to scare the mice away."

We laughed. She did too, standing with her hands on her hips, watching as the cat sprang out of the box to get the measure of his new 'home'.

"Okay, Margarita. I'll let him stay in the *ktima* – only if you promise to come back to the Mani one day," she said, with a shrewd grin.

"Okay, it's a promise."

Poor old Cyclops. I'd think of him in the months ahead. I wanted him to survive here. If this grizzled ball of fur with its one weary orb could survive, so could anything. So could Greece as well.

Tears rolled down her face when we kissed her goodbye. Jim walked ahead of me to the car, not overly fond of emotional farewells. Foteini was someone who seemed too tough for tears, and the sight of her now, overcome with emotion, touched me deeply.

"We've had some fine old times, haven't we?" she said, wiping her face with the back of her hand.

"And I'll never forget them, Foteini."

"You sound like you're never coming back," she said, her big blue eyes full of alarm.

"We will, I promise you," I said firmly.

She stood quietly a moment, biting on her lower lip.

"Dimitris is waiting for you. You better go. And thank you for the present...the cat," she said with a thin smile.

"His name is Kiklopas, after the mythical one-eyed demon..."

"The who?" she crinkled her face.

"Ach! Don't worry who Kiklopas was," I said, remembering our last conversation here about mythical characters. "I hope you'll be friends. And don't give him away, okay?"

Her bottom lip quivered. "I've nothing to give you, Margarita."

"Foteini, you've already given me a great deal – more than you can ever imagine," I said.

She looked blank. I knew she'd be wondering what exactly it was she'd given us, apart from *myzithra* cheese and endless cups of Greek coffee. I squeezed her big hand, marvelling at its size and strength. A hand that had grappled with olive trees, goats ... and mobile phones. There was nothing in the world like it.

But the lack of a gift seemed to be bothering her, I could tell.

Just before I turned to leave she put her hand on my shoulder, her voice cracking slightly. "Remember ... I love you, Margarita."

I was speechless at this shy confession. I could only nod in response, trying also to control a trembling lower lip. It made me wonder if, in all this time, Foteini regarded me as something of a surrogate daughter, a *xeni* one at that, with some strange ideas. It made me think of one afternoon in the *ktima,* drinking coffee, during our first year in the village, when she suddenly announced that she and I were "very much alike". We weren't, of course, but to be adopted by the inimitable Foteini was no bad thing.

I turned quickly and walked through the front gate of the *ktima* to where the car was parked.

She stood at the gate and shouted "*Sto kalo!*" Go to the good!

As we drove away, I could see her reflected in the side mirror. She was still at the gate, waving as we drove down the road towards the village. She vanished as the car jolted round a pot-holed bend on this same dusty stretch of road where we had first seen Foteini, and where our fate had been sealed for the next three years, and where our adventure was now coming to an end.

ⓔⓔⓔⓔⓔ

A week or so before we left Kalamata for the long drive back to the UK, there was one more thing that Jim wanted to do. He had bought a small gift for his father's birthday and wanted to send it off before he left, fearing there would be no room for it in the car. His father had asked for a small replica of a Greek caique, and after hunting all over the city Jim found a beautifully crafted boat with delicate rigging.

After binding it in bubble-wrap and placing it in a cardboard box, we took it to a post office near the marina in Kalamata that we often used. Jim had written 'Fragile' in English on the box and asked at the post office if they could put a sticker on it in Greek with the same word, just in case.

The employee was a woman with good English who had served us many times before. She looked stressed and tired. When Jim asked her for the sticker she just pulled a face.

"No, you don't need it. Everyone in the Greek postal service knows the 'Fragile' word," she said, with a deep sigh.

Jim paid. She plastered at least a dozen stamps on the box and rubber-stamped the delicate package several times. She then did something incredible, hurling it manfully over the top of her head, backwards, without looking. The box sailed through the air and, luckily, landed in a wide-open sack of parcels propped up against a table, without it being smashed to pieces.

Jim and I looked at each other and burst out laughing. That's all we could do. Nothing could have summed up the crisis in such a comical way, if comedy were at all appropriate. Here were pissed-off government employees suffering job cuts, wage cuts, umpteen new rip-off taxes, compliments of the Troika. "Fragile?" her action seemed to say, "I don't give a rat's arse for your notion of fragile!" But she did see the funny side of it, and smiled broadly at her expert throw. As it happened, the caique arrived in one piece and Jim's father was well pleased with it.

The night before we left the Paleohora house for good, we said an emotional farewell to Andreas and Marina up in the house, because they wouldn't be at the *spitaki* in the morning. It had also been a strange and sometimes crazy friendship during a tense time and we knew we'd miss them a lot.

Marina handed me a plastic bag finally and I opened, it expecting to find a bizarre 'pairing', like broccoli and travel sickness pills. But it was a large bottle of ouzo from a Kalamata supplier.

"Peeerhaps you come back one day," said Andreas.

"The house will wait for you," said Marina, in her curious English.

Even before we left the house early the next day it started pouring with rain. The day promised to be stormy. We had started life in Paleohora with a cracking storm – and we were ending with one.

Despite the rain, some of the cats came to see us off, and the new batch of chickens. We'd already said farewell to Zina, now chained at the *spitaki*, yet still she watched us mournfully as we loaded up the car and set off for Patras, to catch the ferry to Italy. She was straining her neck against the chain as we drove out of the property.

"*Yeia sou*, Houdini!" I shouted from the car window.

I could see her shivering in the rain, never taking her eyes off the car. Wallace watched her from his dog bed, perched atop a suitcase on the back seat. He whimpered softly. Was he thinking about their great escape that night among the olive groves? The night that no-one would ever know the true details of. Neither were we to know that we'd never see Zina again and that despite her extraordinary stamina, this winter would be her last.

We got to Patras in the afternoon, with plenty of time for the ferry departure. We weren't too worried about the gathering storm clouds over the city. Jim parked the car outside the terminal building and went in to pick up the pre-booked tickets. He wasn't very long. When he got back in the car he slumped against the seat rather dramatically.

"The nightmare begins, Margarita!" he announced.

"What do you mean?" I asked, thinking of the worst possibilities, like they had no booking for us and the ferry was full.

"The ferry departure's been postponed due to storms over the Adriatic Sea. There are storms everywhere. Just our luck. We won't leave now until tomorrow morning – if we're lucky."

"It's Greece's way of saying it doesn't want us to go," I offered.

"I'm being serious. We could be stuck here for days."

At least we weren't stuck with the hassle of finding a hotel room for the night, as the ferry company was allowing everyone on board for the night ahead of the predicted departure.

The storm passed over Italy during the night and we slept like babies in our 'dog-friendly' cabin. In the morning we went up on deck to watch as the ferry slid finally away from the harbour. Jim had Wallace under his arm, shielding him from a fresh morning breeze. We had a tendency now to treat Wallace as if he were a Ming vase after his health scare. When Wallace started to shiver, Jim said he would take him back to the cabin, but I decided to stay on deck a while.

I watched as the landmass grew smaller, trying to grab on to a final image of Greece that I could keep with me for a while. My eyes searched the rather ugly mass of apartment blocks ringed by low hills, and I finally found what I was after. A small white-domed church on the ridge of a hill, lit by the morning sun and rosy-hued. It seemed like a beacon in the distance and a good omen. I kept my eyes on it until it was just a glittering speck. It was the last piece of Greece I wanted to see before it slipped out of sight forever.

I have had many departures from Greece in my life and each has been a little harder than the one before. I remembered the businessman Tassos at the *yiorti* in Megali Mantineia in 2011 and his question that, apart from sun, sea and a carefree life, "what is it that you foreigners are seeking to find in Greece that you cannot find in your own country?"

It was still a good question, and one that had set me on my own quest to discover what it was about Greece that had kept me coming back again and again, from the early 1970s through some of the country's darkest times.

After three years in the Mani, my longest stay in Greece, I found it was easy to name what I loved about the place, there were so many things, and all of them underscored with simplicity: the sound of an Orthodox chant, the first taste of a ripe fig, an old village *kafeneio* in the shade of a plane tree, a caique slipping across the dawn sea. And, of course, the people themselves, their generosity, their craziness and the feeling that despite everything, they are fashioned to be wise, like the smooth sides of ancient marble warmed by the sun.

It was much harder to say what I had been 'seeking to find' here. I may never know. What I do know for sure is that there is a sense of ease about Greece because it is old, well-trodden and comfortable in its own skin, even in a crisis. When you are enfolded in this space there is nothing more for you to know, or to prove.

The Greek poet Konstantinos Kavafis offers a clue to the power of this country in his poem *Ithaka*, about the Homeric hero, Odysseus, and his long, adventurous return to his Greek island home after the Trojan War.

> *"Ithaka has given you this beautiful journey,*
> *Without her you would not have set out*
> *She has nothing left to give you."*

I had sought a journey once in Greece and found it. But unlike the journey of Odysseus, mine hasn't ended yet.

Sto kalo.

'Go to the good!'

THE END

The prequel

IF you enjoyed this book, you might also like to read the prequel, *Things Can Only Get Feta*. This insightful and humorous memoir explores Marjory, Jim and Wallace's adventure from the beginning as they settle into the hillside village of Megali Mantineia in the Mani, in 2010. It follows their attempts to assimilate into Greek life as the crisis unfolds, with an unforgettable cast of local characters, particularly the irrepressibly unique goat farmer, Foteini. The Kindle and paperback versions are available on Amazon worldwide.

Praise for Things Can Only Get Feta

"Honestly, you won't be able to put this book down."– Maria Karamitsos, reviewing in *The Greek Star* newspaper, Chicago.

"A book to relax into, a wonderful record of Greece's uniqueness, written with wonderment, admiration and wit,

all in equal measure." – Anne Zouroudi, award-winning author of the Greek detective series of novels.

"I respectfully suggest to all wannabe authors of an 'expat life' type of book that you read this book before putting pen to paper. It's an object lesson in how it should be done. Congratulations, Marjory!" – Peter Kerr, best selling author of *Snowball Oranges*.

"Marjory is a very talented storyteller, and many descriptions of events and turns of phrase she used in this book actually made me laugh out loud while reading silently to myself, a feat that until now was only achieved by Douglas Adams and P.G. Wodehouse." – Gry, Good Reads reviewer.

"This is the best book of its kind that I've ever read. It has it all: humour, wit, interesting facts, and a good measure of sentiment. Marjory McGinn is a truly talented author." – Effrosyni Moschoudi, author of *The Lady of the Pier* trilogy.

"Marjory McGinn's style of writing is totally captivating. However, this book is much more than just the adventures of a couple and their dog. It is also a loving and caring approach to Greece at the beginning of the worst economic crisis the state has witnessed since the Second World War." – Spyros Litsas, newspaper columnist and Professor in International Relations, University of Macedonia, Greece.

"A tale full of adventure and wit, delving into the heart of the communities in this area (Mani)... This book might become a future reference source about life in 'unspoilt' Greece." – Stella Pierides, author of *The Heart And Its Reasons*.

Acknowledgements

For this travel memoir, thanks must go firstly to the villagers of Megali Mantineia, Paleohora and Akroyiali, in the Mani, for their friendship and stories, especially the inimitable Foteini. With fond remembrance of the late Nikoletta Kostea.

Grateful thanks to our Kalamatan vet and friend, Evangelos Papadimitriou, whose expert treatment returned Wallace to cheeky good health after a medical drama.

I am hugely indebted to Scottish author Peter Kerr for his publishing wisdom and guidance. Many thanks to Greek novelist Effrosyni Moschoudi for her support, and Greek language advice (any mistakes are mine alone). For his sparkling cover, thanks to artist Anthony Hannaford.

Gratitude to my partner Jim Bruce for sharing our odyssey, and for his expertise in editing and designing this book, (www.ebooklover.co.uk), and also for research on Patrick Leigh Fermor (Chapter 13).

Thanks also to Stavroula Sipsa and her hospitable family in Koroni, Messinia, for providing the village house on a quiet hillside where this book was happily written in 2014.

Lastly, hugs to crazy terrier Wallace for making me laugh, always, and for giving the world a daft new angle on the word 'chicken!'

**Koroni, Greece,
April 2015**